JOURNALS
1990–1992
Anthony Powell

JOURNALS

1990–1992

Anthony Powell

With an introduction by
VIOLET POWELL

Heinemann : London

This edition published in the United Kingdom in 1998 by
William Heinemann

1 3 5 7 9 10 8 6 4 2

First published in the United Kingdom in 1997 by William Heinemann

William Heinemann
Random House UK Limited
20 Vauxhall Bridge Road, London, SW1V 2SA

Random House Australia (Pty) Limited
20 Alfred Street, Milsons Point, Sydney, New South Wales 2061, Australia

Random House New Zealand Limited
18 Poland Road, Glenfield
Auckland 10, New Zealand

Random House South Africa (Pty) Limited
Endulini, 5a Jubilee Road, Parktown, 2193, South Africa

Random House UK Limited Reg. No. 954009

A CIP catalogue record for this book is available from the British Library

Papers used by Random House UK Limited are natural, recyclable products made from
wood grown in sustainable forests. The manufacturing processes conform to the
environmental regulations of the country of origin

Printed and bound in the United Kingdom by
Mackays of Chatham PLC, Chatham, Kent

ISBN 0 434 00423 5

For Hugh Massingberd

Once again I wish to thank Tessa Davies
for transcribing these *Journals*,
and my wife, Violet Powell,
for her assistance.

Contents

Introduction by Violet Powell xi

JOURNALS

1990   3
1991   90
1992   163

Index   228

Introduction

Those familiar with the indoor and outdoor landscape of The Chantry will find that in 1990, while the trees may have grown taller the indoor pattern of life has become more concentrated. Like the pussy-cat in the nursery rhyme, Powell's last trip to London was to visit the Queen. That was in 1987, when HM invested him as a Companion of Honour. He now relies on his friends and his family to supply him with a lifeline of gossip.

Having now no opportunity to visit picture galleries, the Diarist looks through his excellent collection of art books, taking them from the shelf as they happen to be arranged. He thus comes across an esoteric coincidence. When Van Gogh was on a visit to England, he preached a sermon at the Richmond Wesleyan Methodist Chapel. It seems that this, many years later, was where the Q2 Amateur Dramatic Society gave a performance of *The Garden God* by Anthony Powell.

Other reading is, as ever, wide-ranging, with comment and speculation. Powell considers, for example, that Dostoevsky's taste and literary genius would have found the plot of Dickens's *Barnaby Rudge* sympathetic material on which to work. Throughout the years, the rereading of Shakespeare's plays is a *leitmotif*, the *Tragedy of Antony and Cleopatra* being a particular favourite.

A tradition of an annual indoor picnic, brought by Marcelle and Anthony Quinton, together with Evangeline Bruce, has grown up. Writing in 1996, this is a poignant memory. Evangeline Bruce, a former US Ambassadress, was struck with blindness in the spring of 1995 and was to leave friends all over the world to mourn her death in the following autumn.

The offer of a doctorate at the University of Wales is a gratification to the Diarist, though he realizes with regret that the journey across the

Severn Bridge to Cardiff and the ceremony itself would be too exhausting for him to undertake. Powell is all the more regretful because among the Honorands to be installed by the Prince of Wales in June 1992 was to be Neil Kinnock, at that date Leader of the Opposition. As Kinnock came from the Valleys, from whence the men of the Welch Regiment in which Powell had served were largely drawn, it would have been an interesting meeting. In addition a General Election was imminent from which Kinnock might by then have emerged as Prime Minister, though in the event the swing boat of politics found him looking for another job.

The University authorities behave with admirable generosity. A delegation, led by the Vice-Chancellor, comes across the Bridge, bringing with them robes for the ceremony. This takes place in the dining-room at The Chantry, and includes a speech in Welsh by the Honorand. Its success is fully recorded on video.

Soon afterwards there is a dinner party at The Stables to celebrate the eightieth birthday of the Diarist's wife. With three generations of his family and friends coming from afar the evening sparkles, with the Diarist rejoicing in the birthday feast.

During the three years covered by the *Journals* both *Miscellaneous Verdicts* (1990) and *Under Review* (1991) appear, criticism and appreciation from a long career of reviewing. To quote only one pearl fished up from the deep waters of the past, it was surely the happiest of coincidences which enabled the reviewer to compare the two entries in separate confessional albums by the young John Galsworthy and the young Marcel Proust. Favourite Heroine: Galsworthy, Florence Nightingale (who said he knew no other). Proust, Cleopatra (who may well have wished to know no other).

The curtain falls on New Year's Eve 1992, with a tribute from the Diarist to the support and companionship of his family.

Violet Powell
Chantry
1996

JOURNALS
1990–1992

1990

Monday, 1 January, New Year's Day

Not long ago an Austrian, Peter Kislinger, wrote asking for an interview as he was writing a dissertation on *Dance*. I make a practice of refusing such requests. In this case I sent a civil letter back, saying I had been involved in the translation of the Austrian writer Lernet-Holenia, such of whose books as read, I enjoyed. In consequence Kislinger now sends Lernet-Holenia's recently published *Collected Poems* (in German), with a letter saying my reply made him understand Henry James's story 'The Figure in the Carpet'. I could not remember what that was about, so reread it, also 'The Lesson of the Master', equally forgotten. Both stories deal with the relations of a young writer with an older, relatively famous one. In the former, the young writer hears his anonymous review of the older writer's book dismissed by the latter as 'twaddle', not knowing the young man had written it. When he discovers this, the older writer tries, without success, to explain why the well-meaning reviewer, like most others, fails to get the point; something one would very generally agree with. In 'The Lesson of the Master', the older writer warns the younger never to marry if he wants to be a serious artist; then, when his wife dies, marries the younger writer's girl. Even allowing for different behaviour in James's day, described in Jamesian language, both these stories strike one as nonsense in the manner the respective novelists are represented as speaking of their work to each other. I suppose it is just possible that a writer like, say, Meredith or Andrew Lang might talk somewhat in that manner, but if one thinks of the younger writer as, say, Maugham or Compton Mackenzie, neither story suggests in the least James's young writers' attitude to their own writing, tho' in their way both good ideas for story. In what manner my letter to the Austrian made the first clear to him is mysterious to me.

Tuesday, 2 January

Nicholas Shakespeare wants a contribution to a feature in which one is given £25 to spend on three books at one's local second-hand bookshop. V made a recce in Frome and reported there seemed to be no second-hand bookshop as such. However, she put forward one or two possibilities, which I visited this afternoon. I tried first St Aldhelm (Hugh Pincott), Palmer Street, which turned out chiefly new occult books, psychiatry, and so on, only a dozen or so second-hand. The proprietor looked very much the part for selling Eliphas Levi's *High Magic*, etc. I explained I wanted second-hand books only, mentioning I was familiar with Eliphas Levi's work. He replied 'Oh, yes?' in tone of one being told that a customer had enjoyed *David Copperfield*.

Higher up the street, in Catherine Hill, I found The Old Curiosity Shop (R. P. Hackett), which was indeed the old-fashioned type of second-hand bookshop, books in piles everywhere, not too bad a selection. The proprietor, with an impressive double chin, was a little like the late Leigh Ashton, Director of the Victoria & Albert. After considerable roting round, illustrating I thought comparatively comprehensive character of our own library, I bought *Contarini Fleming*, by 'the Right Honourable B. Disraeli', with an Earl's coronet stamped in gold on the cover; W. E. Henley's *Collected Poems* (1907, much reprinted from 1898 edition, with traces of Nineties elegance in title-page). Henley was a not uninteresting, if not particularly pleasant man. Also Walter Scott's *Collected Poems*, which we do not possess and one needs. All useful additions, tho' nothing else one wanted.

Thursday, 4 January

About 2.30 p.m. Henry Mee rang from Nunney, saying he had just lunched there with his girlfriend, could they look in, adding that the girlfriend was quite harmless. I had scarcely hung up when Ania Corless rang from Higham saying Christian Bourgois, having refused to divulge when he is publishing the French edition of *Dance*, had now announced they are producing it in three volumes on 19 January. In addition, *Le Point* magazine wants to interview me next week. Their man, with the striking name of Manuel Carcasonne, is coming on Thursday.

Henry arrived with a girl called Louise, a typical painter's type (Low Countries Primitive, rather than Italy, on the whole, not Rubens/Renoir type). They had been to see Lord Denning at Whitchurch whom Henry is painting. Lord Denning pleased to hear that Louise (Keble) got a First in Law. Henry had a story of two policemen calling on him early one morning with their caps under their arms. He thought some death had occurred at this unusual reverence, but in fact his recently bought, immensely grand Jaguar, parked outside, had been vandalized, which induced this respect in the police.

Saturday, 6 January–Monday, 8 January

V in bed with upset inside, current form of flu. She is starving herself. John coped with the cooking and shopping, nobly staying on till Tuesday.

Tuesday, 9 January

V rose from bed by easy stages. The French journalist Manuel Carcasonne, from *Le Point* (apparently a newspaper more or less of the Centre), came for interview. Due at 10.30, arrived soon after that from the Royal Crescent Hotel, Bath and stayed till 12.30, when he returned to catch a plane from Bristol that evening. He was what one imagined as an archetypal young Frenchman of his sort (from Aix-en-Provence): agreeable, reasonably intelligent, seemed to know my books pretty well. He asked the usual questions. He cheered me by saying, quite unprompted, that he thought *Aubrey* ought to be translated into French and he might well find French publisher. True, Ali Forbes did send me a French cutting some months ago about Aubrey, so he must be to some extent known over there.

Snook arrived at end of the interview, ingratiated himself with Carcasonne, who brought with him copies of the first three volumes of *Dance* in French. They have put a Sickert, a Lavery, a Malcolm Drummond, none of them specially relevant, on the covers, but I suppose they look intensely English. Anyway all pretty. I am variously described as being born in 1903 and in 1905, at Eton and Oxford with Evelyn Waugh (Lancing and Oxford), Cecil Beaton (Harrow and Cambridge), Cyril Connolly (Eton and Oxford), George Orwell (Eton, no University). The first volume is newly translated, the other two are the same translator as when appeared in 1950s.

The proofs of *Miscellaneous Verdicts*, due at Heinemann on Friday, 5 January, as ever, failed to be on time. I delivered a diatribe against printers always being late, my refusal to be bullied by them, as they were late they must finish by the time promised. In the evening Charles Trueheart of the *Washington Post* rang to check on certain points in his interview, the house, my views, etc.

When I recently signed a contract with Lucarini for the Italian translation of *Afternoon Men*, I noticed their office was in Rome. I remembered talking at a party a few years ago with an Italian publisher, Feltrinelli (who eventually incinerated himself climbing up a pylon he was trying to sabotage, quite why I don't know, unless simply because he was a Communist). I said: 'Is your office in Rome?' 'Rome!' he said. 'That's like asking an English publisher if his office is in Aberdeen.' I said: 'Well, perhaps Bath?' He conceded Bath might be nearer the mark. Anyway I do seem to be published now in the Eternal City.

Thursday, 11 January

Proofs of *Miscellaneous Verdicts* finally arrived. John's birthday. We rang him.

Sunday, 14 January

The dotty fan rang about 8 a.m. He was answered by V, who hung up on grasping his identity. Yesterday Lewis Jones of the *Daily Telegraph* obits (assistant to Hugh Massingberd) rang saying Harold Acton was rumoured to be on his last legs, would I write 500-word memoir, and ring him today, after midday, to dictate it. Accordingly, I spent the morning doing this. On ringing the *DT* about 12.30, Jones was not yet in. There was difficulty in finding someone to take the piece down. Jones rang in the afternoon, saying the memoir was just what was wanted, tho' Harold at present surviving. Rather cross at having my Sunday morning disturbed in this manner, as a memoir of Harold was not at all easy to do.

On the one hand, don't want to write in too unfriendly a manner about someone I have always been on good terms with, if not at all close ones, for so long (seventy years); on the other, I am inclined to think Harold an unfortunate influence on the Oxford of his generation. With his brother, Willie, he was certainly an amusing adjunct to Eton life; when older, always prepared to be visited by those who rang up La Pietra from Florence, which not everyone would have been. For instance V and I had pleasant dinner with him and his German boyfriend, Alexander, the last time we were in Florence some few years ago. (When Alexander was out of the room, Harold, characteristically, said: 'He's not nearly so young as he looks.')

At Oxford, Harold's camping about, general silliness, shallowness, conviction that he was himself a genius, made people think that art and letters were the concern only of futile 'aesthetes', occupied with exhibitionism and tuft-hunting. Harold's supposed wit, comic speeches at drunken dinners, could not have been less funny, indeed were exquisitely embarrassing. It was an enormous relief to get away from all that sort of thing to London, to find intelligent people did not behave like Oxford 'aesthetes', tho' Harold himself was always declaring that he hated nothing more than 'aestheticism'. He never delivered the goods intellectually speaking, as did, say, Waugh and Betjeman, even to some extent Robert Byron. At the same time Harold was not a bad old thing; fundamentally, I think, a complete egotist, a cold fish. He knew a certain amount about Italian painting from people like Berenson being habitués of La Pietra since Harold's earliest childhood.

In some ways Willie Acton was the more amusing figure, more genuinely eccentric, so far as their ebullient 'Latin' manner went, and their *diableries*, tho' Willie's pictures must be admitted to have been pretty awful. What exotic blood ran in the veins of Harold and Willie? So far as I remember, their father looked (burly, fair-moustached) much more English than Italian, tho' perhaps the sort of Englishman who has spent most of his life on the Continent. Their mother (whose family came from Chicago, I believe) was a standard American blonde. I believe on her side the family had property in Hawaii. Could there have been a touch of the South Seas somewhere? Neither brother was what might be expected in appearance from the usual Italo-British or Italo-American mix.

I reread *King Lear.* Lear's great denunciation of sex: 'The wren goes to it . . .', really has no bearing of a direct kind on the immediate subject of the play. True, Gloucester had produced the Bastard, who causes so much trouble and has affairs with both Regan and Goneril. These are comparatively marginal aspects in contrast with ingratitude, ambition, and cruelty. In fact, it looks rather as if Lear spoke the feelings in Shakespeare's mind at that particular moment.

Tuesday, 16 January

A letter from Canadian fan, Ellen Charney of Toronto, drawing attention to the Digital Company of Canada using last paragraph of *The Strangers All Are Gone* (Michelangelo's snowman for the Medici) as an ad in the

Toronto Globe & Mail Christmas Number, dated January 1990. I sent this
to Bruce Hunter, suggesting we tease the Digitals about it, tho' not much
hope of getting anything out of them for breach of copyright. Story
appeared in Vasari, the comment is purely mine.

Oddly enough, I had another letter from Canada, Thomas Dilworth
(Windsor University, Ontario), wanting information about my meeting
David Jones, painter, poet, with John Lloyd (The Widow) at Lyme Regis
in 1937. V and I spending Christmas there with The Widow, Wyndham
Lloyd, Brocas Harris and Eve Disher, at the Three Cups, not too bad a
pub, all rather enjoyable. The Widow had asked David Jones over from
somewhere he was living locally to talk about Welsh archaeology or similar
matter. The Widow didn't know Jones at all well. Most notable thing, I
remember, was The Widow, in an aside to me, said: 'David Jones has just
remarked "I can't make up my mind whether or no to stay for dinner" ',
when he had, in fact, only been invited to luncheon. He did indeed
remain to dinner. As it happened, I did not have much truck with him. I
wrote to him at a much later date about some Welsh genealogical or
historical matter; sent David Jones's reply (in several different coloured
inks) to Dilworth, asking him to return it.

Tuesday, 23 January

I finished *Contarini Fleming*, to find that last 100 pages of the volume were
devoted to *The Rise of Iskander*. Although both novels are fairly silly, Disraeli's exuberant style carries the reader on, so that in a way I was quite
interested. After the wildest improbabilities in his early life (apparently
in Sweden, tho' half-Italian), *Contarini Fleming* settled down to being a
romantically approached travel book about the Levant. *Iskander*, founded
on Castriot, a fifteenth-century Albanian, is about a Greek prince, brought
up as a Muslim by the Turks, but secretly Christian and Philhellene. He
changes sides, wins great victories and marries a beautiful Hungarian
princess.

John, looking out of his window at the back of his house in Kennington
Park Road, saw what he thought at first were two large cats sleeping on
the roof of the shed (former pigeon loft) in his small garden. On closer
examination these turned out to be foxes.

Thursday, 25 January

Gales. Many trees down, including the big Luccombe oak in the Park Field just by the house. The garage door was blown away.

I finished W. E. Henley's *Poems*; known ones: 'Out of the night that covers me', 'What have I done for you, England, my England?' (I always vaguely thought was by Browning), the unspeakable 'I was a King in Babylon, and you were a Christian slave'; less known, preferable: 'Coming up from Richmond in the long ago', curious poems about Life and Death: 'She the lodger in the room / He the ruffian on the stair'. One cannot help thinking Henley had in mind a tart and her ponce in the latter, could not say so explicitly, owing to Victorian conventions. I find these last two, with another I thought less interesting, in the Amis Anthology. Henley was an uncomfortable figure, not wholly uninteresting. I always supposed he influenced Kipling, now I'm not sure it wasn't the other way round, although Henley was nearly twenty years older.

Friday, 26 January

John did the round of the property to check trees. There seem to be about a dozen down, not to mention odds and ends of big branches, laurel, Wellingtonia, etc. One has annoyingly fallen from our side across the waterfall.

Saturday, 27 January

Tristram and Virginia at The Stables. I went there to inspect Edna, the new black kitten (two months). She came from some strange religious community, of which Tristram gave an amusing account. Georgia in a bad state from being poisoned by a Chinese take-away, which I thought equivalent of attempted suicide. They had been up to Warwick to see Archie, who likes the place and was acting in a play. He recently turned down a part in a Pinter play being done as too bitty. About 8 p.m. all the lights went out here. Fortunately Spaghetti Arabella was just cooked, but a rather depressing evening.

Sunday, 28 January

The lights went on about 11 a.m. A great relief. Lights fusing is never particularly enjoyable, but one notices that all conceivable toleration of

pottering about with candles in the dark, a faint sense of adventure, goes
with increased age. Tristram and Virginia to midday drinks.

Tuesday, 30 January

I dreamt that Philip Larkin said to me: 'I have just had a letter from Roy
Fuller, which refers to the two fine large oil paintings in his father's
drawing-room. I had no idea Roy's family lived in that sort of style.'

The telephone is now off owing to a tree falling on the wire. There is
a piece in the *New York Review of Books* (to which Tristram subscribes) by
Noel Annan on Michael Shelden's book about Cyril Connolly and *Horizon*.
Like most of Annan's writing, there are patches of good comment. He
seems almost obsessed by this world, to which he himself never belonged,
yet in a way yearns for. Speaking of Maurice Bowra, he mentions survival
of Maurice's voice in Osbert Lancaster, his taste for litotes
(understatement) in my writing. I don't think I got that from Maurice.
Hubert Duggan and I used to converse that way while still at school.

Saturday, 3 February

Peter Mumford came on Thursday to see the tree damage. I had a letter
this morning from English Heritage asking to report damage as owner of
'registered historic house park garden'. A letter from a French fan, saying
there had been a lot of favourable reviews, which is cheering.

Monday, 5 February

V sold two review copies at the Hunting Raven bookshop, Frome, with the
proceeds of which she bought Lees Mayall's privately printed memoirs,
Fireflies in Amber, and a pair of pyjamas for me. Henry Mee rang in evening.
He is being given eight minutes on Channel 4 News for his show, with
which he is very pleased (certainly that's quite generous, if it isn't cut),
in which he wants various of his sitters to appear, including me. He
suggested filming should be next Monday, to which I agreed if that could
be arranged.

I reread *Pericles*. Of course the only scenes that are really any good deal
with Marina in the brothel. These are very good indeed.

Sunday, 11 February

I lately received letter from Philip Nokes, who has just moved into Stoney Lane Cottage, saying he was compiling a Register of Dauntsey's School, Wiltshire (450th anniversary in 1992, but Register to go back only to about 1890), asking if he could use for epigraph remark in *Books Do Furnish a Room* about Septimius Severus being a notable enemy of the Old School Tie in having had a man scourged for mentioning fact that they had been at school together. Nokes also made complimentary remarks about *John Aubrey and His Friends*, something always popular with me. We asked him and his wife in for drink on Sunday morning, but the wife turned out to be away for the weekend. Nokes (said to have wished to be ordained at one moment) is tall, bespectacled, somewhat schoolmasterish figure, middle thirties, intelligent, apparently a policeman's son from near Devizes. He is some sort of ecclesiastical bureaucrat in the Wells Diocesan Office. We chatted away quite enjoyably. Snook took a great fancy to him.

Tuesday, 13 February

The Congressman (John Monagan) sent a signed and inscribed (to me) photograph of General Colin Powell, the 'black' Chief of Staff of US Army, responsible for the recent invasion of Panama. This must be acknowledged to be a good joke, even tho' General Powell is the palest of pale shades. I have asked John Monagan how I should thank for it. Mr Trueheart of the *Washington Post* wrote to say he received a considerable fan mail from his interview piece. He forwarded certainly a most flattering example saying that the BBC office in Washington should be picketed until *Dance* is put on TV screen. My French publisher, Christian Bourgois, suggests visiting us in spring.

Friday, 16 February

Peter Mumford (who joined us in a cup of tea at breakfast) came to deal with the question of trees down after the gigantic gale of 25 January, some of which need urgent attention, one on other side of lake, one leaning on the power line. A tall poplar has fallen against a big beech opposite The Stables.

I agreed to review a book on Fielding for the *Washington Post.* I found that when I read *Tom Jones* (with enjoyment) aged seventeen–eighteen, just after leaving Eton, when we were living in The Close, Salisbury, my

father a Lieutenant-Colonel in the Welch Regiment, Fielding also lived in
The Close just after leaving Eton, his father recently appointed Colonel
of the Regiment of Invalides (newly formed unit mostly made up from
Horse and Foot Guard veterans of Marlborough's campaigns). The Inval-
ides later became the 41st Foot, then the first battalion of the Welch
Regiment.

I was cheered by a letter from Bruce Hunter quoting enthusiastic
endorsement of *Miscellaneous Verdicts* from Dorothy Olding, my American
agent. She is going to offer this to Houghton Mifflin, none of my previous
US publishers having much to recommend them at the moment. However,
placing the book will be the thing, which I suspect may be difficult with
contemporary American publishers. Letter from an Iraqi living in Basrah:
'I would be most pleased if you would send me some of your books with
your nice dedication.'

Monday, 19 February

A Marathon day. Heavy rain all day. During the morning Octavio Rocca
rang to confirm coming tomorrow for the *Washington Post* interview. This
was followed by a call from Martin Cleever, Associated Press, taking photographs for the interview. After luncheon the telephone rang, which turned
out to be Lord Denning. Denning is one of those to speak about his
Henry Mee portrait on Channel 4 TV (others appear to be, in addition
to myself, the actor John Mills, Lord (Harold) Wilson, Daphne Park, head
of Somerville). Lord Denning wafted waves of genial egotism down the
line in accents of a stage peasant. He said the camera crew was on its way
to me now, that they were a very nice crowd, did I now live in Nunney? I
agreed I lived only a mile from Nunney. Lord Denning then related that
he had an ancestor called Newdigate Poyntz, a poet, who lived at Nunney
in a large house or castle, two or three centuries ago. He continued for
some time to ramble on about such themes. I must be one of the few
people in the country prepared to listen with comparative interest to this
sort of thing, and take it in sufficiently to pursue the matter further. In
short, Newdigate Poyntz does not figure in the *DNB*, nor any other biography available of literary men.

However, V and I, when the dust had settled, which was not much
less than forty-eight hours later, did trace something of the sort. Quite
extraordinary how people, even those of intelligence, love phoney gen-
ealogy, while hating the real thing. It turned out that the Poyntz family,
one of great antiquity (the Cliffords, including The Fair Rosamond, were

originally called Poyntz), at one stage intermarried with the Newdigates. Several of the Poyntz family were called Newdigate Poyntz, including one who lived at Nunney (b.*c.* 1740). No connexion shown with the Dennings, but that could have been through, say, an unrecorded second marriage, or simply unrecorded births. There also seemed to be illegitimate issue by the Duke of Cumberland. I found no record of any Poyntz living at Nunney Castle as Lord Denning alleged, when I told him there was a castle there). The castle had indeed been bombarded during the Civil Wars, therefore uninhabitable during the eighteenth century.

Lord Denning's call was followed by several from the driver of van bringing Henry Mee's picture, and the camera crew, as to how to get here. I warned the vanman that a big van should not come up the drive, which Henry himself had mentioned to them, when he saw earlier how huge the van was. Inevitably the most vast van ever seen did make its way up the drive, fortunately just managed to get out again without damage. A large camera crew, together with two scene-shifters for the picture, Henry himself in his very grand car. At first I did not greatly care for the general demeanour of the camera crew, but later came round to them rather more. The reason for this initial difference from usual camera crews that turn up here was, I think, revealed by a cameraman, whose name I asked, saying my son was TV producer, would like to know if cameraman was one he knew. The cameraman's name was Alan Florence. He replied: 'Oh, I'm just a newsman,' implying grander persons than he did documentaries and were the sort of cameramen Tristram would employ. This probably applied to the rest of crew.

Their technique was different from some, that is to say taking a long time to set up, then not bothering about changing the way I sat, which way I looked, something taking hours to settle with some crews. Two girls not bad either, Margaret (I do not remember surname), producer; Fiona Murch, interviewer. The latter said she was brought up in Nigeria. I asked: 'Was your father a DO?', which seemed to surprise her, the answer being affirmative. Quite attractive, with that slightly African look, loose limbs, even features, regions impose after some years, like Miranda Hayward developing a faintly Indonesian appearance after living there for seven years, previously plump Liverpool girl. The present girl referred to my 'rather naughty' captions, which I had not thought specially so.

The Mee portrait is far better in actuality than it looks in reproduction, really surprisingly so, coloured photographs distorting Mee's colour values more than most painters. I was greatly relieved by this. It is pretty big, not less than 5' × 4', I should say. Snook was much excited by all these people.

At one moment I carried him in for a shot, but I am so inured to cutting, myself only appearing for a split second, that Snook could well not appear. They seemed pleased with interview, even spoke of using some for 'Voice Over'. If all this appears on 22 May it would make a good moment for *Miscellaneous Verdicts*, supposed to be published on 21 May. V gave them all tea. Less tired at end of day than might have been expected, also happier about colour, composition of the portrait, really quite an impressive picture.

Tuesday, 20 February

Octavio Rocca, the *Washington Post* man, arrived about 10.30 a.m. with an Associated Press photographer, Martin Cleever, travelling together in Cleever's car, certainly the most sensible manner of coming, but usually beyond journalists' logistics to arrange. Rocca was of Spanish extraction, his long dark overcoat, black hair close to skull, only a cocked hat needed to make him a Goya *majo*, a bullfighter perhaps out of uniform. He is the paper's music critic, just returned from Russia, which he seemed heartily to have disliked, saying it was a great relief to taste English food again, even English weather, in fact drizzling, windy, but sentiments which sounded heartfelt. He was familiar, of course, with Constant Lambert's music, and seemed reasonably intelligent, knew my books (including the early ones) well. It will be interesting to see what he makes of the piece.

He said he was looking for a copy of *Afternoon Men*, as the germ of *Dance*, which he was bright enough to grasp. I said I would give him a copy, then found I did not possess one, so inscribed the English edition of *Wheel* for him, as having the Barbara Ker-Seymer jacket, an important feature. I was rather exhausted in the evening after two days of it.

I finished Walter Scott's *Collected Poems*, bought in Frome when doing *DT* feature on local second-hand bookshops. Reams of boring stuff, tho' one feels Scott *was* in his way a poet, and an attractive personality. There remains 'Look not thou on beauty's charming . . .', some of 'Marmion', 'Brignall banks are wild and fair', several others. Anyway Tennyson, Macaulay, Burns (perhaps a certain amount of vice versa with the last) helped themselves fairly liberally.

Saturday, 24 February

Timbermen were functioning the last two days. They made various muddles, including not returning the keys of Stoney Lane gate. The tree in the wood opposite the lake threatening the cable was dealt with, presumably by the Electricity or the Telecom people.

I reread *Midsummer Night's Dream*. Theseus and Hyppolita (Queen of the Amazons, captured by Theseus, if I remember right) enter in hunting dress to the sound of hunting horns. Hyppolita remarks something to the effect that she remembers a wonderful run she had with the Quorn (so to speak), with Hercules and Cadmus, when hounds gave tongue with just the same musical baying. One suspects this was deliberately put in by Shakespeare to raise a laugh from hunting members of the audience.

Tuesday, 27 February

Storms still, thunder in the night, a light fall of snow. V was going to London and wisely put that off. I finished a considerable Balzac read and reread. English paperbacks, French in small half-calf volumes belonging to my grandfather, Lionel Wells-Dymoke. One wonders what he made of them. He was not 'literary', but said to be fond of *Hudibras*. My own Balzac objective is to obtain a better grasp of the linked-characters side. I have never read enough in bulk to get the hang of these: *La Fille aux yeux d'or* (we have a copy with Conder illustrations); *La Duchesse de Langeais*, *Père Goriot*, *Les Treize*, *Les Illusions perdus*, *Eugénie Grandet*, *Ferragus* (Fr), *La dernière incarnation de Vautrin* (Fr), *Un Prince de Bohème* (Fr), *Les Comédiens sans le savoir* (Fr), *Un Ménage de garçon* (Fr), *Le Médecin de campagne* (Fr), *Gaudissart II* (Fr), *La Cousine Bette*, *Le Cousin Pons* (some of the untranslated novels have varied titles in same volume).

The chief impression left is Balzac's colossal vitality (he died at fifty-one, having written over ninety novels, not counting his other stuff). Apart from that, one is struck by the immense social impact of the Empire on France, ten years during which fortunes made, fantastic careers carved, by persons starting from nothing, thereby leaving a section of society unassimilated for at least a century. The linked characters are followed up in most of the novels, but quite unsystematically, producing utterly implausible situations (*La Fille aux yeux d'or*, Vautrin's adventures, and others are really fairy stories, at which Balzac is often at his best, all mixed up with meticulous financial descriptions, detailed accounts of how businesses like agricultural holdings are run).

Unlike Dickens, Balzac knew the ways people can make money. He is always good on technical, if often boring, details. On the other hand, he did not know about smart society; his great nobles, ladies of quality and dandies are often absurd to a degree. All the same, the overall effect is tremendously impressive, especially things like Vautrin's homosexuality, Cousine Bette's passion for Mme Marneffe, subjects which could not be written of quite openly, are enormously well handled. The 'good' people are always absurdly stupid in behaviour, everyone else (even allowing for taking a low view of human behaviour, which one certainly does) is perhaps rather over-scheming in their conscious evil. One feels the average person does not take so much trouble, as Balzac represents them doing, to swindle someone else; possibly more true in France.

When Balzac does punish his evildoers (he doesn't always, they often triumph) it is not enough to send them to prison, kill them, they have to die of some appalling disease known only, even then rarely, to negroes in South America. The theme of *Cousin Pons*, a poor man who builds up a marvellous collection of pictures (the sort of thing Balzac lets himself go on about, Titian, Rembrandt, Van Dyck), all swindled from him, is crude in the total imbecility of Pons's German friend Schmukke (extraordinary early nineteenth-century view of Teutonic simplicity and kindness). If less improbably conceived, this might have provided a good Henry James novel, a similar valuable collection made by the despised cousin of rich, grand Americans, who suddenly discover its worth, intrigue to get it against others (possibly Europeans), who have their eye on it, in fact Balzac's plot is more intellectually presented. Anyway a rewarding Balzac read.

Wednesday, 28 February

David Moore came round yesterday evening, pointing out that the poplar nearest to the garage is heaving ominously, might fall, do damage, so I took the car out. I rang Lang Brown early this morning, who was somewhat harassed by work in consequence of the hurricane. He will do what he can. Another interesting fan letter consequent on *Washington Post* piece from William Claire complaining about *Dance* not being on TV, suggesting he gets up protest against the BBC, picketing their Washington office. I wrote thanking for the letter. Lang Brown's men came, took down the poplar by the garage. That was just as well, because heavy gales followed. Patrick Taylor-Martin rang saying he was reviewing *Miscellaneous Verdicts* for the *Sunday Times*, asking for an interview for some other paper, he didn't yet know which. He will ring again in March or early April. An encouraging interest in the book.

Thursday, 1 March

Anne Lancaster rang to enquire the name of the gallery (Judd Street Gallery) where Virginia's show taking place. She said she was suffering from trees blown down in gales. In the afternoon James Knox came to talk about Robert Byron, whose life he is writing. I did not particularly look forward to this visit, as Robert was never a great favourite of mine, tho' one must admit him an unusual and forceful figure. I saw nothing of him in later stages of his life, so thought I should not have much to say. However, Knox turned out as unusually nice and intelligent, in short I thoroughly enjoyed talking with him. He runs the business side of the *Spectator*, but is now leaving to start up his own art company. An Etonian, thirty-seven, married (his wife née Owen, half a Heygate, the latter an amusing point).

Knox (a distant relation of Ronnie Knox) has been interested in Robert Byron for some time and thinks him a specially important figure in the architectural sphere. Various people (three, I think) wanted to write this biography, but were frozen off by Robert's sister, Lucy Butler, widow of Ewan Butler (and now wife of his cousin Rohan) who keeps guard over the Robert Byron archive. She has made a sort of museum of everything Robert bought. The Byron grandfather was apparently extremely rich, 10,000-acre property in Surrey, hideous Victorian house, never passed on to Robert's father for some reason, something going wrong. My feeling about Robert Byron is that he was certainly gifted, but hard to define exactly how.

There was a touch of Betjeman, an immensely strong personality, vastly ambitious, tuft-hunter, but unlike Betjeman always prepared to have a blood row on slightest provocation. Henry Yorke was greatly under Byron influence in early days. Henry told me that Robert was once in a cinema queue and some altercation took place with the man in front. Eventually the police were called in and Robert spent the night in the cells. He was anxious to keep the incident quiet. That was in the early 1930s, I think. James Knox has considerable charm. Pleasant afternoon.

Sunday, 4 March

I read in some paper that Kingsley Amis was dedicating his new book *The Folks that Live on the Hill* (Primrose Hill) to Peter Quennell, which at once aroused thought this might be to alleviate Quennell's own appearance in the novel. Perhaps an unworthy suspicion. Saw lorry marked SOUTHERN

BULK, no doubt some form of carrier, but one pictured Marseillaise female–procuress type.

Tuesday, 6 March

I reread *Treasure Island*. Like all novels with boy heroes (*Kidnapped, Kim*) it is impossible to avoid certain pederastic undertones, hard to know in Stevenson's case (as opposed to Kipling) how near the surface. Like Conrad, Stevenson is first-rate at describing action, while the plot itself lacks ingenuity and careful working out. For instance, the narrative is suddenly taken on from the Doctor's point of view, which could easily have been avoided, or, alternatively, used to explain how the stockade and plan of the hidden treasure were given up to the pirates, with whom some sort of a treaty was made. This is never made clear.

The blind man, Pew, is an excellent and original character. He is killed far too early on. That might have been avoided. Pew is well worth preserving as a sinister, implicitly homosexual figure; and a pity to lose him after devising so striking a personality. Long John Silver is said to be modelled on Stevenson's friend W. E. Henley. As a character Silver is not up to Pew, but also good. If the identification is true, one feels that Stevenson got off a few Old Friend scores *vis-à-vis* Henley. One notices extraordinary similarity in the manner of all Scots who write autobiographically (self-applauding), one wonders how much this is tradition (begun by Scott), how much due to national character. It seems to me that Pew and Long John Silver might well have been combined in one sinister blind figure.

Wednesday, 7 March

When I opened up the house this morning about 7.40 a.m., to my great surprise Snook on the doorstep. I had myself carried him to bed the night before, and earlier bolted the back door with two bolts, put up catch on the door of scullery. Bolts, remaining still drawn, had been forced without undue damage, the same with the catch of inner door. Drawers, cupboards, were all open in kitchen, scullery, nothing taken, not even the radio. Double-doors into dining-room (owing to the kitchen being a former chapel, one bolt up, one down) not attempted. I at once rang the police on 999. PC Isom arrived just before 8 a.m. and took notes; he said he was from Bristol. He remarked to my question: 'It's a rare name, said to be Greek.' He was a big man one could picture as an evzone.

On Monday, 5 March I had noticed bricks, stone, fallen away from a hump of ground outside the kitchen lying over the former domestic offices in the basement, leaving an open aperture through which a child, or animal, might have penetrated. The area known as the Minoan loo. This falling-away could have been caused by decay, wet, gale damage, but looked a bit as if assisted by the hand of man. I asked Mr Millard to plan repairs yesterday. It is now clear it was a try-out for burglarious entrance. There are three bolts to the door of the old kitchen leading to this area, also bolts to old kitchen door, two locks and a bolt to the door at the top of the stairs, but bolts don't seem much good.

About midday Scene-of-Crime Officer (SCO), Nick Pile, called with a mysterious box of gadgets to detect fingerprints etc. He took samples of splinters from doors. He somewhat resembled Derek Erskine at Goodhart's (Eton), with me, later a magnate in Kenya, where he appeared in the background of the Erroll murder. One felt Erskine might well have become an SCO had he been born into another world. Similar break-ins took place recently at Curry Rival and West Compton. Mr Millard's merry men arrived later in the day to renew bolts and fill up hole leading to basement. Mrs Lloyd was concerned that Snook's nerves might have been upset by felonious entry into kitchen.

Duncan Fallowell (who wrote piece about me in *Time Out*, repeated this in American *Vogue* or like glossy) rang for possible information about Alastair Graham, on whom he is writing piece for the *Daily Telegraph*. I used to see Graham in the Hypocrites my first term or two at Oxford, but never really knew him except as the acknowledged great love of Evelyn Waugh. He possessed Dresden shepherdess good looks, nothing much to say for himself it always seemed to me, possibly a type of narcissus incapable of dealing with anyone not in love with him. He retired in comparatively early life to a remote village in Wales where he died a year or two ago, after existence there as a hermit.

The publishers sent me the abridged volume of Virginia Woolf's *Diaries 1915–1941*, which I have been reading. What a dreadful woman she was, humourless, envious, spiteful, the embodiment of all the Victorian prejudices against which she was supposed to be in revolt, hating servants and 'poor people', while attending the Labour Party Conferences every year. She talked of the troops in army exercises of 1938 as 'idiotic young men playing soldiers on the Downs for which I am paying', while not showing herself exceptionally courageous when the Blitz was under way. She did latterly go so far as to express satisfaction when German aircraft were brought down. Of course all this can be excused by pleading that she was unhinged mentally.

One tries to be fair about her good points. David Cecil said she was agreeable to discuss books with, did not talk nonsense ('Hardy has genius but no talent', etc.). She never mentions any contemporary writer with approval except perhaps Eliot (laughing a good deal at him) who was not Bloomsbury. For instance, she never says a word about *Mr Norris*, although a friend of Isherwood's. She had a definite taste for queer young men. Although efforts have been made to pretend there was 'no such thing as Bloomsbury', she was always writing 'All Bloomsbury are here', 'He is anti-Bloomsbury', 'I hope Bloomsbury will', all the time trying to starve out any writer or painter who did not qualify as 'Bloomsbury'.

She had an extraordinary sense of personal social inferiority, yet her father had been a relatively distinguished man of letters, also her grandfather. The previous generation was captain of a trawler in the North of Scotland or something of that sort, which has a certain romance one might think. Uncongenial as the Duckworths were, her half-brother, the connexion was perfectly respectable so far as it went. She was abject to 'aristocrats', notably Vita Sackville-West (with whom, of course, she had a lesbian affair), tho' almost always spiteful about her, also any other upper-crust figure she came across, e.g. David Cecil himself.

All the same the *Diaries* are on the whole extremely good, readable, infinitely better than her novels. I have always thought this (her letters are also good), tho' one sees what she wanted to get away from in Bennett, Wells and Co., French realism in short. She herself lacked all sense of pattern in novel writing (even compared with such 'experimental' writers of the period as Proust or Joyce), she herself never progressing beyond material that does not rise much above (if at all) that of, say, E. M. Delafield, who really handles similar stuff better in an unpretentious manner.

As I had not read any Virginia Woolf novels for ages I took *The Waves* and *The Years* (both unread) out of the library. The former, to use a favourite word of her own, is twaddle. I can't imagine what Cyril Connolly was thinking about (just hedging his bets, I suppose) when he said in *Enemies of Promise* it was a masterpiece. In general Cyril did not hold a high opinion of Woolf novels, causing her always to refer to him as 'that little pimp Connolly'. *The Waves* has all the artificiality of a Compton-Burnett background, without any of the wit, willingness to grapple with real human problems, general grasp of novel-writing material. To do

Virginia Woolf justice she was very jealous of Ivy Compton-Burnett and did suspect how good she was.

The Years is more down to earth, but no one in their senses could suppose it a better novel than, say, The Old Wives' Tale, in spite of her patronizing attitude towards Bennett, who was touchingly humble to her. The Years characters are of the purest cardboard. The fact was she had not the slightest idea how other people lived or earned a living, but produced all the clichés, old colonels, sage dons, dignified dowagers, jolly schoolboy getting 'swished' (her term, Virginia Woolf was always rather keen to emphasize whipping). True, at one moment a man exposes himself (at least one assumes that was what happened), but in general no effort is made to record or narrate real, perhaps sinister, human problems, the whole thing vaguely tailing off into a more or less unsatisfactory fate for everyone concerned.

The abridgement of this Diary edition was done by someone other than the writer, so of necessity that gives a special view of the Diarist herself, tho' I doubt if it is a substantially incorrect one. There are first-rate glimpses of the English countryside, good exterior vignettes of individuals met (Vivien Eliot, Osbert Sitwell and Hugh Walpole), but one feels understanding never penetrated at all deep, nor was wished to do. Leonard Woolf does not sound particularly nice (he was fantastically stingy), among other things rude to servants 'because not a gentleman', his wife says. He was a good memoir writer and had an immense amount to put up with. One would say there is evidence that they certainly went to bed on several occasions, notwithstanding her dislike of sexual relations. She regrets that they might have had children 'if she had shown a little more self-control'. For instance, when on her birthday he 'slipped into my bed', giving her some present (incident she refers to many years later), also when she speaks of 'antics' at the end of one evening, when, I think, they had more than usual to drink. Presumably she was a virgin into her thirties. One is staggered to be reminded that, when she drowned herself, her body was not found for three weeks.

Thursday, 8 March

An amusing letter from Patrick Murphy enclosing a photograph of the drawing-room at The Elms, Melton Mowbray, my grandparents' house, with members of the Murphy and McCraith families (the latter relations of Mrs Murphy) in a group having tea. Presumably the house had been let or lent to them. The photograph might well have been taken by my great-grandfather, William Adcock, an early photographic enthusiast. 'Baba' McCraith, my grandfather's partner in the surgery, generally recognized as my grandmother's lover *en titre*, who married a Greek girl from Smyrna. Mr Murphy's letter reveals a Levant Consular/Indian Civil/ Medical Service world, throwing light on my grandparents' considerable foreign/overseas connexions. We have a signet ring bearing (I worked out from reference books) supposed McCraith/Magrath crest (a bird of some sort).

Friday, 9 March

Steve came from Mildav to put additional locks and bolts on the doors.

Saturday, 10 March

Evangeline Bruce rang. She is returning to the US and hopes to come here during the summer. She had seen the piece about me in the *Washington Post*, which she did not think particularly good. I told her I was like Conrad, who said he took a footrule to what was written about him, rather than reading it. Evangeline said she thought an American writer, Larry McMurtry, funny, not everyone did. He got the Pulitzer Prize and she recommended him rather hesitantly.

V, John and I lunched with Tessa and Joff Davies at Whatley House for the traditional party celebrating Tessa's and V's birthday on 13 March. I gave Tessa the Italian translation of *Venusberg* as she likes reading Italian. Lucinda present without husband, John Sunnucks, who has broken his collar-bone by fall from a horse out hunting. Mary Anne and Richard Charrington, Michael and Isobel Briggs. Michael Briggs told me Monet had been a member of Beefsteak Club, put up by Whistler, Sargent. Luncheon local catering: crab mousse, beefsteaks, two sorts of pudding, fizz as aperitif (did not partake), white wine, Chianti (latter V and I slightly aware of the following day). Pleasant party.

Monday, 12 March

Marvellous spring afternoon. Later John Rush, of Higham, rang, saying a new man doing *Desert Island Discs* wanted me to do a repeat (previous choice perhaps twenty years ago). I agreed, provided recording was done here. Rush also said he hoped soon to announce an offer from Thames TV to do *Dance*. This is cheering, tho' I replied that I was like a woman who had been seduced so often with promise of marriage that I now despaired of ever coming to the altar, at least very sceptical about it. We celebrated V's birthday (tomorrow) with caviar, Bollinger '83 (given by Heinemann, for my own last birthday).

Tuesday, 13 March

V's seventy-eighth birthday. I gave her gloves bought by John to her instruction. Georgia is over from Oxford for a night. She has plans to ski at a French resort, while reading Plato. I supposed Frome is the last resort of miniskirt, but they seem to hold out in Oxford too, notoriously home of impossible loyalties. We had Breton smoked chicken for dinner, with Château Gressier Grand Poujeaux, Moulis '79, which Archie gave me last birthday, not too bad, less body than might be expected from age, pleasant, slightly astringent aftertaste, I think tannin.

I reread the *Collected Poems* of George Herbert. One gets a shade tired of all of them being devotional on just the same note, even if the high standard struck is always maintained. Herbert is usually regarded as superior to Henry Vaughan, whom I greatly prefer, anyway at Vaughan's best ('I saw Eternity the other night', 'My soul there is a country', 'They are all gone into the world of light'). Having recently linked my Vaughan ancestors to the main line (even if probably illegitimately) the Tretower branch, the poet's, can be included as distant relations: I'm not saying Herbert isn't pretty good:

> Lovely enchanting language, sugarcane,
> Honey of Roses, whither wilt thou fly?

also:

> Lay out thy joy, yet hope to save it?
> Would'st thou both eat thy cake and have it?

Was Herbert the first to ask that extremely pertinent question?

Friday, 16 March

Modern Painters arrived, containing my piece about sitting for various painters, including Henry Mee, whose portrait was to be reproduced, together with ones by John, Lamb, Moynihan, for comparison, Henry's intended to be of larger size than the others. By some brilliant editorial muddle they managed to make the large portrait, supposedly of me, that of the PRA, Roger de Grey, putting a small of myself on the following page as de Grey. I rang Henry to tell him of this and got an answering service, so he is probably away. I don't particularly mind, as obviously the large portrait is of a different person from three small ones, but it does seem a piece of incompetence. I wonder what de Grey thinks.

Tuesday, 20 March

I reread Kingsley Amis's new novel *The Folks that Live on the Hill*, which John tells me is name of a jazz tune, used here by Kingsley for his neighbours on Primrose Hill, round the corner from which Kingsley lives in Regent's Park Road, a residence I have not visited. I laughed aloud once or twice; Kingsley is never boring, tho' approaching that in *Difficulties with Girls*, on which this is a slight improvement, tho' nothing like as good as *The Old Devils*. The book rather tails off, without much construction, vaguely sentimental, happyish ending.

Wednesday, 21 March

Adrian Andrews asked if he could put up a (movable) shelter for his lambs, about thirty feet long, by wall on west of Park Field, probably near opening into next field going west. I saw no great objection. Farm buildings are on the whole inoffensive, anyway this one would not be permanent. I consulted Mr Joyce, who will write letter to Andrews covering conditions when arranging for the grass-feed contracts next month. I informed Adrian Andrews.

Saturday, 24 March

A curious fan letter from John Larrett, who was rereading *Dance*. During this period he took his two terrier bitches, German and Daisy, for a walk one evening, losing Daisy in a copse. He thought she had got stuck in a rabbit hole, but it was getting dark, so he had to come home. He was worried because Daisy had young puppies, with which his wife sat up all night. He retired to bed with *Hearing Secret Harmonies*. Almost at once he came on the incident of Mr Gauntlett losing his bitch, Daisy, and being told by Murtlock to seek her in the spinney. Mr Larrett felt all would be well. He slept for five hours, rose at first light, and went to the copse from which Daisy immediately ran out on his calling her.

I reread *As You Like It*, probably my favourite among the Comedies, although (in spite of championing Shakespeare's clowns against many attackers) I don't find Touchstone very funny. What tremendous camping about must have taken place with Rosalind, played by a boy, then dressed as a man, but telling Orlando to pretend she is Rosalind and make lover's speeches to her. Then she faints when told that Orlando has been mauled by a lion. How extraordinary Shakespeare was about the names he gave his characters. Having designed a somewhat stylized character called Jacques, a melancholy man, who is a distinct feature of the play, Shakespeare then brings in a third son of Sir Roland de Boys, calling him Jacques too.

Friday, 30 March

I sent Mr Patrick Murphy (who appears to be Baba McCraith's great-nephew, is also descended from Baba's sister, in fact two McCraith relationships) the signet ring with the McCraith/Magrath crest, which undoubtedly belonged to Baba McCraith, possibly a token given by him to my grandmother (who always referred to him as Băbă rather than Băbă). A white hare, with a few black markings, was sitting or loping round the house for several days (a Mad March Hare?).

Sunday, 1 April

V, John and I watched the Tristram-produced TV film *Kremlin Farewell*, written by Nigel Williams (a young man who interviewed me some years ago about Orwell). The plot: the son of Bukharin, an old Bolshevik executed by Stalin, is sent to an orphanage, but eventually manages to get away. The boys were excellently played by British schoolboys. Nigel Williams is said to be Left, but this could scarcely be more effective anti-Socialist propaganda, except that Bukharin himself was made to look like a matinée idol, rather than an infinitely cunning terrorist with a small beard. The Russian scenes shot in this country were convincing. It must have needed a lot of producing/directing, as dependent on presentation, rather than dialogue or situations.

Friday, 6 April

An advance copy of *Miscellaneous Verdicts* arrived. It seems all right, at least I didn't immediately open it on a misprint as one usually does. V answered the front door to Mr Moss, itinerant repairer of drives. She said, 'Oh, it's

Mr Moss, isn't it?' 'Yes,' he replied, 'tall, dark and handsome.' I told him to do £100 worth of work on the drive, where heavy vehicles have cracked surface. This seems to have been effected satisfactorily.

Tuesday, 10 April

Archie with two friends, Daniel Barraclough (Warwick), Justin Abbot (Lincoln, Oxon), were at The Stables yesterday. Archie is apparently staying about a week, the friends uncertain.

I reread *The Folks that Live on the Hill*, which V says is an exploration of the mini-cab civilization. It really is not good, Kingsley is never exactly boring, but the writing is dreadfully slipshod, determination not to be pretentious developing into a form of pretentiousness.

Bob Conquest rang in the evening, on his way to Russia with Liddie, a TV assignment. I asked what he will do. Bob said: 'Stand in front of the Winter Palace, say: "This is the Winter Palace".' He has been suffering from a spinal nerve, painful, now a bit better. He is writing an article on Lenin for *Isvestia*.

Wednesday, 11 April

As nothing has been heard for a month, I rang John Rush to ask if any movement had taken place on the part of Thames TV. As always, some hitch, in this case the basis nerves about the TV Bill going through in two years. This is thought to threaten commercial companies by putting the industry up to the highest bidder, accordingly only rubbish likely to be provided. A producer interested in *Dance*, Abrahams, did Olivia Manning's *Fortunes of War*, which I thought far from exciting, chiefly because the novel itself lacked form after the beginning. Also its supposedly funny White Russian (main character) was immensely unfunny. I asked John if doing the first half, then the second, had been suggested. It had, also a third at a time. I prefer the former to doing the whole thing right away. Three is also worth considering. As usual one can only hope for the best. My own keenness on TV showing, which might well be mediocre, even bad, is the importance of effect on ordinary book sales. TV is almost a necessity nowadays for establishing a novel like *Dance*. I have, curiously enough, a feeling the situation might recover.

Archie came to luncheon. I gave him a pair of spats I dug out the other day, which I thought might be useful for P. G. Wodehouse parts. In fact

Archie may use them for playing Autolycus in *The Winter's Tale*, which rôle he is sustaining at Warwick.

I read two volumes of Theocritus (also contained a little Bion and Moschus), translated by Andrew Lang, with frightful illustrations by Russell Flint, Medici Press cardboard covers, etc., an Eton Prize. It seemed a production of untold beauty at time of choosing. I didn't much care for Theocritus, from which all the worst sort of Amaryllis stuff seems to derive. I reread Arthur Mizener's *Twelve Great American Novels*, picked up by chance. Arthur's criticism on the whole is extremely competent and well expressed, when he deals with good writers (tho' I can never take Faulkner, whom he thinks the best American writer of twentieth century), with such as Cozzens, Warren. I suppose Arthur's patriotism as an American gets in the way, exaggerating their attainments.

Good Friday, 13 April

Tristram came up before dinner. He talked of his new Michael Palin film (a forebear of Palin's, an Oxford don, married an American girl and had to give up his Fellowship, dons not being allowed to marry in 1860s). This is to be 'for the big screen', rather exciting, because, if success, goes everywhere, after being tried at, say, the Curzon, then TV. Tristram is just back from New York, which he had enjoyed. Archie borrowed several Milton books for his work. I gave him a leather-bound *Collected Milton* (1858), of unknown provenance.

Monday, 16 April

Joff and Tessa Davies, Richard and Mary Anne Charrington, Tristram, Virginia, Georgia, to drinks midday. We talked of the supposed nuclear gun held up by the British Customs on the way to Iraq. Joff (his subject) said undoubtedly something fishy about the careful working of the barrel, possibly satellite, rather than rocket-launcher.

I asked Richard Charrington, as a regular soldier, whether when the Last Post is played at funerals, having stood to attention, that position ceases on the change to Reveille. He said he was uncertain, Lancers reversed their lances during former, reverted to normal at the latter. He thought it safer to remain at attention. He described something as 'too surreal for words'; shades of the Victorian cavalryman. Later Gerry Bowden with daughter Kate, lunching at The Stables, dropped in for tea. Gerry is an extremely nice man, one of the few MPs who rises above that difficult condition. He said some recently created peer, uncertain which door to go through at division, asked the peer in front of him, Lord Salisbury, who replied: 'Well, all the Bishops have gone through the other one, so probably we'd better go through this.'

Wednesday, 18 April

Patrick Taylor-Martin, who is reviewing *Miscellaneous Verdicts* for the *Sunday Times*, asked for an interview. He was staying with a friend at Rode near here. Aged thirty-five, looks somewhat older. He is a slightly untidy version of the actor Peter Bowles, who was in *Afternoon Men* years ago, now celebrated for playing gents, cads, a nice man, if not always specially convincing in these rôles.

Taylor-Martin chattered away and appeared fairly bright. He had read everything in the way of modern fiction, this making V think him to possess touch of Maclaren-Ross, perhaps also conveyed by his double-barrel, making a living off reviewing, literary odds and ends. He said he thought *Agents and Patients* would make a first-rate TV film. I agree, indeed . somewhat because the *Beyond the Fringe* crowd actually negotiated about that, but what a hope.

It turned out he had an ambition to do 70,000-word book about me, possibly for Viking-Penguin, for which he appears to work. I told him Bruce Hunter (whom he knows) recently asked if I wanted to do a book of that length about Sachie Sitwell (refused), which interested Taylor-Martin, who had met Sachie and would like to write about him. He said he would make enquiries as to whether some such series was in process of formation, possibly offer a piece on me if that were so. I did not discourage this, in case worse befall in the way of biographers in that sort of line (as has happened in the past). A short thing for the British Council, students and others, might not be undesirable.

He said he thought Peter Quennell had been staying at Weston when Sachie died (*aet.* ninety-one or so). Sachie had large photograph of his wife, Georgia, and Pearl Argyle (both dcd) in the drawing-room; also Moira Shearer, but his housekeeper, who treated him latterly more or less as a child, made him take Moira Shearer away.

Archie came to dinner. He had written essays on Milton and Lorca. As it happened I read Lorca's poems in translation a short time ago. I can't say I really made much sense of him. Endive in ham was good; Château Bernard Raymond '79, not put forward as specially interesting, except as ordinary drinkable wine eleven years old.

Thursday, 19 April

The Catalan translation of *A Question of Upbringing/Buyer's Market* in one volume arrived, to appear in series *Great Twentieth-Century Novels*. This does not prejudice the whole sequence appearing in Spanish or Catalan.

Hugh Montgomery-Massingberd for the *Sunday Telegraph* interview. He came by taxi from Bath or Westbury, bringing a present of a bottle of Moët et Chandon '83, and three large packets of smoked salmon. It was really very kind, one can only hope set down to expenses. We had a glass of sherry and he then gave us luncheon at the Bridge House. Hugh's appetite is renowned. I was therefore anxious that enough to eat should be provided. Hugh had Creole soup, beef and mushroom pie, gooseberry crumble, so with a couple of slices of plum cake at tea one hopes he kept from fainting before reaching the restaurant car on the way back. We had usual glass of wine or two at the Bridge House, white or red to taste.

Hugh in great form, produced much amusing gossip. The memoirs of the cartoonist Nicholas Garland (some such title as *Only a Few Killed*) has been widely reviewed, always with hints of spiteful recording there of colleagues' remarks, tho' never revealing what actually said. Even Hilary Spurling did not more than indicate that.

Hugh spoke of the Spencers' house Althorp, pronouncing it 'Althrop'. I said: 'You can confirm it's called that, can't you, because I always supposed so, then someone insisted the other day it was pronounced as spelt.' Hugh said it was indeed called that in the past, but he alleged that the present Lord Spencer, bowing to the public that visits the house, has thrown in the sponge, calls it Althorp; for the same reason the Duke of Bedford has ceased to call Woburn 'Woo-burn', as traditionally pronounced.

Friday, 20 April

Three ladies from the sub-contractors of English Heritage came to see storm damage, take notes about history of the house, grounds, grottoes, etc. Firm called Task Force Trees, Jane Wade (more or less in charge), Lara Holmes (trees as such), Tess Canfield (history), last apparently American, cat fan, liked my Memoirs giving account of house (also our cats). V showed them round. All impressed by the place, grottoes. I do not despair of getting some sort of grant.

Monday, 23 April

William Leith came for an interview for *Tatler*. He proved quite bright and asked sensible questions. He had been at Warwick University (of which he gave a favourable account). Then went on to Corpus, Cambridge. He said he reread *Afternoon Men* every year. This greatly cheered me, combined with Patrick Taylor-Martin speaking well of *Agents and Patients*, as one likes to feel those early numbers are not utterly forgotten. Leith said he wanted to talk to someone who knew me, so I put him in touch with Henry Mee, about whose show he might also say something.

I am struck by the difficulty of estimating the abilities of those who come to do interviews. As often as not I make an entirely wrong judgement. For instance, I supposed the character called Rocca from the *Washington Post* was reasonably intelligent, but his piece turned out of the utmost banality. The Congressman sent it (Rocca has not, up to date, as promised), who said he heard it had been 'loused up' by editors. My chief objection is being represented as using the ludicrous word 'gay' for homosexual (which I'm told American queers themselves dislike now), a term I abhor. I suppose no US paper dares use the word 'queer'. What a craven race they can be in such respects. On second thoughts perhaps we are just as bad, or anyway becoming so rapidly.

Tuesday, 24 April

V and I lunched with Lees and Mary Mayall at Sturford, where Anne Hill (née Gathorne-Hardy, widow of the Mayfair bookseller Heywood Hill) is staying. She had recently been in motor smash (her own fault, she said), accordingly pretty decrepit, tho' V thought less silent than usual, a characteristic shared with her late husband. Alex Mayall (who has suddenly become rather large) was also present, helping with cooking. She disappeared from time to time. She alleged that she could tell from outward appearance that Ferdie Mount lived in North London; Tristram in South.

Thursday, 26 April

I made a curry for a luncheon party of eight persons: Pamela Harlech, Selina Hastings, Anthony Hobson, Vidia and Pat Naipaul, John (who helped with odds and ends like salad). Anthony (leaving for Venice tonight by car) arrived rather early. He said Pamela Harlech's father was a high-powered lawyer representing Park-Bernet, auctioneers of New York, now more or less merged with Sotheby's. Selina (whom we asked to 'bring' Pamela Harlech) is off to Hawthornden next week to write her book on Evelyn Waugh. She said David Holloway (who saw the MS for serial publication) remarked that Hilary Spurling's *Paul Scott* was the best biography he had ever read. Pamela Harlech has a distinct look of Pam Berry. We put her next to Vidia, who was in great form and gave her tremendous lecture on all sorts of subjects. He is off to Czechoslovakia almost immediately.

I opened the magnum of Santenay '83 Ferdie Mount gave me for Christmas, also Tristram's burgundy (Nuits St Georges '85), having some doubts as to whether the magnum would be enough for seven persons (John not drinking). On the contrary nearly half a bottle was left over, everyone consuming so much less these days than they used, partly, I suppose, owing to age, partly more care taken about drink-driving. Vidia had come in his new car. Good party.

Rather appropriately in the light of the Harlech marriage (Pamela apparently finding David Harlech's taste for racing a trifle unsympathetic), I finished Edith Wharton's *The Buccaneers* (1938), her last (uncompleted) novel, which she seems to have played about with for some years. I admire Edith Wharton at her best, which is an extremely able best. This, however, is far from her best, possibly always the case when she is not dealing with Americans. The theme is girls, not of what Mrs Wharton herself would regard as 'good' families, although rich, who marry English noblemen in the 1870s. The American opening is all right (though one must remember one is not American, so hard to judge, and Henry James used to demur at his friend Edith's novels (tho' that may have been jealousy, from which James certainly suffered).

When the author gets to England it all becomes terribly stylized, both favourably and unfavourably, the beautiful old houses their owners have lived in since time immemorial and aristocratic stiffness of manners. One doesn't doubt there was a lot of stiffness, but hardly as she presents it. The potentially intellectual young American, Nan, marries the Duke of Tintagel, who is looking for a bride not hoping to entrap him as a duke. He is under the sway of his conventional mother and the marriage does not go well.

Mrs Wharton planned Nan was to run away with the only son of a baronet, in an early version a Guardsman; in actual book he has made some money in Brazil, where they would presumably go after elopement. Although Mrs Wharton knows her British social stuff up to a point, there is much stereotyping of English aristocrats and society, among other things surprisingly objecting to American high spirits, boisterousness, in such things as dancing a dance called the Virginia Reel. But surely horseplay is one of the objections that might be levelled at *British* society of that or later periods? Had she, for instance, never seen Sir Roger de Coverley danced at a Hunt Ball? Of course Edith Wharton was getting on in age, shows the dangers of writing novels when the author is growing out of touch.

Monday, 30 April

A big, rather inarticulate young photographer, Andrew Crowley (one felt certainly no relation to The Beast 666), half-Irish, half-Cornish, his grandfather a fisherman, came for the *Sunday Telegraph* picture. He had the virtue of taking only three-quarters of an hour.

I reread *Romeo and Juliet*. 'O, here's wit of cheveril [kid leather] that stretches from an inch narrow to an ell broad.' Yet another indication that the writer's father was a glove-maker? I find the scene funny where the Nurse's man, Peter, has a row with the musicians. Indeed I can't understand people who say Shakespeare is never funny, tho' admit I don't care for Touchstone. I also reread a classical anthology translation *Voices of the Past* (ed. James and Janet Maclean Todd). When given Hon. D. Litt. at Oxford, the Chancellor, Harold Macmillan, compared my work with Menander's. There is an extract from one of Menander's plays here about a malicious slave who unsuccessfully attempts to put his master against his wife. I suppose this could be fitted into my works *mutatis mutandis*.

Tuesday, 1 May

Penny Perrick, Fiction Editor of the *Sunday Times Book Supplement*, came for an interview in afternoon. As her mother, Eve Perrick, had some name as journalist (*Daily Express*, I think) we expected a career-woman type; on the contrary slightly comic appearance that is also attractive, with fluff of hair, not bad looking, baby-doll voice. She knew my books well, including *Aubrey*, having said a word about the paperback and reviewed *The Album*. She, too, had seen Hilary Spurling's *Paul Scott* MS, also thought it brilliant ('very scandalous'), recommended it for *Sunday Times*. Interesting to see who gets it.

Penny Perrick had views of her own, which is always refreshing, liking neither *The Raj Quartet* nor the same as TV *The Jewel in the Crown*. She spoke of my having remarked that when I appeared on the London scene

'all articulate young men were writing a novel'. She said nowadays that is
no longer the case, young people are not interested in the arts, but politics.
No doubt true, though such things are always to some extent taking place
underground unknown to world at large; that the young men of the
Twenties who were writing novels accepted fact only in circles where that
was taking place.

Thursday, 3 May

One of the three English Heritage ladies (Jane Wade) rang last night to
say the organization might make a grant up to fifty per cent for hurricane
damage in January. This is cheering news. I asked her to confirm on paper.
Today I alerted Lang Brown (in fact Mrs LB) to extract the big oak from
lake. V says that, if analogy of *Macbeth* is followed, Birnam Wood is being
taken away *from* Dunsinane, rather than reverse.

Bob Conquest rang. He had just returned from Russia. Indescribably
bad food, discomfort, but he himself was much lionized. In one place the
KGB man gave a girl in the crowd his camera, saying: 'Take me standing
beside Robert Conquest.' Bob was shown scenes of various violent events
like the murder of Rasputin, Kirov, tho' he did not quite manage to get
inside the Lubyanka. I told him to take care next time, when he does
get in, they don't shut the door (as they did on the Polish officers visiting
Russia 'on his honour as a soldier' of Marshal Zhukov during the war).
Bob wanted to get someone on the telephone (no Leningrad telephone
book, of course), after a Russian girl tried a block of flats for ages. She
told him he must either give exact number of flat in the block, or, alternatively, the date of the person's birth. Liddie said she felt like the slave in
the chariot of the man having a Roman Triumph reminding him that he
was mortal. There was a fearful shortage of petrol. Bob asked why that was.
He was told it was all being smuggled into Lithuania.

We watched some of the TV film of Bruce Chatwin's *On the Black Hill*.
The opening scenes in Radnorshire were not too bad. Gemma Jones is
always good, one noticed her at once, as a parson's daughter who marries
a farmer. I was, however, much struck, when 'Cwm Rhondda' was played,
the farmer represented as black Welshman. How very different the Radnorshire people really are from that sort of Welshness. It is always said that
the Welsh regard Radnor as English, the English as Welsh. That does not
come out in the film – or rather was missed. General effect of the whole
was not particularly striking. I always feel there was something a bit phoney
about Chatwin.

Friday, 4 May

Author's copies of *Miscellaneous Verdicts* went to Roy Jenkins, Roy Fuller, Hilary Spurling, Anthony Hobson, Tessa Davies, Roland Gant. A letter of thanks arrived from Rupert, which indicated, I was glad to know, they had gone out. Rupert is writing his autobiography.

Tuesday, 8 May

I returned my claim to English Heritage for tree grant, also notified Peter Mumford this had been done. Christopher (Simon) Sykes, with his remembered silent retainer, Wayne Vincent, arrived in the afternoon for *Tatler* photographs. CSS is bigger than I recalled, with that slightly awkward air that gradually works off, so that one finds him very agreeable. He took a lot of photographs. Some of me, some of both of us, one with a billiard cue. I felt rather guilty about that, as I haven't played slosh for years, tho' admittedly used to do so. Sykes said he might use those that did not appear in *House and Garden*, copy of which he had not, in fact, seen and we showed him.

He is a friend of Hugh Massingberd, of whom he told various stories relating to Hugh's prodigious appetite. They went to Scarborough together, where Hugh was ravished by rows of whelk stalls, which he cleared out, also eating a whole lobster. On some occasion Hugh, on journalistic location, caught a tropical intestinal complaint in Africa and had to starve for twelve days. He asked Christopher Sykes to celebrate luncheon with him coming out of this state. Apparently Hugh and his wife Caroline (never met, as it happens) always eat out and watch a lot of TV, the box being rigged up above their bed, on which they have to lie to do this. The photographers left about 5 p.m. A shade exhausting.

Wednesday, 9 May

A letter from Roy Fuller thanking for *Verdicts*. He is in bed awaiting 'tests'. In that somewhat similar connexion I saw Southwood. OK, in fact he said I need not come again unless something amiss. He was at his most Widmerpoolish. His initials are WFWS. Could the two Ws both stand for Widmerpool? I was much relieved at this clearance, as going there always hangs over one a week or two before.

In the afternoon Sally Soames came to photograph me for the *Sunday Times*. As Emma Soames, daughter of the late Christopher Soames, edits

Tatler, the name suggested some connexion in glossy paper world, turned
out a little woman in trousers, mackintosh, gym shoes, with slight air of
the Near East or suchlike. She arrived about ten minutes before the stated
time, 2.30 p.m., out of the house by 3 o'clock, something to be applauded.
All the time she kept up a patter of rapid-fire talk, rather like a fortune-
teller. She said she had son of twenty-seven, who was going bald ('You
have much more hair than he has'), tho' she sometimes told people he
was only twenty. She had photographed for the *Sunday Times* for twenty-
four years. So she must have been in her early fifties, tho' hardly looked
that.

   She talked about various people she had photographed. I asked if she
had done Kingsley Amis, who was a friend of mine. She made a face. So
far as I could gather she had photographed Kingsley twice for the *Sunday
Times*, then was sent to photograph him for his publisher. She arrived too
early (her estimate four minutes, Kingsley's twelve), so he told her to go
away until right time. She then made enquiries, found her watch was fast,
Kingsley's must be slow. Returned, told him this, an altercation took place,
resulting either in her walking away, or Kingsley slamming the door, which,
not altogether clear. Anyway, Kingsley is alleged to say he will never again
be photographed by a woman. Kingsley (several people have remarked
lately) has begun to look oddly like Evelyn Waugh. He now seems to be
behaving rather like Evelyn too. One wonders where it will all end. When
Sally Soames left (she had kept her taxi) she kissed me, saying: 'Thank
you for being so nice.'

Friday, 11 May

A woman called Mrs Denning rang the *Telegraph*, asking if I could tell her
anything about Gerald Reitlinger, as she was having a show of his pictures.
Some girl then took her number and passed it on to me, instead of giving
her mine, or just telling her to write. I rang the number, inevitably Mrs
Denning was out. Place apparently the Halkin Gallery in Halkin Arcade.
Mrs Denning rang me in due course. I told her such information as I had
about The Squire was in my Memoirs. She seemed quite uninterested in
this and said they had an Introduction to catalogue already. Did I know
where all the Reitlinger pictures were? Anyway, she had no time for further
material about the painter himself, as the show was coming on in June.
Why she should suppose I knew where all The Squire's pictures were I
cannot imagine. She said she understood some were 'in the Caribbean'.

In the circumstances it seems rather late in the day to enquire about the pictures.

It would appear the show being put on at short notice by the Ashmolean. Possibly something of the sort was conditional to inheritance of the Reitlinger ceramics. Mrs Denning sounded rather as if her interest in the subject was waning. One sees it all as typical of The Squire's unhappy stars pursuing him beyond the grave: muddle, unsatisfactory arrangements, even a certain lack of geniality.

There have been several reviews in the papers of a biography of Tom Driberg. They made me reflect on the fact that I knew him on and off for a long time and could never see the point of him, except as undoubtedly grotesque figure. Most people found him amusing, or were appalled by him. I first set eyes on Driberg my last term at Oxford when someone took me to a party of his at The House. They described him as 'a most bogus man'. I had drunk a good deal and remember nothing about the party, nor Driberg.

Then Edith Sitwell hailed him as a promising poet, who was earning a living as a waiter in Soho (I think). Thence he graduated to being 'William Hickey', gossip writer of the *Daily Express*, of which he more or less laid the foundation and made a success. We were always on perfectly good terms, indeed I believe he put in something about *Afternoon Men*, to give the book a boost, for which one was naturally grateful. Constant Lambert thought him amusing and used sometimes to talk about him. Evelyn Waugh had been at Lancing with him (tho' appreciably older in school terms), which to some explains their relationship, but Malcolm Muggeridge (who might be supposed to hold Driberg as frenetic homosexual, extreme Leftist, in utter horror) easily tolerated him, I suppose as a 'good journalist' and politico. In short, a great many intelligent people thought Driberg amusing, which I never could see. Had I disliked him that would obviously have been another matter. He was always perfectly civil.

At a much later date, when doing a radio programme on Constant Lambert, he lunched here (brought down by a BBC character, Derek Dreischer, Roy Plomley's retainer on *Desert Island Discs*). It was a stiflingly hot day. Driberg, who did not look at all well, was covered with flies at luncheon. Again we got on all right, but he asked questions of the utmost banality, never produced anything of the faintest interest; one would have thought almost an impossibility for someone who had seen much of Constant. Perhaps Driberg's boringness was really the secret of his success. Driberg himself died soon after. V always said she suspected we had contributed to his decease by that luncheon, with the heat and flies.

While on the subject of supposedly amusing intelligent persons for whom everyone fell (using the phrase both sexually and merely intellectually, socially) I would add Goronwy Rees. True, I never knew Rees at all well, but him too I came across occasionally. Again we got on perfectly well. Why, for example, did F. M. Montgomery immediately pick out Goronwy when on his staff, ask him to come in in the evening to talk. One cannot see. Maurice Bowra also somewhat fascinated by Rees. In these examples one may be up against homosexuality, either admitted or crypto, and of course Rees undoubtedly attractive to women. I find Driberg and Rees interesting as usually one sees just what fascinates people in adventurers of that kind, even when not in the smallest degree susceptible oneself.

Wednesday, 16 May

Sarah Bradford came to talk about Sachie Sitwell, whose biography she is writing (not the 70,000-word job regarding which I was recently approached). I reviewed a readable book by her about Cesare Borgia some twenty years ago. She is an attractive blonde in her middle forties. Her own information, together with later research, revealed that she was née Hayes (daughter of a brigadier). Her first husband, Anthony Bradford, lived in Lisbon (which she greatly liked), doing some work connected with American PR. V remembers meeting her, then heavily pregnant, at dinner with the Mayalls, when Lees was *en poste* there.

Her second husband, William Ward, is heir to Lord Bangor. The latter (Lord Bangor), V says we met dining with Arthur Duckworth at Orchardleigh some years ago, Bangor then married to his fourth wife. I have no recollection of this. Sarah Bradford met Sachie once or twice in the 1960s. She said it was thought that some of his loves (such as Pearl Argyle, Bridget Parsons, one or two others) had been consummated, but no one seemed to know which, or for certain. Also there is divided opinion as to whether Sachie greatly resented Georgia's goings-on, or did not care a damn (more correctly dam, a small Indian coin). One of Georgia's boyfriends, known as The Copper, was a Chief Constable.

I asked if the Duke of Westminster (Bendor) was keen on Georgia, as Sachie Sitwell used to stay with him and go on trips. Sarah Bradford said the general view was that Georgia supposed so, in fact the Duke liked talking to Sachie, having an unexpected intellectual strain. I have heard this before. Most of Sachie's letters are in Texas and her visit there is contemplated with apprehension owing to the expense. At present no grant is on offer and large sales certainly unlikely. I was not able to produce much, but we had quite an enjoyable talk, as Sarah Bradford is bright. She complained she was insufficiently clued up about Sachie's poems, for that matter his prose (as well she might be, both obscure enough). In the contemporary Sitwell family all is much as ever, periods of no one friendly, no one being on speaking terms with any of the others.

Sarah Bradford also wrote a book about George VI, who had an affair (probably his introduction to sex) with an actress, Phyllis Monkman, whom I well remember seeing when young in musical comedies (*The Co-optimists*, etc.). She is now dead. Her brother has a collection of jewellery given her by the Duke of York, including a miniature of himself in a small leather case.

Sarah Bradford used to write accounts of auction sales of books for the *TLS*, which I remember thinking rather good. She was then sacked by the then editor 'in a tantrum', as she said, about her 'mentioning another newspaper'.

Thursday, 17 May

Roland and Nadia Gant, on the way to stay with the thriller writer James Leasor before returning to France, looked in this afternoon. They had been in Russia (I think doing research on this book they are writing together), bearing out the awfulness of the food being beyond words, otherwise enjoyable. They attended the Heinemann Centenary Party, 700 guests, crowds of people, even Tom Rosenthal scarcely able to get in. One cannot imagine what Roland does on the top of a mountain miles away from publishing gossip, which was his whole life.

Friday, 18 May

I received a letter from Jeremy Treglown apologizing for having sent *Miscellaneous Verdicts* to 'a reviewer who wasn't as enthusiastic as I [Treglown] would have been myself'. The *TLS* arrived on the breakfast table under his letter, so it was revealed that the reviewer in question was P. N. Furbank, who wrote a book about E. M. Forster, also edited Forster's Letters (I can't remember whether or not the latter have appeared). When Furbank appealed for Forster letters I sent my Forster note apologizing for workmen making a row in his flat (under mine at 26 Brunswick Square). I remember that although this was utterly trivial, sometimes such odds and ends provided information about dates. (Forster might have mentioned fancying a workman in his flat, on which this would have thrown light.) I did not add the latter, but did say that although I did not care for Forster's novels, I thought Furbank had written an excellent biography.

In his review of *Verdicts* Furbank grumbled that I thought Forster, Virginia Woolf and D. H. Lawrence overrated, accused me of pomposity, also of 'pococurantism', term with faint whiff of pomposity perhaps itself, it might be supposed. I am interested in Treglown's behaviour. Literary Editors often like to cushion the fall after handing out a book to a reviewer who they know pretty well will not like it, but this conjecture may be unjust. That could also be true of Frederic Raphael (in one of his letters to Roy Fuller) saying 'The Editor of the *TLS*' held as low an opinion of my (AP's) Memoirs as he, Raphael, did. One just notes these things as of psychological interest.

Monday, 21 May

Publication of *Miscellaneous Verdicts*, for which Heinemann sent in celebration a bottle of fizz, which we drank at dinner (De Courcy, not listed in Cyril Ray's *Champagne*, so one can only hope for the best tomorrow). Reviews in the Sunday papers were satisfactory (*Sunday Times*, Patrick Taylor-Martin, made some quite good points; *Observer*, Anthony Burgess, also polite; I did not expect anything in the *Sunday Telegraph*, owing to Hugh Massingberd's interview the previous week). These should repair any potential damage by *TLS*. Henry Mee sent an immensely grand illustrated catalogue, with my 'long captions', also piece about Painters and Sitters, for his show.

In the afternoon Peter Mumford and David Brabon appeared to survey plans for extracting the large oak from the lake, and other tree matters after the hurricane. Brabon had heard the disc jockey John Peel say he would take *Dance* to his island in *Desert Island Discs*.

Tuesday, 22 May

In the evening V and I watched Channel 4 News, on which eight minutes was promised to Henry Mee for his show. Knowing the habits of TV, I supposed this might be severely cut, perhaps omitted. On the contrary, Henry was done proud, not to mention myself speaking about my portrait, after which were shown those of Lamb, John, Moynihan, my 'long caption' about the Queen's picture was read out. Lord Denning and the actor John

Mills also appeared, the former in his nineties, the latter not much short of my own age but very spry.

Mills said Henry charged £10,000 for a portrait. Lady Denning did most of the talking, which caused V to say it made her additionally glad she herself refused to appear. Frank Whiteford, lecturer at the Royal College of Art, a figure with Old Bill moustache and bluff manner, spoke with mild disapproval of Henry's painting. I did not think him too unsympathetic a figure, while the sort of thing he said prevented the programme from seeming too much of a set-up affair. The journalistic line is that Henry Mee is not cared for by the National Portrait Gallery nor the pundits, at the same time is pet of 'the Establishment', including Buckingham Palace.

Thursday, 24 May

Sheep-shearing is taking place in the fields round the house. For some reason Snook greatly disapproves (tho' the sheep did not make appreciably more row than usual). Snook went out in the morning and immediately returned to the house, from which he refused to move for the rest of the day. Possibly feared his own whiskers might be trimmed.

V brought Noël Coward's play *The Vortex* from The Stables, which neither of us had seen or read, tho' I remember a great fuss about its 'decadence' when played in 1923. It's terrible stuff. I was unprepared for quite such rubbish.

Tuesday, 29 May

V and I drove into Frome this afternoon for me to have an eye-test (not done for eighteen months), while she took car to get right-hand mirror replaced, damaged in entering the garage, which is a shade too small for the car. At Dollond & Aitchison I was tested by same young man (perhaps Pakistani or partly) who did my eyes last time. Gave excellent report, very slight deterioration due to age, could still read small print with specs (£12.25).

Wednesday, 30 May

Lees and Mary Mayall to luncheon provided by the Flying Casserole, service provided actually in Chantry. We tried it before when alone, Boeuf Stroganov and Boeuf Créole. This time we had Chicken Cacciatore, quite good. One realizes that, similar to all restaurants, indeed up to a point all

cooks, only one taste. The Mayalls were in good form. They gave a favour-
able account of Sarah Bradford when in Portugal (where her husband
Tony Bradford does indeed seem to have had some marginal form of
Intelligence job). When the Mayalls were in Japan, Sachie and Georgia
Sitwell, travelling with John Foster and Princess Somebody-or-other
(Russian name, 'not Imeritinsky,' Lees said), the party was asked to
luncheon at the Embassy. Georgia Sitwell rang Lees to say that she thought
he ought to know that John Foster was having an affair with the Princess.
This was of course a very tiresome thing to do as it was nobody's business.
However, Lees dealt with it tactfully, no one was in the least interested
and they came.

Thursday, 31 May

Curious dream: I was walking down the Burlington Arcade, where the
shops were more like those in Carnaby Street, full of trendy clothes, almost
a souk, with proprietors standing at their door. The Arcade was crowded
with people. A middle-aged woman I knew, rather like Diana Cooper, but
I could not remember her name, was coming towards me. She stopped to
speak to a younger woman standing at the door of one of the shops. She
said: 'Talking of feudalism, would you care to take charge of the fête at
Longleat?'

Mark Amory rang about 9.30 a.m. asking if I would review for the
Spectator. He himself is going away for three months to write a book about
Lord Berners, of whom we talked for a while. His job is to be temporarily
taken over by A. N. Wilson. I agreed in principle to do this occasionally.

Hilary Spurling rang. The Spurlings had an extraordinary time in Russia,
where they stayed with a 'dissident' painter's family, painter had been
locked up for a time before the Gorbachev era. John Spurling is writing
book about Modern Russian painters.

Sunday, 3 June

To my surprise a longish piece in the *Sunday Times* about reviews of *Verdicts,*
written as first of series, by Harvey Porlock, obviously *nom de guerre,* which
I suspect covers in this case Patrick Taylor-Martin, who came here the
other day. He made the good point that rather dull respectful notices
might have been expected for a book of occasional writings of that sort,
on the contrary quite a lot of reviews had been cross. This is most satisfactory, because the reason I resisted for so long making a collection of such

pieces was the prospect of getting a few boring reviews that would go no way in selling the book. Now the stuffiness of several papers has made *Verdicts* a news item. As Edith Sitwell once said to me: 'It's wonderful being able to make people so angry when one is so old.'

Tuesday, 5 June

Alison Lurie, having taken a train from London arriving at Westbury 12.46, turned up 1.15, more punctually than expected by me, not by V. The taxi-driver had apparently severely interrogated Alison as to whether or not she had 'an appointment', evidently regarding her in a somewhat sinister light, the newly ash-blondeness of her hair perhaps raising suspicion as to her respectability. We took her to the Bridge House, Nunney. Luncheon very good (tomato-lemon soup, beefsteak-mushroom pie, spiced cake/apple/clotted ice-cream, glasses of wine). Alison is now drinking little or nothing. She brought a box of Black Magic chocolates, a name she never gets over, also her book *Don't Tell the Grown-Ups*.

The Bridge House is partly an antique shop, so after luncheon Alison bought some cutlery for her London flat. She was in excellent form. These days one is occasionally aware, quite how it would be hard to say, of the Professor of EngLit. V thought this episode would probably appear in a novel, as Alison noted that Mr Edgeley (Mine Host of the Bridge House) wore a shirt the same pattern as the wallpaper. Enjoyable if slightly exhausting day.

Wednesday, 6 June

Virginia to dinner. Archie hopes to be going to the US for two months, New York, Washington; Georgia to Mexico, Guatemala, with another girl. Warning Virginia she was to be made subject of experiment, we drank Nuits St Georges '85, given me by Tristram, then opened, not drunk, at luncheon party some six weeks ago, resealed with vacuum stopper John gave me. The wine had become rather thin, flavour remaining good. Artichokes (our own), Breton cold smoked chicken.

Thursday, 7 June

Vidia Naipaul rang with regard to a letter I forwarded to him at the request of a character called John Summers, a Welsh journalist who interviewed both of us years ago and is now living in retirement in

Carmarthenshire. This Summers is apparently related to the Revd Montague Summers, an odd, even faintly sinister, clergyman of some sort, who wore eighteenth-century clothes, edited Restoration plays, said to practise Black Magic. I never met him, but in early life both Evelyn Waugh and Cyril Connolly were offered a job as his secretary.

Vidia said he had greatly enjoyed *Verdicts*. I asked what he was writing, he said nothing. He thought he would give up writing. V suggested he is now a feudal knight. I thought more Kipling's Indian knight, who gave up everything, going to live among the animals and becoming a saint. Vidia's book on India appears in September. Enjoyable talk. He is extremely intelligent.

Friday, 8 June

Examining the books at The Stables, V found a paperback of *The Reef* (1912) by Edith Wharton, never read by either of us. Interesting plot, not (it seemed to me) well worked out, even accepting conventions of the period. Darrow, a Secretary at US Embassy in London, is invited to stay at a French château by Anna, widow of another American, to whom she was unhappily married. It was always understood that she would marry Darrow if her husband died. The château is owned by her mother-in-law, also an American of the Old School, widow of French nobleman through second marriage. Darrow is abruptly put off at last moment by Anna and decides he will go to Paris anyway as he has ticket. Falls in with an American girl on the channel boat, Sophy, a governess, and has a brief affair with her in Paris. Later, after having had the explanation why Anna put him off, Darrow goes to the château, he finds Sophy governess to Anna's child, also secretly engaged to Anna's stepson Owen. Darrow and Anna now set about getting married (apparently going to bed), but the relationship is broken up by Darrow's affair with Sophy coming out, also Sophy's engagement to Owen. At least outcome seems uncertain. All is treated with a maximum of heavy weather and some obliqueness as to what happens. Edith Wharton was perfectly capable of humour, a touch of which would have immensely gingered up what is in itself a good story. Perhaps this might have made a better play, even if everything had gone wrong, which nowadays would certainly be felt unnecessary.

Tuesday, 12 June

Letter from Bevis Hillier, now editing Sotheby's magazine, *Preview*, asking for a piece about Connoisseurs, with especial reference to Gerald Reitlinger. I shall take this on. A. N. Wilson, who is standing in as Literary Editor at the *Spectator* for three months (while Mark Amory writes his book about Gerald Berners), is in touch on subject of reviewing.

Saturday, 16 June

A Knighthood for Kingsley Amis in Birthday Honours. Hilarious. Old and New Selves once more prominent. Delighted and wrote.

V and I watched Trooping the Colour. We had been invited to dinner at the George, Nunney, by my agent Bruce Hunter, who was staying there with his friend Belinda Hollyer, an intriguing accompaniment to the invitation. Bruce then rang, a muddle had been made by the George, so now the Bowlish House, Shepton Mallet, is the venue. He himself would ferry us there and back. Belinda turned out a jolly, square-set lady, of New Zealand origins, bright, employed on children's books side of publishing. She is thinking of setting up on her own. The Bowlish House is distinctly smartened up since we went there some twenty-five years ago with Brian and Nancy Horrocks (the General and his lady having stayed at Bowlish before moving to the still unreconstituted Chantry Stables).

Dinner in principle not too bad, perhaps a mistake to order Barbary duck, sauce good, if duck rather tough, with rather disgusting *nouvelle cuisine* dish of vegetables. My soup excellent, V's asparagus soufflé too, both of us having some form of syllabub, also good. I drank white wine (Alsatian?) before, throughout, dinner; V had Campari soda, claret, latter she said not bad, if not exciting. Enjoyable evening in which good deal of gossip, business, dished up. I mooted the question of a second volume of occasional writings to follow *Verdicts*, which Bruce thought possible. He also spoke of some American character, to whom John Rush had already referred, prepared to put up money in conjunction with BBC or commercial company for TV *Dance*. I should prefer the latter.

Sunday, 17 June

Bruce Hunter and Belinda Hollyer to pre-luncheon drinks. Bruce is an able agent, most happy when talking shop. He was, however, interested in Ramsay of Bamff Charles I cap, gloves, scarf, etc., as he himself has Ramsay

Monday, 25 June

After the William Wake interview, the tape turned out not to be working, so he turned up here again, doing that with sufficient address to make a second visit tolerable. The timbermen dealt with the Luccombe oak satisfactorily, removing large chunks to side of field, then levering the stump back into its hole, where it will now become a feature.

I am reading a proof of P. G. Wodehouse *Letters* (ed. Frances Donaldson) for the *Spectator.* Wodehouse was a curious figure whom I cannot altogether rationalize even to myself. The jokes, verbal antics, often make one laugh aloud. In many ways he speaks understandingly about writing, well aware of his own limitations, at the same time unexpectedly sensitive about reviews. His behaviour in both wars was open to criticism, tho' of course outrageous that he should have been attacked in the actual manner he was regarding the disastrous German broadcasts. His desire to be liked caused him ultimately to become friendly with William Connor (Cassandra), responsible for leading the pack of journalists against him. I remember mentioning this to Frankie Donaldson, who said in explanation: 'It was Plum's wish to be considered a good fellow.' I had not realized how far such feelings went. He even wrote to Evelyn Waugh, who was doing broadcasts to prove Wodehouse's innocence, requesting Connor should not be attacked.

The paradox is that the sort of 'good fellow', 'old boy', Wodehouse wanted to be would surely have made, for instance, some apology about listening to the German news radio (which Wodehouse mentions) when held in Germany, which must have reported such news as 'Seven enemy planes down', i.e. British ones, yet Wodehouse never suggests this could have been painful to him. The excuse made always is that he was entirely apolitical. No doubt that was true, but even after the First War he made some remark to the effect that he might be locked up when he returned to England. He never showed the smallest effort to be prominent in organizing British war charities in the US or anything like that.

After the Second War fuss, he wrote that he had no self-pity, having made an ass of himself, which was certainly true. It is very hard to know what he felt about this asininity in relation to his own code of 'good chap' behaviour and heartiness. He perpetually complains about the boredom of the reading matter that comes his way, yet always lacking that additional effort that books even a shade highbrow require, being unable to cope with, say, Balzac. One would entirely agree such books need an effort, but that is usually repaid.

Wodehouse was, however, a great Shakespeare reader, it would appear developed during periods of being locked up. He certainly preferred the company of unintellectual, on the whole philistine, people, tho' those involved various forms of writing, such as musical comedies. He had the Victorian dislike for explicit sex, reinforced by his own undoubted sexual oddity. One sees a slight parallel with Max Beerbohm, whose work, in principle, Wodehouse did not like, though he admired *Seven Men* (undoubtedly, with *Christmas Garland* parodies, Beerbohm's best writing). This well illustrated Wodehouse's literary stance. I was for a moment surprised by his attraction to occultism, then remembered he had a brother involved in such things. I found the *Letters* intensely interesting.

Wednesday, 27 June

I dreamt I was giving dinner, probably at the Travellers', to Roy Fuller, Nicko Henderson and Mr Bailey, the alcoholic antique dealer, who used to have a curiosity shop in a kind of cave in lower Wardour Street, he later moved to a grander, more ordinary shop in one of the Piccadilly arcades, probably arranged by a young man sometimes helping there. Mr Bailey contributed (with Christopher Millard) something to Mr Deacon in *Dance*.

Monday, 2 July

Tessa Davies to tea after the WI. When sitting last week as a magistrate, she told man on £70,000 burglary charge he was remanded, at which he shouted 'Oh, no, I'm not', jumped from the dock and threw a tear-gas bomb. He was with difficulty overpowered. The CS bomb had been given him by his girlfriend (where would one obtain such?), also a get-away car waiting. Such gas must not be treated with water, which makes burns more painful to the eyes, so there was a considerable amount of disarray. A good example of scenes from provincial life. Tessa had very nobly made her way to the Hop Exchange to see the Henry Mee show, whereabouts of which was hard to find, in fact not far from Southwark Cathedral.

I finished *Roman Fever*. Edith Wharton's excellent line of her own possibly is worsened rather than improved by Henry James influence. One feels Stuart Preston, famous social figure in London during war, usually spoken of as Jamesian figure, would perhaps have been more suitably treated by Wharton, the Jamesian verbiage getting in the way of a fascinating study.

Tuesday, 3 July

Michael Thorp, vet (the Longleat lions rather than our cats), married to Heather Manley, rang to say Heather's mother had died. Edward and Marion Manley (she very Scotch, formerly District Nurse) lived many years in The Lodge, an unusually nice couple. Mrs Manley, who 'did' for us, suffered at end of her life from softening of the brain, had been (as said locally) 'to Wells', where she lived for some years not knowing what was happening. This will probably make things a trifle easier for Mr Manley, now in the housing estate at Nunney, a figure much respected locally, and really exceptionally nice, exceptionally 'good' man. In afternoon I saw Lister about the lower plate, wrong again. He is going to get a longer stud, so I see him again on Tuesday.

Thursday, 5 July

Anthony Hobson rang to ask us to luncheon on 29 July. He had been staying with the Fergussons at the Paris Embassy, and taken to super-smart ball at château formerly owned by Diane de Poitiers, amazing toilettes of ladies. Anthony (who can chatter away in French) remarked on the extreme rudeness of the French: he was introduced to about fifteen people, who always turned away after introduction.

Friday, 6 July

Mrs Manley's funeral at the Methodist/Wesleyan Chapel, Nunney. The building (1812 over door) is part of a block just by Castle, undistinguished outside, more impressive within, rectangular room with high ceiling and box pews. I never attended a nonconformist service before. The two ministers who officiated the simple rites were sympathetic, tho' regrettably the dreadful modern Bible used. Hymns: 'In heavenly love abiding', 'The Lord's my shepherd, I'll not want' (Scottish paraphrase of XXIII Psalm, for contemporary popularity V says the Queen responsible), 'All things bright and beautiful'. Verse about rich man in his castle, poor man at his gate, omitted, which in fact would have been unusually appropriate in this case. About a hundred in the congregation. One might have expected more, Mrs Manley being very popular, but funeral of youngish woman at Mells no doubt reduced numbers.

A sweet letter from Selina Hastings, expressing regret I was leaving the *Telegraph*, saying her mother (Margaret Lane, who wrote for the paper) also sorry, wanted her to convey that. I don't think Margaret Lane and I met since she and Jack Huntingdon (then Hastings) dined with Alec Waugh before the war when V and I were the other guests at some hotel-restaurant in Clarges or Half Moon Street.

Saturday, 7 July

John suggested giving Betty Walker a copy of the Henry Mee catalogue, as she had seen the TV programme on his show. John is shooting it in himself on Nunney Court as the Walkers are away. Betty rang this evening, seemed delighted, a good idea on John's part.

Going through the art books I came on *The Chelsea Song Book*, illustrated by Juliet Wigan (O'Rorke), inscribed to me 1931, nearly sixty years ago. I felt a slight pang, not so much of past love (always startling), as regret that her indolence, vanity, egotism, allowed her to let her drawing slide. She had a real wit in her time, charming pictures of their genre, all lost in a morass of narcissism and, one imagines, latterly pretty sordid affairs. She nearly cried when I brought up the subject of her drawing the time she was here a year or two ago. I also recalled (as antidote to such sentimental twinges) that I inscribed two of my early books to Juliet, 'with Love', which both turned up at Sotheby's in the 1960s (going, so far as I remember, for about £70). They were bought by Bill Davis. When we were staying with him and Annie at La Consula, I reinscribed them respectively: Sotheby's with date, 'I too have had my dreams and met / Ah, me, how many a Juliet' (Arthur Symons), and 'So how now, Juliet', said by the Nurse in *Romeo and Juliet*.

Sunday, 8 July

Just as we were sitting down to luncheon, two characters, one of them called Colonel Something-or-other, arrived to ask if they could destroy mink (admittedly a pest), hunting them (as I understood it) with two couple of hounds by the lake. They had only just discovered it was owned by me (why?), they would otherwise have written, as they usually did. They were dismissed without ceremony, arriving at this inopportune moment, and told they could not, as one cannot know what hunting there with dogs might lead to. About 6.30 p.m. a fan from Toronto arrived on doorstep with two females in a car. He said we had corresponded, name Teddy Moran(t?), belonged to AP Fan Club there. He was coming over here to work at Canadian Broadcasting, himself a writer. I talked to him for a few minutes at the door and told him he could take his party round the lake if he wanted. The thing that makes one despair is for someone to have read the twelve volumes of *Dance* and at the end of this suppose its author the sort of person who wants to be called on by a total stranger without warning on a Sunday evening.

Tristram rang before going to Switzerland to shoot *American Friends*, also to describe the Chatsworth Ball. Powells, Mounts, Lennox-Boyds more or less took over one local hotel, Alice Boyd was wearing a tiara at dinner. Dancing in the marquee, the central court roofed over, dark ceiling, stars. Archie did not attend, as already in the US.

I reread Proust (fourth or fifth time, Kilmartin translation now). Combray, early Swann, remain splendid, Françoise, etc., tho' already Swann's jealousy shows sign of causing tedium, much as one likes Cottard, Norpois, or Bergotte. I had forgotten how fascinating are period details of Odette's Art Nouveau drawing-room. Bloch, Saint-Loup, Charlus, all very alive.

Sex transposition begins to show awkwardness with entry of Albertine. The little band, as such, might be girls, but their behaviour, conversation, always sounds more like boys, also Marcel's talk of so many successful pick-ups, hardly likely unless straight tarts. Milkmaids, fisher-girls, improbable unless homosexual transpositions. *Cities of the Plain* almost consistently good (except perhaps for theorizing on subject of homosexuality), Legrandin, Verdurins, the lift boy etc. Elstir never quite comes off either as man or painter.

One might generalize that everything about Albertine is boring; everything about Charlus good. Brilliant set pieces from the start continue into *The Captive*, but dreadful longueurs in *The Fugitive*. *Time Regained* shows definite signs of exhaustion. I came to the conclusion I really do not understand Proust's 'unconscious memory' theory. Its effect seems no different from conscious memory. You bite into your tea-soaked brioche, think of your childhood, or trip on a paving stone, which happens to recall something. If Marcel was born about 1880 (as most recent commentators lay down, certainly making comparative chronological sense of earlier sequences), he would have been only about forty when he 'reappears' in Society, where everyone else is now in their dotage, complimenting him on looking so young. Groups remain comparatively unchanged except for certain surprises such as Mme Verdurin having become Princesse de Guermantes. Otherwise Marcel is able to judge Society with much the same eye as when he entered it, which one would

have thought scarcely possible in contrasting 1890–1900 with 1920s, tho'
that may have been less difficult in France.

Often one feels the generalizations do not make sense. Over and above
all this one is struck by perpetual emphasis on Marcel's popularity, charm,
good looks, women who fall for him, confidences given him by 'great
aristocrats' of both sexes. I have always held that, as a matter of technique,
it was better to say the Guermantes were immensely kind to the Narrator
(rather than waste time describing how he managed to ingratiate himself
with them), so that he could get on to describing Guermantes life itself,
but the author's egotism, narcissism, does to some extent run away with
him. All the same the dazzling side of the novel makes up for a certain
amount of dullish, even silly, stuff, while longer life would probably have
given time to correct some of the repetitions, dying as he did at fifty-one.
I still feel that the novel (all novels) should be presented as it is in its
entirety, not cut about into selections. One notes that Marcel more than
once remarks that his relations with Albertine were 'never complete'. Did
(either in life or fictionally) Proust ever have 'complete relations' with
anyone? Perhaps saying this is to excuse the sex transposition.

Tuesday, 10 July

I took a taxi into Frome to see Lister, who is relining the lower plate. It
now seems much improved. I returned to base, whence V and I drove to
Kilmington to lunch with John and Suzanne Keegan. A small rambling
manor house beside the Church, the arms of a Cornish family, Paynter-
Cromden (second name uncertain), over the front door, tho' nothing like
the original owners of the place. The Keegans' daughter Lucy, with a small
child, other members of the Keegan family appearing after luncheon.
Guests, Terence Brady and Charlotte Bingham, he an actor and writer of
plays, TV scripts, which they do in collaboration; she a popular novelist
(under her maiden name). Her parents, Lord and Lady Clanmorris, are
also writers. I have corresponded with the latter about biographies she
writes which I reviewed.

Terence Brady is lively, amusing especially about the TV world; she quite
agreeable. They live over by Alfred's Tower, west of us, where they breed
horses and have had a few modest racing successes, she said. The house
haunted by banging doors, steps in corridor, and so on. She (not her
husband) is an RC (like Keegans), so hangs a rosary on the outside handle
of her bedroom door. The rosary always on the floor by the morning.

Keegan said at Quatre Bras the French cavalry charged, while the 69th

(2nd Battalion The Welch Regiment) was forming square, the Regimental Colour was lost and ensign, age fifteen, cut to pieces with innumerable wounds still holding King's Colour. The Keegans have two cats, Edgar (a Maine Coon), huge, only eight months, will grow bigger; Oscar, black half Siamese. Food good, new Burgundy (which I quite failed to recognize, supposed something like Chinon, as having slightly raspberry taste, even Spanish, but wisely kept that conjecture to myself). On return, owing to something John Keegan said, I found he was Balliol man, age fifty-six.

In desperation for something to read, decided to try the paperback of *Gargantua and Pantagruel* (tr. J. M. Cohen), probably pinched from *Punch* when I was there. My first brush with Rabelais was when I was about twelve or thirteen, staying with Henry Yorke at Forthampton, when we found a copy of Urquhart and Motteux's translation of Rabelais, whose name we both already knew in relation to obscenity. Since then I have occasionally dipped into the two-volume edition, illustrated by Heath Robinson (bought by my father), but never got very far. This time I read the whole thing with mild enjoyment, taking 700 pages chapter by chapter. I had not realized what a devastating attack it was on the Roman Church under guise of boisterous scatology. Much tedious stuff about eating and drinking (from which Belloc, Chesterton, Beachcomber, etc. derive), occasionally amusing, the surrealism is striking in descriptions, in a sense perhaps birth of Surrealism itself. The fantastic erudition and physical energy of Rabelais himself as writer could not be more impressive. I was interested to find that he was, in fact, the first to say that hunting was the image of war. Did Jorrocks read Rabelais? Undoubtedly Surtees must have had a copy (with no doubt other outspoken works) in his library. I wrote Cohen (now eighty-seven, I see from *Who's Who*) a fan letter.

Wednesday, 11 July

Virginia at The Stables for gardening. V and I dined with her. She gave us an enlarged account of the Chatsworth Ball. All ages from twelve upwards. Georgia and friends stayed dancing until 7 a.m. Edna missing in London.

Thursday, 12 July

Hilary Spurling (who nobly came by train) to luncheon. She was on great form. She said she had seen the Bill Pye head and it was an excellent likeness, in fact she was enthusiastic about it. I have asked her to enquire price of a bronze cast, perhaps smaller size, as the head itself seems larger than life. We talked of her Paul Scott biography, which appears in October. I told Hilary about Bruce Hunter (also her agent) turning up with a girlfriend, to which Hilary replied she had met one or two girlfriends before. The Flying Casserole (food agency in Chantry) luncheon (Boeuf Stroganov, slightly less good than before, if all right) drank Château Fombrauge, St Emilion '78 (given by Alvilde Lees-Milne, when Jim asked himself to lunch), from Berry Brothers, not madly exciting. Enjoyable visit.

On the principle of having another look at books one habitually runs down, I reread F. M. Ford's *The Good Soldier*, which to my great surprise Hilary liked (tho' read a long time ago and had forgotten all about it). Once more I found it deplorable. I can understand Graham Greene's passion for *The Good Soldier*, indeed all Ford, because he is full of Graham's sort of baggage, RC problems, everyone lapped in self-pity, but Hilary, for that matter Cyril Connolly, inexplicable (tho' Cyril also pretty hot on self-pity). The story is narrated by an American wholly unlike any American one ever met, about a good old English squire and cavalry officer, the background completely cardboard, who sleeps with every woman he meets. The last is believable enough, at same time immensely heavy weather made about it all. Finally he commits suicide in orgy of Ford's Teutonic sentimentality. The superlatively good review of *Verdicts* in the *London Review of Books* by Barbara Everett had light thrown on it by Hilary, who knew Barbara Everett, an academic, who would have liked Hilary's life as a 'literary lady' (Hilary's phrase), while Hilary (to my great surprise) said she always longed to be an academic. Enjoyable visit.

Friday, 13 July

ARC Quarry is making trouble trying to close Mells Lane. This preposterous project is to be resisted to the hilt. V was so horrified by the tattered cuffs of shirt I was wearing at Mrs Manley's funeral that she sweetly gave me a new one chosen by John in fine pink pattern.

I reread *The Taming of the Shrew*, which I always think funnier than generally allowed, tho' The Bard does not make identification easier by calling one character Gremio, another Grumio. Obviously a great deal is omitted that might have made a better-constructed play, at same time remarkable what a good show *Kiss Me Kate* was with minimum of alteration from original.

Tuesday, 17 July

Bob and Liddie Conquest to luncheon. Both in good form, if Bob looking trifle tired after filming in Russia, which must have been gruelling. In any case this hot weather is extremely exhausting. Bob said when Philip Larkin was in hospital towards the end, Monica Jones accidentally was announced as 'Your wife', at which Philip started from the bed: 'My wife! . . .' Strange *histoires* about getting Liddie's daughter married. Apparently you have to take what comes in America as to who performs the service. Bob was to 'give Helen away', but the deaconess in question refused to have these words said. Various other formulas suggested, 'present', etc. all refused, so Helen in fact was never actually 'given away', Bob going on to read the Lesson. This sort of contemporary inanity really seems to reach its climax in the US. Luncheon by the Flying Casserole: Boeuf Créole, rice, quite good. Liddie had a glass of lemon barley before lunch, with V, half-bottle of Maso Lodron. Bob (who apparently drinks half-bottle of Californian champagne every night at home for dinner), bottle Frascati before and during meal, less one beaker drunk by me. Enjoyable day.

Thursday, 19 July

I have had trouble trying to find anyone who will repair my electric typewriter. Finally, through the good offices of Tessa Davies (pulling rank as a Butler & Tanner director), National Technical Equipment, Sunbury-on-Thames, sent Mr Turnbull, a gloomy figure, who took the typewriter away, prophesying little hope owing to age. Apparently they last only about ten years, of which I have had some seven. This seems to have been one of the first of its kind. They seem to have no exchange value like cars. As it happened, Mr Turnbull came from Coleford, location of our local surgery. 'Awful place,' he commented, with some truth. V much occupied with arrangements to thwart ARC's plot to close Mells Lane.

Friday, 20 July

Georgia rang to say goodbye before setting off this afternoon for Guatemala for a month, then Mexico. I tried to reread *Three Men in a Boat*, but finally broke down.

Tuesday, 24 July

Evangeline Bruce, Tony and Marcelle Quinton brought the traditional picnic, arriving just before 1 p.m. Weather warm, fortunately not so hot as Friday, which would have been overpowering. Evangeline a bit quiet, I thought (how her legs are thin, like Prufrock, tho' no doubt more elegant). Tony Quinton, as normal, in bursting form. He is very different from Maurice Bowra, while sharing the same overwhelming flood of talk. More general than Maurice's, often subjects one would like to pause over, carried away on the torrent. At same time he has Maurice's appreciation of what other people say. He had been reading Denis Healey's Memoirs, which he described as a book 'ghosted by the author himself'.

Tony has the most extraordinary powers of memory, reeling off pages of Wordsworth, Arnold, popular songs of the 1930s, etc. in amazing manner. He loves all Wordsworth (as to whom I am a bit lukewarm, once one has admitted he is a great poet) including the 'Ecclesiastical Sonnets', which really amount to a kind of History of the Church of England. These he quoted hilariously. He gave us his 'Tribulations of Authors', an address to the Royal Literary Fund. I mentioned *The Fisher King* had gone into French, Italian, Spanish, Portuguese. Tony remarked: 'The lash of impotence makes all men brothers.' I gave them Henry Mee catalogue. Evangeline brought Memoirs of Sondra Gottlieb, former Canadian Ambassadress in Washington (fan of mine, famous for slapping her secretary's face on TV), in which Evangeline is compared with Lady Molly in *Dance*. (Evangeline is certainly richer.)

The picnic consisted of smoked salmon, chicken pie, potato salad, gulls' eggs, Quinton chutney (excellent), *Sachertorte*, blue Stilton in pot, all first-rate, tho' V persuaded Marcelle to take back some of the chicken pie, which she thought otherwise would last us too long. We drank Château Bernard Raymond, Bordeaux Superieur '79 (light, smooth, if not madly exciting, good with picnic food), of which Tony, V and I (Evangeline a tiny drop) consumed bottle and a bit. Evangeline previously had a mild vodka and tonic (which I think she left most of), Marcelle (who is very keen on *Verdicts*) nothing, except perhaps a little water. Tony was determined on the way home to explore bookshops of Frome, chiefly on strength of reading my feature on local bookshops in the *Telegraph*. The girls perhaps rather less keen. Enjoyable day, less exhausting than such occasions sometimes turn out these days.

I reread the *Collected Firbank*, dismayed to find it somewhat tedious, tho' Firbank's grasp of dialogue technique is undoubtedly original, not to say seminal. One likes different books at different periods of one's life. That is quite reasonable. The Lang Brown's people came for a final clearing of the hurricane damage.

Wednesday, 25 July

Penny Perrick, *Sunday Times*, rang to ask if I would review Frances Partridge's latest *Diary* (1960–63), to which I agreed. They pay better than the *Telegraph*. I arranged with Mr Millard to construct three steps from V's sitting-room on to the terrace, making less likelihood of falling on one's face.

Friday, 27 July

V attended the ARC conference about their new quarry proposals, closing of Mells Lane, etc., regarding which I wrote a formal letter of protest to the Mendip District Council. In this connexion found an entry in Leland's *Itinerary* (*c.* 1530), describing Leland going from Mells to 'Nunney Delamere' through 'enclosed hilly grounds', evidently Mells Lane. This might come in useful at later stage of the anti-closure campaign.

Sunday, 29 July

Driven by John, we lunched with Anthony Hobson at Whitsbury. Guests: Elizabeth Jane Howard (late Amis), Vidia and Pat Naipaul, Lady (Suzie) Walker. V supposed Vidia might be upset by this morning's disturbance in Trinidad, where Black Muslims seized hostages. Vidia, on the contrary, was taking it all in most easygoing manner. He said trouble made by gangsters, nothing to do with political parties or local respectable Islamic Trinidadians. It is sinister they should be given money by Gaddafi, at the same time an element of carnival about whole affair.

Jane is now moving to an area in North London west of Highgate. She said some few years ago, attending a Literary Prize committee, she had a car, so offered lift to James Pope-Hennessy. He mentioned an address in Ladbroke Grove, where she herself used to live. The house he named had the reputation of being haunted, a peculiarly grisly murder having once been committed there, screams sometimes heard. James Pope-Hennessy replied that was quite true, screams were sometimes heard. One became quite used to that sort of thing. (Just what Henry Mee remarked about his Jamaica Road house.) Somewhat macabre that Pope-Hennessy was himself murdered there some years later by male prostitutes.

I gave Anthony Hobson the Henry Mee catalogue, having a spare one or two, also one to Jane. I told Vidia I would send them one later. Excellent '82 Saint Emilion (I missed the Château). Good party. When Anthony was recently in New York thinking to sound American, he told the taxi-driver an address in Park *Avenoo*. Driver replied: 'What sort of a Bond Street cowboy are you anyway?'

Arrived home about 5 p.m. Later V and John went downstairs to play snooker. I was about to go up to my bath at 7 p.m., when there was a knock on door. This turned out to be Henry Mee himself, accompanied by a girlfriend introduced as Jane, saying: 'I've brought a present for you.' This was another huge portrait of myself. Most generous. It is better, I think, than the previous one, same size, somewhat lighter in tone, the expression what I imagine to be characteristic. This came as utter surprise. Henry is always a trifle enigmatic on first arrival, the girl perfectly agreeable but silent. Drinks were refused (they had come from London, to which they would return), so we gave them coffee. They left after about half an hour in the large van Henry used to transport picture. The portrait will pose certain problems in hanging, as there is not room, generally speaking, for a postage stamp on the walls of this house. A letter from Evangeline Bruce saying that at the Chatsworth Ball, Debo referred to Andrew Devonshire's cluster of former girlfriends as 'Andrew's fiancées'.

Thursday, 2 August

Intensely hot. Mr Millard in person, with his son Anthony, came to hang the Mee portrait on the stairs, where it will take the place of the copy of Van Dyck's Prince of Barbançon (bought by Lionel Wells-Dymoke as portrait of a Lord Pembroke, original full-length at Althorp), now moved to the right. The Mee looks splendid, the red of my shirt taken up by the red of the wallpaper. Mrs Lloyd (to our great relief) is ravished by it, Mr Millard himself repeated 'Super, super'. As V pointed out, everyone these days has the advantage of hearing persons like herself talking about pictures on TV. In afternoon Mr Mosley brought the new car, the Clubman. I'm glad to say it seems all but identical with last one.

Sunday, 5 August

Slightly cooler, heat having reached a peak on Friday, which equalled the heat of August 1911, when we were at some seaside place, where I well remember having frightful upset one night, combined with nightmares about Guy of Warwick killing the Dun Cow, the story being read to me at the time. This was regarded as an exceptional occasion, as I was noted in childhood for not being frightened by horrifying stories. Alleviation of the heat was greatly welcomed, as it gets me down.

Letter from John Keegan, who noticed from the Mee catalogue my middle name was Dymoke, and asked if related to John Dymoke, who was instructing at Sandhurst when Keegan was teaching there. He said he had particularly liked him, and that he wore scarlet and a spiked helmet at Coronation, the Championship having been abolished owing to law against duelling. This I knew, it was when John carried the Standard of England. I dispatched *Infants of the Spring*, which explains all. Richard Cobb's review of *Verdicts* in the *Spectator* at long last, good but referred to my 'mildly ticking off' Conrad for calling Maupassant's *Bel-Ami* a masterpiece, which it was. Complete misunderstanding on Cobb's part. *Bel-Ami* is one of my favourite books. I said I was 'surprised' at *Conrad* liking it, because of his own buttoned-up treatment of sexual matters, enjoying anything so highly sexed, unromanticized. Extraordinary how even intelligent people like Cobb can get hold of the wrong end of the stick; tho' Cobb, rather like Hugh Kingsmill, is immensely expert in limited areas (far more, of course, than Kingsmill), less so in certain other ones. For instance Cobb wrote in his review that the last sixty pages of *Verdicts* were all about Proust, and still did not persuade him he ought to read Proust, yet Cobb otherwise is steeped in everything French, in which one would have thought Proust unavoidable.

Tristram and Virginia are at The Stables, having had an enjoyable week in Spain. La Consula, Bill Davis's house, where we stayed once or twice, is now owned by the King of Spain, always available for him, but used for odds and ends, recently a dog show.

Alan Watkins sent *A Slight Case of Libel*, an account of an action brought against him by the Labour MP Michael Meacher, who claimed to be 'son of an agricultural labourer', which Watkins made fun of in his column. Meacher's father, like himself, was educated at Berkhamsted School (not to mention Graham Greene, Peter Quennell, Claud Cockburn, Mark Boxer), had a nervous breakdown after trying to be an accountant, and a private income, owned a farm on which Michael Meacher himself worked.

Alan Watkins (whom one suspects of being a frustrated novelist) is good on small points, clothes, etc. Both V and I laughed a lot. Meacher must be a monumentally humourless ass. Watkins rightly won the case, tho' at moments thought he was not going to.

I sent him a postcard of *Rorke's Drift*, by Lady Butler, where 24th Regiment (later South Wales Borderers, now Royal Regiment of Wales) won five VCs. I suggested *Michael Meacher* would have been an excellent name for Dickens novel, in which Alan Watkins would be the villain, oppressing the ill-used eponymous hero. The story full of Dickensian names, Moonman, Millinship, Mick Priggen, etc., Sergeant Buzfuz in fact quoted as an epigraph of one chapter.

Wednesday, 8 August

Former cruise friends from Kansas, Bill and Virginia Robinson, rang from London, after a cruise in the Baltic with their grandson. This did not include Tallin (Reval) and Riga, which one would have liked to hear about these days. They seemed in excellent form, no mention of Bill's heart trouble.

I read Lord Denning's *Autobiography*, which Gerry Bowden sent (having two copies) in return for the Mee catalogue that John gave him. Denning presents an extraordinary paradox of ability combined with a kind of mental laxity. The Dennings were five brothers, sons of a draper in Whitchurch, two of whom were killed in First War. The remainder became respectively a General, Admiral, Judge, Denning himself Master of the Rolls and Life Peer. His book contains every cliché and hackneyed quotation the mind of man could conceive, and an overwhelming egotism, yet (like his brothers) a constant history of worldly achievement. He has no conception whatever of putting book together as a 'work of art', at the same time he himself is not an unsympathetic personality, even if one doubts his having much grasp of circumstances when making the Profumo Report. Lord Denning and Henry Mee must have been wonderfully funny together.

Thursday, 9 August

Billy Chappell rang in evening and talked for a time to both of us. He said he had been having trouble with his emphysema, which goes up and down, at the moment a bit better. He might appear here one day if someone drove him, possibly Selina Hastings. Selina herself with difficult parents on her hands, her mother (Margaret Lane) suffering from Alzheimer's disease, I think, and father also rather under the weather these days. I sent Billy the Mee catalogue, which he said he would like.

Sunday, 12 August

Mrs Laurie Adams Frost, Toney, Alabama, sent *Reminiscent Scrutinies: Memory in AP's Dance, etc.* (Whitson Publishing Co., Troy, NY). This was more intelligent than general run of theses, dissertations, etc., saying with truth nothing of much value had been written about *Dance*, except Hilary Spurling's *Handbook*. Mrs Frost emphasized references to Nietzsche, adding the friendship with 'Captain Alexander Dru' caused the philosophic influence of Kierkegaard. That would have greatly amused Alick.

Monday, 13 August

Philip and Vivienne Nokes, Stoney Lane Cottage, came to evening drinks, primarily to discuss the campaign against ARC's attempt to close Mells Lane, and in a lesser degree to talk about my letter saying I had traced sources of the story about Septimius Severus having had a contemporary scourged for mentioning they had been at school together, the latter I could not recall exactly. He had looked up the Septimius Severus references (*Scriptores Historiae Augustae*, Loeb Classics). *Contubernalis* (comrade-in-arms, intimate friend, mate) who so unwisely embraces SS, when Proconsul in Africa (not Emperor). The chronicle does not say specifically they were at school together, but that would certainly be likely. I'm sure someone told me so, probably a lecture by Mortimer Wheeler, making the story more picturesque, when we were at Leptis Magna, Septimius Severus's home town. I would hardly have got it from Anthony Birley's biography as that appeared in 1971, same year as *Books Do Furnish*, in any case incident barely mentioned. The fellow Old Boy, if Old Boy he were, had been 'beaten with clubs'.

Nokes also looked up Mr Tylee (former owner of The Chantry) in Burke's *LG*, noting a Tylee forerunner lived at Seend, Nokes alleges in Joan Sumner's house, the lady Aubrey got into such a mess with. The Tylees were bankers in Devizes and inhabited this part of the world since mid-seventeenth century. Snook pressed his company on both Nokeses. Enjoyable talk. Some rain at last after prolonged drought, which always makes me feel much better.

Thursday, 16 August

Michael Rogers arrived 2.30 p.m. to talk about Gerald Reitlinger, on whom he is writing piece in Macmillan's *Encyclopaedia of Oriental Archaeology*, intended to become something like Grove's *Dictionary of Music* (he said). He was in his late fifties, white hair, bright blue eyes, biggish, dark-blue blazer, flannel trousers. Rogers belonged to David Pryce-Jones's generation at Oxford, he said, RC, intelligent. He began life teaching Philosophy at Oxford, then taught in Egypt, now deals with Islamic matters at the British Museum. Rogers already knew The Squire, so it was not necessary to start from scratch. Apparently the Museum had an eye on the Reitlinger ceramics for a long time, someone being deputed to stay with The Squire every six months or so to keep in touch, lots being drawn as to whose fate that was to be, owing to the legendary discomfort at Woodgate. In the end the ceramics went to the Ashmolean.

Possibly Henry Reitlinger, The Squire's elder brother, also a collector, had earlier left some to the British Museum. Rogers said David Piper may have exaggerated value of the Gerald Reitlinger Collection, because the top rank of collectors insist on perfect condition, which, characteristically, The Squire did not. In fact he rather liked pottering about mending slightly damaged pots himself. Well one remembers this. However, Rogers said, even if the market value was perhaps shade less than estimated, no doubt whatever that, for breadth of representation, the Reitlinger Collection was the best in the world.

Rogers, who learnt fluent Russian during his military service, talked of Pushkin, and the impossibility of translation owing to the subtlety of language, which everyone always emphasizes. Had known Maurice Bowra, that gave evidence of possessing some taste for smart life. He surprised me by saying that The Squire was quite aware before he died that the ceramics were scarcely at all damaged by the fire at Woodgate, but on the other hand he was greatly upset by loss of First Editions, which had been burnt. I didn't know Gerald was greatly interested in these, which, Rogers said, included inscribed copies of my own works, good general assembly of Twenties/Thirties novels, etc. I knew the art books were outstanding and I suppose the others grew in rarity value over the years. An interesting talk.

During last few days everyone to whom V spoke on telephone, or wrote, mentioned a piece in *Tatler*, which we alone had not seen. These included postcard signed B & B from (presumably) hotel near Bruton, which V diagnosed (I agreed) as 'Bruce [Hunter] & Belinda [Hollyer]', which later turned out not the case, so it remains a mystery. *Tatler* piece by William Leith was satisfactory.

Friday, 17 August

John sent a copy of the Mee catalogue to his friend, Peter Hall, Ambassador in Jugoslavia, who wrote a most agreeable fan letter, which arrived at breakfast this morning. I was just reading a sentence enquiring whether any further steps had been taken regarding the adaptation of *Dance* for TV, when telephone went. This turned out to be Katie Nelson, who took Tom Wallace's place at Norton, with whom I dealt during production of the American paperback of *The Fisher King*. She was ringing from France (Bergerac) and explained that her husband, Harry Brown, was source of John Rush's words some months ago about an American who had been in touch with BBC on subject of *Dance* for TV.

Higham gave no hint of this Katie Nelson connexion, tho' Bruce Hunter said a word when we dined with him the other day that vague stirrings were taking place. There was some uncertainty as to when the Browns arrived in England, but, after various subsequent telephone calls, it was announced that they would touch down at Heathrow on Sunday, 19 August, hire a car and drive straight down here to discuss matters, as they were returning to US on the Monday. Heaven knows whether they will bring this off, but V wisely suggested getting in a cold Breton chicken in case it meant supper. One cannot help feeling it would have been simpler to give some warning of all this at an earlier stage, also an outline of what is planned, but that is not in the nature of those concerned with anything to do with films. One notices this when hearing accounts of even Tristram's business dealings.

Sunday, 19 August

In spite of some scepticism on our part, also rain in sheets (the weather having broken), the Browns turned up about 6 p.m. I had not been told that Katie Nelson of Norton was wife of American interested in *Dance* TV, as she had only recently left publishing, unknown to John Rush. She was not at all what I expected, which was toughish female publishing executive. Slim, attractive, what might perhaps be called schoolmarm chic, long black loose dress, as she was eight months gone, something I always fail to notice. Harry Brown, fiftyish, at Oxford (Magdalen, Marshall Scholar), where Iris Murdoch was his tutor. Son of a Hollywood producer (whom V thinks she remembers reading of when we were in Hollywood), therefore the background second-generation Hollywood, parallel with, say, Budd Schulberg.

Harry Brown, Jr I took to at once. Energetic, amusing, much charm, immensely keen on getting *Dance* done on TV. Had been in touch with Alan Yentob, now head of BBC2, once Tristram's boss. Brown knows the novel extremely well. It is of course difficult not to take to someone who displays these qualities, which I am only too well aware can cover a multitude of lettings-down. All the same I am determined to get what fun I can during my declining years out of such possibilities as this. They stayed to dinner, moving on to the Royal Crescent Hotel, Bath.

Monday, 20 August

John, who possesses an encyclopaedia of movie people and movie matters, rang with details of Harry Brown, Sr, who started life on the stagecraft side, progressing to production, and did many Westerns, also several films one knows vaguely by name. In earlier days had arranged lighting for Stroheim's *Foolish Wives*, my favourite picture ever. Harry Brown, Jr was in fact born 1934. They bunched us from Bath, nice gesture, flowers always delighting V. John Rush rang from Higham later in the afternoon after a talk with Harry Brown. Rush is rightly always cautious, having had so many rebuffs in this field, saying he was chronically a bit suspicious of sons of Hollywood directors, TV in US, etc.

However, Harry Brown will be in London again in September (presumably after she has had her baby), when real business will be discussed. The point is that having secured some sort of option (if Rush thinks that feasible), Brown will have to raise the money. Brown thought the film might have to be edited a bit for the US. When they were down here he was much taken with the suggestion that *Dance* should be done in two bits (Ken Taylor's idea), which I'm sure there is a lot to be said for. Meanwhile, I propose to retain a modicum of euphoria, while totally accepting everything will probably fall through as always before.

Tuesday, 21 August

A young man from Burges Salmon, the solicitors, returned the title deeds of The Chantry, which we thought best to get back, as they might be required for maps, etc., in connexion with English Heritage matters.

Thursday, 23 August

George Lilley, Librarian of St David's University College, Lampeter, who is working on a bibliography of my works, wrote to ask if he could come here again for research. I cannot really interest myself in bibliography. Told him that as politely as possible, sending the Mee catalogue.

Sunday, 26 August

Tristram and Virginia at The Stables. We discussed Harry Brown possibilities with Tristram. Like John Rush, he was extremely circumspect about prospects.

I reread *Twelfth Night*, never a great favourite of mine. Maria is lively, but Sir Toby Belch and Sir Andrew Aguecheek don't really come off. The Duke is rather a sympathetic character. 'A sentence is but a chev'ril glove', another reminder that The Bard's father was a glover.

Wednesday, 29 August

We refused the last Roy Jenkins invitation on the grounds East Hendred a bit far for luncheon at the age one has reached, at the same time making them promise they suggest themselves for lunch here, which they did for today. We invited Anthony Hobson when at the Glebe House a month ago. Then V had the brilliant idea of getting Jilly Cooper as a spare girl, Jilly having written an article recently in a *Sunday Express Colour Magazine* complaining about Leo's roving eye and the fact that men were asked out on their own, ladies never. I sent Jilly a letter saying we had both cried so much over her piece that we hoped, greatly as we loved Leo, she would come on her own to the Jenkins luncheon. This was accepted, in fact it turned out Leo would not have been able to come anyway.

Anthony arrived first, so we were able to ascertain that Suzie Walker, met with him, is not a widow as earlier put about, but in process of divorcing her husband, Lt-Gen. Sir Anthony Walker, Deputy Chief of General Staff, quite a grand job in army terms. The Jenkinses were coming from Honiton in Devon, where Jennifer was on some National Trust business, whether or not to buy a house. Before lunch Roy drank gin-on-the-rocks with dash of sherry, somewhat exotic taste. He is in process of approaching publishers with his Memoirs. Jennifer is always a trifle sad, one feels, tho' obviously greatly enjoys her National Trust stuff. Jilly was wearing shorts (for which she is perhaps getting a shade too grown-up), in great form, bringing a box of chocolates; Anthony too in good form, more or less dating Jilly before leaving. The Jenkinses and Coopers are to meet again (not previously knowing each other) in a week or two's time at Plàs Newydd, Leo being Henry Anglesey's publisher for the latest volume of the *History of British Cavalry*. I had not known that Heinemann (or rather Octopus) had sacked Leo's subsidiary from their cartel. The Flying Casserole produced Boeuf Créole, rice, to which we had added green salad, gâteau, plums. Château Latour '64 (given me by Tristram, Moulins du Cadet '78 (bought some years ago from Wine Club – a single bottle left over for some time). I thought the former immensely good, with tremendous body, almost like burgundy; the latter good too, if expectedly lighter. Anthony thought the Moulins du Cadet possibly preferable. This may indicate my own taste for heavy wine. Snook jumped on the table at the end of lunch, which would have greatly shocked Alison Lurie. Interesting party, if a shade exhausting. Everyone seemed to make a great noise talking, but that may be only increased age on my part. Rain in the evening, which relieved the intense humidity of the day.

Thursday, 30 August

Peter Mumford arrived with English Heritage forms to sign for the hurricane grant, which should be £1,000 against bill for £2,300, if all goes well.

Friday, 31 August

Large coloured picture of Jilly Cooper on front page of the *Daily Express*.

I reread *Ulysses* in the Bodley Head edition, 1986. One wondered if normal book production would affect enjoyment, or French jobbing printer's typeface, printed on lavatory paper, is in some way essential part of the book. It turned out that one soon became used to normal print. The first 200 pages or so are splendid, begin to tail off into a sometimes pointless unintelligibility. The dramatic form in the brothel scene, sometimes effective, goes on much too long. It would certainly have been preferable to have written this in the naturalistic style of, say, the Martello Tower. Bloom's wanderings, told in cliché style of his own thoughts (one presumes), are sometimes amusing, but the self-conscious manner of writing ultimately becomes rather tedious. Earlier naturalistic styles allow plenty of scope for the occasional 'experimental' phrase if so desired by the author. The question-and-answer section about Bloom is remorselessly boring, as well as often unintelligible.

Molly Bloom's reflections are a *tour de force*, tho' I never feel satisfied that is how a woman's mind works. I think it is how a man thinks a woman's mind works. Once that is admitted the section imparts an enormous amount of information about various characters in the novel. The book ends on a sentimental note, to which there is no particular objection, tho' one feels sure that the sentimentality (which Joyce's poems show) was a characteristic Joyce was always fighting against, even if admissible here within the terms of reference. On the whole I greatly enjoyed this rereading, even if it did not change view already held that *Ulysses* is a book unique in its effort to create a new way of writing, wonderful in its picture of middle-class–lower-middle-class Dublin, but written with a pedantry that handicaps in competition with the greatest novelists. Joyce's command of words and phrases is much superior to his mastery of form, even when the form is 'revolutionary'.

Tuesday, 4 September

A letter from Jilly (crossing one from V) thanked us for the luncheon party and added that her daily, having done the shopping which included ox's heart for the cats, left a note: 'Your money's in the envelope and your heart's in the freezer.'

I am in process of rereading one of my favourite books, *The Education of Henry Adams*, the Introduction to which inspired getting out of the London Library (via John) his novel *Democracy*, described there as brilliant picture of Washington political life. The title is a bad one, but the novel itself holds up extremely well. A rich, pretty young widow arrives in Washington in the late 1870s, with her younger more frivolous sister, anxious to make a marriage that will bring her power. In the end the political corruption disgusts her, she sets off for Europe, tho' there are indications that the younger sister will marry one of the elder one's cast-offs. Some amusing characters and set pieces like the ball at the British Legation for a German Grand Duke married to a British Princess. The phrase 'Kitchen-Cabinet' occurs. A book well worth reading.

Wednesday, 12 September

Helen Fraser, of Heinemann, to luncheon to talk about another volume of journalism. This went extremely well, no question of stalling about doing it. Helen even spoke of a possible third. She made good suggestions about arrangement, which cleared my own mind on the subject. She is nice and intelligent, also very funny about Leo Cooper when part of the Heinemann combine ('I don't want to teach my grandmother to suck eggs, but', etc.). Helen had not found him particularly sympathetic as a colleague, so was amused at his role in the current matrimonial row. The Flying Casserole: Chicken Cacciatore, vegetables. Millefeuilles and blackberries picked by V. Helen Fraser does not drink in the middle of the day. She said that she much regretted that Heinemann (before her reign there) had refused to give £25,000 for Hilary Spurling's *Paul Scott*. She was reading second volume of Anthony Burgess's Memoirs, better, she thought, than first. Successful visit.

Tuesday, 18 September

John and Ros Anderson to tea. He, fan of long standing, was formerly Lower Master at Eton, where he was known as Jack the Ripper, from a tendency to 'tear over' exercises. He has on occasions had extracts from my books done at 'Speeches'. The Andersons had suggested looking in, as in neighbourhood, apparently to attend AGM of Wessex Water, in which he holds shares. Both talked a good deal. Just before he left Eton, Anderson saw an inconceivably ill-dressed boy in the street, to whom he said: 'During my thirty years at Eton I have *never* seen a boy wearing such scruffy shoes. What is your name?' 'Solzhenitsyn, sir.' Schoolmasters' wives develop a curiously similar look in later life. Gave John Anderson three copies of Mee catalogue, one for himself, one for School Library, one for the Head Master, Eric Anderson, as John Anderson is going to Eton in near future. Charles Pickthorn presented me with Surtees's *Analysis of the Hunting Field*, done by the Surtees Society.

Thursday, 20 September

Mr Eastwood, who has a second-hand bookshop at Puriton, a village north of Bridgewater, came to buy about a hundred books we were getting rid of (£250). Said he usually did well at Book Fairs. John brought down some new slippers for me from Simpson's, was able to get same ones striped red and black, called Achilles, one would have thought inappropriate name for any footwear. *Spectator* sent Hilary Spurling's *Paul Scott*, full of interest.

Tuesday, 25 September

Virginia's birthday. We rang her. They were going to celebrate at a Spanish restaurant. V to the Bath Clinic for her check-up with a new surgeon with Dickensian name of Mr Umpleby. All well, but he took an X-ray as she hadn't been seen for about eighteen months owing to Mr Lloyd Williams's retirement.

I finished Hilary Spurling's *Paul Scott*, very good, also another book about him by Robin Moore. In the latter interesting comment by John Bayley to the effect that *The Jewel in the Crown*, *Staying On*, made such excellent TV because Scott relies almost entirely on documentation, rather than 'creating a world of his own'. This is a most apt comment in general, about TV as well as Scott, but it must be added that Merrick, the homo-sexual sadist police officer, with his discomforts social and sexual, seems to some extent a phantasm of Scott himself. Merrick, who could have been doubtful in the novel, certainly makes the film memorable. Bayley thinks the rest of the book needed TV to fulfil itself, with which one would wholly agree.

Friday, 28 September

Diana Beaufort-Palmer rang to say she would be in the neighbourhood, could she come to see us, so invited to tea. She was, in fact, going to Corsham to buy a peacock from Lord Methuen (£75), mate for her peahen. In the event the agent said Lord M did not want to sell until later in the year. Diana is now eighty, well turned-out. She poured out a mass of stuff about her early life, much of which I did not know. Her father, a barrister, lived in Hampstead and they never saw anybody, so at the age of nineteen she went to Universal Aunts to offer her service for job. Her only qualification was knowing Spanish, as she had an aunt living in Majorca. This aunt played some considerable part in her life, eventually leaving her a house there.

Varda of the Varda Bookshop had gone to Universal Aunts to find someone to look after her daughter, Minka, during the holidays. Diana took on this job. She was henceforth launched into a world of extreme racketiness, culminating in marrying Bobby Roberts. This marriage, of course, broke down completely after a year or two, but the account she gave of Bobby during his period managing Sadler's Wells showed him perfectly capable of doing this, getting on well with Lilian Baylis, organ-izing the hiring of stools for theatre queues, etc., when sober, which admittedly he wasn't very often. Diana greatly liked Miss Baylis. After divorcing Bobby she married George Beaufort-Palmer, brother of Francis Beaufort-Palmer, who used to give a lot of low-level parties in the 1920s. Another brother married a Turk.

I never heard anything of George Beaufort-Palmer, reason being he was apparently somewhat louche figure, gambler, existing for the most part on being boyfriend of Mrs Paul Phipps, mother of Joyce Grenfell and Tommy Phipps. Mrs Phipps then sacked him in favour of Lefty Flynn, a B-movie actor playing cowboy parts, whom she married and who then decamped to the US. George B-P then married Diana. This also lasted only a few years. Diana, who now lives near Newbury, was driven over by her 'lodger', a gnarled, horsy little man with a white moustache, by no means young, who was not allowed by her to come into the house (parking somewhere, he returned to pick her up).

Diana herself really didn't seem in at all bad form, speaking of various marital disasters with complete objectivity. The Beaufort-Palmers, as a family, seemed less bogus than one had formerly imagined, being descended from some admiral named Beaufort, who had been connected with Maria Edgeworth's family, with which the Pakenhams also had links. Diana's house in Majorca was next door to that of the Bolkonskys (Volkonskys of *War and Peace*), she sold it to the Prince and Princesse d'Orléans, the former, son of the Comte de Paris, French Pretender, who I believe disinherited him after his divorce. Anyway he does his own cooking. A certain amount of rather fascinating information emerged, but as with so many people who cannot stop talking, impossible to get a word in edgeways to clarify various points. Exhausting, but not uninteresting. I had intended to give her a Mee catalogue, but forgot to do so in struggle of her bringing over a bunch of herbs, books to sign, etc., so will send one.

Monday, 1 October

I reread *The Merry Wives*, never much thought of, but I always rather enjoy. In the duel to be fought between Sir Hugh Evans and Dr Caius one is surprised that the former never pleads his Orders as making impossible to accept challenge. Perhaps his acceptance is part of the contemporary joke, or did clergymen ever fight duels? 'A beard like a glover's paring-knife', The Bard's glover father again. We had salmon and fizz (Veuve Clicquot Ponsardin '82) for dinner to celebrate our engagement anniversary, actually previous day, 30 September.

Wednesday, 3 October

I reread Philip Larkin's *Required Writing* (reviews, etc.). This includes a curiously unfriendly piece about *Books Do Furnish a Room*, although declaring himself a fan (which he is described as in Anthony Thwaite's Introduction to *Larkin at Sixty*). Kingsley Amis said Larkin did just the same to him, Kingsley attributing such occasions simply to Kingsley and me being able to write novels, Larkin not. I am always unwilling to accept this reason, being minimally envious of other writers myself. I also feel a critic of Larkin's ability should put objective criticism first. It is, however, true that Larkin himself says he regards novel writing as a higher activity than poetry, and does speak of his own regret at ceasing to be able to do the former. Some of his objections suggest a niggling attitude to the novel which could account for his own conking out.

For instance, that the words of 'South of the Border' are incorrect, which they well may be, but I was not reproducing the libretto, but roughly what the troops sang. Again, complains of use of place names for characters, specifically, Isbister, Ada Leintwardine, Widmerpool. I didn't know Isbister was a place name (Orkneys, four villages, I find) when I used it, but there were several persons of that name in the London telephone book. Ada Leintwardine I would admit to being rare. I came across the name several times in the seventeenth-century Welsh Marches documents, liked it.

The Widmerpool family took their name from the Nottinghamshire village, where they lived, were numerous for several centuries. Incidentally, pondering what were actual names of painters like Isbister, I thought of Frank Salisbury, tho' that did not occur to me at the time. He remarks that General Conyers and General Liddament lack the substance of Waugh's Ritchie-Hook. This seems to me to show a taste for very coarse texture, as I wouldn't regard Ritchie-Hook as one of Evelyn's best creations, tho' of course that's a matter of opinion. Larkin's criticism is always capable on poetry, but his extreme enthusiasm for Barbara Pym and Julian Hall (Eton contemporary of mine, I must be one of the few who remember his two or three decidedly low-keyed novels) seems to indicate a taste in Larkin for lowish vitality in the novelist.

Barbara Pym has a lot of good points, chiefly inventing a world wholly her own, which she never fully developed. She would have been the first to recognize her own limitations. I think this rather inhibited taste is to some extent due to Larkin's chosen strait-jacket of anti-sophistication, 'abroad', exoticism in any form. This, I think, was partly a sense of inferiority for being 'provincial', partly self-protection. The strait-jackets writers force themselves into (Hemingway, Waugh, to some extent even Amis) are always interesting in the way they bring a certain later retribution. Incidentally, Larkin sometimes transgresses his own rules, quoting '*Où sont les neiges d'antan*' as example of a poetic line, sometimes using a word like *dégringolade*. One sees that a wish for non-affectation, revolt against Eliot's saying modern poets must be obscure, like a breath of fresh air first of all. Eventually, if carried too far, becomes a sort of tyrannical puritanism. Talking of poets, I always got on well with the three Sitwells, liked them all in their different ways, but when I sent them copies of *Caledonia*, none of them acknowledged it, I suppose disapproving for one reason or another, possibly thinking I was getting above myself. Looking through a second-hand book catalogue today, noticed a lot of Sitwell items. Highest price asked for anything, Edith £55, Osbert £30, Sachie £42. I reflected that not so long ago an American bookseller offered *Caledonia* at $3,000 (say £2,400).

Monday, 8 October

When I reread *The Education of Henry Adams*, one of my favourite books, I did fall down a bit on the longueurs towards the end. The first two or three hundred pages remain infinitely readable, especially the English experiences, while he was Secretary under his father at the US Legation. The latter part of the book tails off into romanticism about science, putting the world right, showing an utter lack of grasp in such matters as how Foreign Affairs would eventually turn out.

Adams was born in 1838 and died in 1918, his great-grandfather had been second President, his grandfather sixth, father Minister to St James's. Adams didn't much care for the English (but then he didn't much care for the Americans either). He was extremely acute about both countries, especially Bostonians, of whom he was one. He describes English society as it was in his day (in certain ways, *mutatis mutandis*, continues to be), and his description is better than anyone else's I could mention offhand of either nation. When he taught at Harvard he said the undergraduates there were 'ignorant of all that man had ever thought or hoped'. He used the phrase 'glittering prizes', no doubt whence Birkenhead culled the cliché in first instance, to whom it is usually attributed.

Thursday, 11 October

At long last my electric typewriter has returned from the National Technical Services (Weston-super-Mare), where it has languished since July. It behaved eccentrically at first, but does now seem to work.

I reread *Portrait of the Artist,* most of it first-rate, tho' Joyce suffered from a failing endemic in the craft of fiction of not knowing (or not caring) when he is being a bore. On the other hand, he is particularly good on such things as a family row about Parnell, conversations between students, etc. Discussion (more truly Stephen's views) on Aesthetic much too prolonged and tedious. The termination of the book with brief diary entries is out of key with rest.

In going through the art books I have been looking at the Arthur Rackhams, of which we possess quite a lot, my father collecting them; V also was given several Rackhams as a child. How good Rackham was, a genius at his best. The pictures are usually beautifully designed, the comic subjects required for the story executed without the least facetiousness. Fairies and such are treated with a delicacy that always remains right side of sentimentality and whimsicality. Edmund Dulac on the whole avoids these failings too, but with much less originality of fantasy. Kay Nielson, Willy Pogany, Brunelleschi produce what are often close to fashion design, in any case with minor talents. George Barbier is a good artist, again bordering on stage designing. Rackham remains a pure illustrator with invention, humour, a touch of the macabre added by such work as the Nibelungen or the Demon blowing the castle-horn in *The Ingoldsby Legends.* I believe Rackham often inserted a portrait of himself into his pictures, but do not know which figure he is.

Monday, 15 October

V, feeling under the weather, upset inside, stayed in bed, starved. Mr Lavender (one thought of Earl Lavender in John Davidson's novel) from the Mendip District Council, called to see The Stables and establish whether to pay Poll Tax as two flats, or house occupied by only one family. I gave him the keys, having, I trust, persuaded him of the latter. He was agreeable, on returning keys gave impression he was convinced. One hopes for the best.

Thursday, 18 October

The redoutable Mr Moss appeared and repaired a patch of the drive down to The Stables, which has worried me for some months, also patches in front of the house (£130). Commissioned him to renew chippings in front of garage (£130). Mr Moss was suffering from a nerve in the back of his neck. He informed me had just become a grandfather.

Wednesday, 24 October

Georgia came over from Oxford, arriving about 7.30 p.m. for the night. Dinner from the Flying Casserole (vegetable curry, quite good). Georgia looking very well in spite of being in dock for amoebic troubles, now cured, she said she was feeling better than ever. Her travels in Mexico, Guatemala, Honduras, Belize, were on the whole successful and enjoyable. She recently stayed with the Cotterells at Garnons, Herefordshire, owned by the grandson of my school contemporary (barely known). She took about half a dozen hardbacks, and same number of paperbacks, of my works, now sorted out for distribution among deserving cases.

The Congressman wrote that he lunched with Norman Sherry in Washington. Sherry is researching the second volume of Graham Greene's biography. Sherry described Graham as a 'sly old fox', an understatement. All the same, one is glad he has grasped at least this, as was by no means apparent from his first volume.

Monday, 29 October

V, John and I watched the first instalment (of three) of Kingsley Amis's *The Green Man*, about an innkeeper of (represented in film as too grand) a haunted country pub with a reputation for good food. This is one of the best of Kingsley's books, though I always felt the appearance of the ghost should result from the *exact* licentious behaviour of innkeeper to whatever sinister seventeenth-century murder Dr Underhill did. That is suggested, but never quite worked out in the novel. Ghost parts are well done in film (but ghost should never be shown without someone seeing him), also the rest, tho' Albert Finney was a shade too heavy both physically and morally for Kingsley's character. The minor parts are also good, except all the women looked alike, same age, so they were difficult to sort out. On balance excellent performance.

Thursday, 1 November

Harold Caccia obit, my twin, b. 21 December 1905, tho' (for astrological purposes) in India. Harold was immensely good at everything, Captain of the Oppidans, XI, Field, head of the Foreign Office, Life Peer. He was also (by rotation chiefly) President of the Lit. Soc., where I always liked him. A man of great innocence in spite of all this. At Eton there were some most sinister characters in his house (Kindersley's, later Slater's), of which one is sure he was quite unaware. Harold had an ancestor mentioned in Dante's *Inferno* so perhaps hereditarily used to sinister company. A dotty woman rang up about 7.30 p.m. to ask if I could tell her origins of the Fisher King legend. I informed her that writers do not like being telephoned and any encyclopaedia would give the information. If that failed, send me a letter.

Friday, 2 November

Death seems rambling through Etonian 1905-ers, as Hugh Smiley dcd today. The *Telegraph* rang because V had been bridesmaid when Hugh married Nancy Beaton. As *The Pageant of English Poetry* had been quite enjoyable to read in bed, I tried during the day *The Pageant of English Prose* by same Editor (R. M. Leonard, 1912), also Eton Prize (from Goodhart) my second half. This was boring beyond words.

Monday, 5 November

Tristram and Virginia at The Stables. They had a splendid time in the Veneto. Vidia Naipaul rang as I had sent him a line about his *India*. He said Heinemann was pleased with the way the book was going. Good sales in India, where the paperback was marketed at about £8. This a big change from Vidia's first book on India, part of the economic revolution, he says, now taking place. Tremendous changes are on the whole good, he said, it will be about fifty years in developing. This means movement away from the old Gandhi meditation, lying on beds of nails, etc. There is an immense broadening of the base where power and money are concerned. Vidia had been in the US recently. He was going to revisit places seen about thirty years ago, Trinidad, Guiana, where apparently the Jagans and Burnham are still in power, only place in the world (except China) where Communism still functioning, tho' no doubt their sort of Communism something rather on its own. Anyway should make interesting pieces for the *Telegraph*.

The second episode of *The Green Man* (V decided she would allow herself the luxury of skipping it), less good than first. Finney is getting his head down in awful way actors do, putting in dreadful little bits of business, like tossing eggs in the air when making breakfast. I consider it technically wrong that Dr Underhill (the ghost) should be shown on his own, not with someone seeing him. It implies the ghost was actually there, so to speak, in the flesh, not an illusion. I admit this raises all sorts of complicated questions. This begs a question which should not be put, cf. old movie rule that no one should be shown speaking on telephone without also showing person at other end.

I reread *Love's Labour's Lost.* The beginning is amusing, also the obvious connexion with Sonnets, Dark Lady, etc. The later part is too full of contemporary jokes now to be intelligible. Armado was said to be Ralegh. One wonders if Ralegh talked at all like that as a caricature. 'Infants of the Spring' used here as well as *Hamlet.*

Tessa Davies to tea after WI.

I reread *The Real Charlotte,* Somerville & Ross novel (1895), which V took thirty years to make me read in first instance. Going through the story again I find it better than ever, perhaps a shade stagey at the end but extraordinarily well put together, balanced in pattern, all the characters alive.

Wednesday, 7 November

Rodrigo Moynihan obit. He was eighty. Henry Mee wanted to paint him as the artist in his 'Eminencies' group, started, but Rodrigo showed little interest, so Henry gave up. Rodrigo possibly was feeling rotten, tho' painters are always tricky about each other. I should like to have seen more of Rodrigo, but we met late in the day. He never managed to get down here to inspect the portrait *in situ.* V is having trouble with a tooth. She is seeing Mr Joy again this morning.

Saturday, 10 November

I have corresponded for years with a musical enthusiast called K. Harvey Packer, who has almost an obsession about Constant Lambert, tho' no doubt could not be more admirable in promoting him. He has recently been trying to organize a Lambert exhibition in Bournemouth. He tells me that Flo Lambert died last year, leaving quite a bit of money (presumably settled on her by Kit, possibly from Kit's royalties), with which she has endowed a scholarship at the Royal College of Music. What an extraordinary story, one from Balzac, dating from the day she opened the door to Constant at the house of the Russian pianist in St John's Wood, Constant telling me after he had been admitted by 'the most beautiful creature you ever saw'. Balzac would also have enjoyed the fact of her being coloured, coming from an unknown family in the East End, possibility of her official (as opposed to actual) father being hanged for murdering his wife on account of latter's penchant for coloured sailors (whether or not that was true, Balzac would have loved its picturesqueness). Flo had terrible ups and downs, poor girl, she had some very good points, but I'm glad she ended with enough to live on.

Sunday, 11 November

V and I watched a few minutes of the Cenotaph ceremony. In the evening John and I saw the final episode of *The Green Man* (V saying she was too frightened after the first ghost scene). It was all rather a muddle, beginning with a threesome with a wife and mistress, then appearance of 'The Visitor', apparently God, a quietly dressed young man, who gives Albert Finney a cross. All a shade embarrassing. Then Finney meets Dr Underhill again, who tells him he will show him 'Marvels'. This boils down to exhibiting Finney's father (Michael Hordern), who died a few days before, and a lot of naked ladies writhing about, including at one moment his own daughter in the shower. Finney gets the trendy parson (the good actor who played Anthony Blanche in *Brideshead*) to exorcize the inn. The trendy parson complains that ghosts are all mumbo-jumbo.

This seems to me improbable, because however trendy and sceptical, he would surely not have become a parson unless he liked doing that sort of thing. Finney makes him repeat the performance (in his surplice) in the woods where various sinister things have happened. There is a great explosion, smoke, the parson falls into the hollow. That is all mildly funny. Finney's wife apparently goes off with his mistress (tho' that was not made absolutely clear). Then a new beauty arrives at the hotel. On balance I quite enjoyed it all, except the fucking, which is always terrible on the box. I also thought more care should have been taken to make the ghosts subjective matter to whoever saw them. V is still having trouble with her teeth.

Tuesday, 13 November

Mark Amory rang from the *Spectator* to say Malcolm Muggeridge was on his last legs, would I do a piece about him. I refused on the grounds that the situation had become too complicated between us to deal with in small space. I felt rather discomposed about this. In any case it is not improbable that Malcolm will recover, as he did a short while ago after receiving Extreme Unction.

I finished reading Lady Cranborne's Symposium about David Cecil, which V ordered from the Hunting Raven in Frome to give Pansy for her birthday. V said the book got her down. I quite agree. For some reason all that mainly aristocratic sweetness and light was too much, more than one could reasonably bear. The contribution of the Salisburys' butler, Mr Tunnell, was far the best, recording among other anecdotes how David, on the way to a wedding from his parents' house in Arlington Street, had entered a taxi, found he had no buttonhole, so got out of the taxi from far door to buy one from the lady selling flowers outside the Blue Posts in Bennet Street. The taxi-driver, unaware his fare had left, drove on. Reflecting on what made this story so vivid, I decided it was the flower seller outside the Blue Posts (which runs into Arlington Street at right angles), frequented by Mr Sponge, where I too have consumed an occasional sandwich myself. Later Tristram rang to explain that at Lady Cranborne's party for the book he had been given two copies, one for me, which he will hand over next time he is down.

Wednesday, 14 November

A wonderfully warm autumn day. For a time we even turned off the heating. In the morning David Thomas, Editor of *Punch*, rang to say Malcolm Muggeridge had died, would I do a piece for *Punch*? I explained again in rather more detail than to Mark Amory why that was difficult, indeed got a certain amount off my chest by talking to him about Malcolm's editorship of *Punch*. Later in the morning the *Daily Telegraph* ('Peterborough', Susanna Herbert) rang to try for some story about Malcolm. I repeated my explanations. She said something to the effect that 'Bill Deedes was not back from lunch yet', so matter was left there.

In the evening the *Standard* ('Londoner's Diary', John McIndoe) rang on same quest. McIndoe addressed me as 'Anthony'. I asked if we had met, he said no, calling me Anthony seemed 'easier'. I told him it was not easier for me and did my stuff again. McIndoe rang later asking for the date of Muggeridge review of *The Valley of Bones* (1964), as that might make a story. He ended with perfect journalist's piece of sanctimoniousness: 'Anyway, I'm sure we all wish him well wherever he may be.' I replied that must remain a matter of speculation. Finally, American National Broadcasting Company (which the girl who rang described as 'like Radio 3') asked me to say a few words about Malcolm to Robert Figel. This I did, tho' doubt anything will result.

The whole business rather shook me up. If it were possible to say something on the lines of 'Well, we had our differences, but in memory, etc. etc.' it would be easier, but so far as I was concerned I supposed we were on the best of terms. Nothing came as more of a surprise than Malcolm's review. V says (I'm sure with truth) that Malcolm resented my making no comment about his outburst against the Queen, which he certainly knew was unsympathetic to me. He lacked any form of self-control. Incidentally, Malcolm had said to me not so many months before that outburst, 'You know I may be having a hand in composing the Queen's speech at Christmas next year.' I presume that was probably in some way connected with friendship with Ann Fleming, whose cousin Martin Charteris was Secretary (or whatever he was) to HM.

When I gave Malcolm an excellent notice for his *Diary* published in 1981, he wrote thanks, but I had the impression I was piling up yet more bad marks by not having taken the opportunity to be disagreeable, thereby making myself vulnerable. The legend that we never spoke after Malcolm's review is untrue. We had, in fact, corresponded recently before this. I have thought a lot about him. Malcolm had marvellous qualities. Wit, charm, sympathy, genius for making his *vis-à-vis* feel that he reflected genius for reflecting whatever his *vis-à-vis* wanted to find. What I never grasped in early days was his unbridled envy, tho' he would sometimes refer to that failing in himself (saying, for instance, in one of the marathon telephone conversations we would have when the Muggs too lived in Regent's Park, 'It's been an awful day, this, that, and the other having gone wrong, now I hear Graham [Greene] has won the American Book of the Month.'

I always thought he was joking on such occasions. He would disparage everybody and everything, having a peculiar grasp of individual weak points. This was related to his ability to make the dullest Parliamentary measure sound amusing in the way he talked about it, detailing how every MP would react. If we had not fallen out in the private field as we did, I should have found his later public behaviour most distasteful. The much advertised religiosity, revivalist-sermon manner of making public statements, all had no end but self-promotion, the attacks on humbug power merely a form of expressing power in itself. His moral standpoint was dreadful humbug. The religion he wanted to advance was Muggeridge-ianity, which had certainly a few basic tenets, such as use of contraceptives being forbidden, tho' otherwise not easy to follow. Things began to go badly wrong, I think, when he got away on his own, first at *Punch* as Editor, then in his TV pronouncements. This was somehow based on fearful disappointment (I suspect) at finding himself 'uncreative'.

As it happened, Malcolm too had possessed (possibly also as a school prize) *The Pageant of English Poetry*, which has as frontispiece small oval portraits of five poets (Shakespeare, Milton, Keats, Shelley, Tennyson). Malcolm and I were looking at this once, and he said: 'You know, when I was a boy, I used to lie musing on these pictures, wondering which of them I should be.' His uncertainty about what he felt led to his personal unreliability and hysteria. This uncertainty was illustrated by his saying to me on some occasion when telling about his womanizing: 'You know, the extraordinary thing, looking back, is how unenjoyable most of it was.' On another occasion he said, speaking generally of his past life: 'I really feel the only thing in it was the women.' This all combined with immense immediate kindness to people. Malcolm and I have had enormously enjoy-able times together, talks, laughs, serious discussions. His death leaves me with the oddest sensations. V wrote to Kitty.

Friday, 16 November

Tristram rang in evening, when V and John were playing snooker, to announce Ferdie Mount had been appointed Editor of the *TLS*. I have always thought Ferdie's gifts more political than literary, but he might well ginger the *TLS* up. We talked of Malcolm Muggeridge's death, also of Lady Cranborne's Symposium about David Cecil. Tristram himself contri-buted to the latter (chiefly David on TV as arranged by Tristram). I asked why Jonathan Cecil was not represented, as (unlike most actors) he writes distinctly well. Tristram said Jonathan had begun writing something about David's great love for the theatre which had been one of the causes of Jonathan becoming an actor, then it was all too complicated to describe what he, Jonathan, felt about his father. Tristram was interested in the story in my contribution about David meeting Henri Bernstein, the French dramatist, because Tristram greatly admired a film called *Melo* made from one of Bernstein's plays, brilliant French froth, he said, all about nothing.

George Lilley wrote to say that the St Paul's Press is prepared to publish his bibliography of my works. This is satisfactory.

I reread *Hudibras* fairly (in fact very) perfunctorily, pretty boring, I can't think how I ever managed to get through it to review the book. My maternal grandfather was said by my mother to enjoy *Hudibras*, as a favourite book.

Sunday, 18 November

Alan Watkins did (on the whole) a good piece about Malcolm Muggeridge, in the *Observer,* where he spoke of 'falling out' between Malcolm and me, which he linked with Bagshaw in *Books Do Furnish a Room* (1971) being supposedly modelled on Malcolm, which he never was, tho' I now see that might have appeared so for a number of reasons. I sent a line to the *Observer* saying break due to Malcolm's tone in reviewing *The Valley of Bones* (1964), which indicated deliberate policy on his part to end our relations; also Malcolm himself would recognise the fascination with Marxist heresies Bagshaw possessed as a characteristic of Malcolm's friend A. T. Cholerton, which Malcolm himself described to me.

In the 'Mandrake' column (Frank Johnson) in the *Sunday Telegraph* was an item saying Malcolm's *Winter in Moscow,* probably his best book, never republished owing to its anti-Semitism. Thinking it over, one sees this perfectly true (Frank Johnson always worth reading). Malcolm was not exactly anti-Semitic, but he was somehow obsessed with Jews, saying all sorts of people were Jewish when there was not the faintest reason to suppose that: e.g. A. P. Herbert; Ernest H. Shepherd, the illustrator; Hamish Hamilton, the publisher; lots more. Contrariwise, I was astonished by Hugh Kingsmill once saying to me that he was certain Malcolm himself had a lot of Jewish blood. This had never occurred to me. Apart from his preoccupation with Jewishness, I should have thought most improbably. His mother's name was Bool, I think; one would think North Country version of Bull, tho' I suppose it could have been Buhl. Anyway Malcolm's dominant strain seems to have come from his father's side. He thought his Muggeridge grandfather an undertaker and a bad lot (Malcolm said), otherwise knew nothing of him.

Thursday, 22 November

I reread *The Green Man* to check on the TV production. The novel has good points, never quite sufficiently worked out. The hero's occult experiences are so extraordinary that they would make anyone famous (anyway in the occult world), if described in a book. Might, I think, have been described a trifle less improbably. The Kingsley Amis tiresome woman always has certain similar characteristics, funny here in case of the mistress, which did not come over in the film, thereby causing a relationship to appear a bit too easy. Kingsley's inner horrors, semi-religious, semi-aesthetic, interesting.

Owing to the insane antics of the Tory party Mrs Thatcher has resigned, impossible not to comment *quem deus perdere vult, prius dementat*.

Friday, 23 November

I had a look at Malcolm's review of *The Valley of Bones* to make sure I had not exaggerated its unpleasantness at the time, but it was indeed extraordinarily sour. Pondered whether I had trodden on any of his corns. He said that I admired Stendhal (which he knew merely as a friend, nothing to do with reviewing the book), that Stendhal had been scarcely known in his day, was famous a hundred years later, I had received contemporary 'acclaim', but *Dance* would come to dust. It then occurred to me to examine *The Valley of Bones* jacket. Am now certain this was the root of the trouble. As my sales have always been extremely modest judged by anything like real bestseller standards, I could not understand what Malcolm meant by 'acclaim', but the quotes on the back, *NY Times*, Kingsley Amis, L. P. Hartley, V. S. Pritchett, are certainly laudatory. I am always unwilling to attribute malice to straight jealousy, especially in someone of whom I was as fond as Malcolm, but I'm now pretty sure that was the cause: a sudden burst of hysterical rage, induced by envy, which sometimes used to assail him. Indeed Malcolm himself used to refer to it at times.

Sunday, 25 November

I wrote to Mrs Thatcher expressing regret at her resignation, saying that at one of the dinner parties where I met her she had spoken of Dostoevsky's *The Possessed* (in Russian *The Devils*), i.e. those that entered into the swine, which then rushed over the cliff. This seemed a perfect example of what had happened to her, the swine being her betrayers in the Tory Party.

Tuesday, 27 November

Mandarin paperbacks sent passages from the *Dance* volumes which they propose to put (according to their custom) at the beginning of each book.

These seem well chosen, whetting the reader's appetite without giving anything away. I was glad I had not been asked to suggest these myself. Norman Sherry rang, which was kind of him because I was a shade brisk in *The Balliol Register* about his first volume on Graham Greene (which he had read in *Verdicts*). He does not seem to have taken offence at that. He has done about 65,000 on his second volume, but is worried about threatened publication of a book on Graham by [Anthony] Mockler. It looks very much as if at some stage Graham gave Mockler some encouragement, tho' apparently is greatly against him now. Sherry's views on Graham are naive to say the least, but he himself is a nice chap. Sorted the last few months' press cuttings, among which I found a *Times* 'profile' of John Major (11 October, before the Thatcher crisis), saying Major was sometimes compared with Widmerpool by fellow MPs. From the News tonight it seems clear that Major will become Prime Minister.

Thursday, 29 November

We celebrated our wedding anniversary (in fact 1 December) with smoked salmon at dinner and a bottle of fizz (Veuve Clicquot Ponsardin '82).

Friday, 30 November

Peter Mumford of Lang Brown's came at 2.15 p.m. to go round the work done on trees with representative of the Countryside Commission, Ginny Cator, who rang that she had started half an hour late, then ran into a bus, arriving about 3.30, thereby buggering up everyone's afternoon. She appeared to be a shade gnomelike, rather than a straight witch, but I only saw her for a moment with dusk coming on (no doubt her natural element). Hope this will result in a Heritage grant. Mumford checked on a few trees that may or may not need attention.

Sunday, 2 December

Tristram and Virginia at The Stables. They attended Gerard Irvine's seventieth birthday party, owing to his incumbency, at the Jerusalem Chamber, Westminster Abbey, where Henry IV died and the Little Princes were taken from their Sanctuary. As might be expected, many stratospherically High Church clergy. I photographed Ashbey and Eleanor, brought down for the first time.

Thursday, 6 December

Brigitte Mitchell (her husband brother of the writer Julian Mitchell) came to talk about my time at Oxford for the French quarterly-type magazine *Autrement*, which appears at irregular intervals, devoted to subjects like Towns, Countries, periods, etc. The Mitchells live at Dyrham Park, he employed by the National Trust doing the job formerly undertaken by Jim Lees-Milne, whom they knew well. Mrs Mitchell, a big Frenchwoman, late forties one would say, out of picture by Manet. She is a Professor at Lille, going there to teach once a week. Lively, amusing. Difficult to say much about Oxford, as the *Brideshead* legend is now so established. I tried to give a less unreal picture, but hard to know what the French can take in, as she herself said, they (the French) hold the oddest views about this country. Alvilde Lees-Milne recently had a heart operation, now, it seems, is all right. Brigitte Mitchell said Alvilde (her gardening expert rôle) took the Mitchells to luncheon with a Greek called Stephanides (met with Clarissa Avon), also in that line. On arrival Alvilde was rather sniffy about cars outside, 'Doesn't look much of a party'. At that moment manservant appeared at the door, said: 'Do you mind not parking there, the place is reserved for Princess Margaret.' Brigitte Mitchell occasionally takes a grandson of Comte de Paris out from Downside (he is son of one of the Bourbon daughters), so probably *bien*.

Hilary Spurling rang in evening to thank for wine sent for Christmas. We had a long talk about her Paul Scott book. She had become totally identified with Scott in the course of writing (understandable), taking badly those reviewers who said Scott wasn't a first-class writer, tho' the reviews I saw seemed excellent, all things considered, after some difficulties in the initial stages with Roland Gant, who instigated the project, then became sticky about giving information (anyway left the country). Roland wrote Hilary a wholly appreciative letter, saying ninety per cent of the book was entirely new to him.

Friday, 7 December

A fatuous piece in yesterday's *Times* by Bernard Levin about Malcolm Muggeridge and myself, the gist of which was that it was absurd of me to quarrel about a review, which merely meant the reviewer took a different view of the book from myself. I have thought Levin's journalism greatly deteriorated during the past decade from what he could do earlier, this was particularly missing the point. Levin clearly has no glimmering of

Malcolm's complexities and had certainly not read the review. He showed no grasp of the implications of Malcolm's sudden hysterical outbursts. In any case it ill becomes Levin to imply that reviews 'don't matter', as he sent me a most obsequious letter (17 September 1970) saying of his own book, *The Pendulum Years*, 'It would give me immense pleasure, and a good deal of gratification, if you would consider reviewing it,' followed by another (9 November 1970) saying, 'What a generous and handsome review . . . You were very good to me.' In consequence of this attack I have had to write to *The Times* saying Levin must learn that you can't believe all you read in the papers (e.g. that Malcolm and I had not spoken for seventeen years), there is still time to do that as he is only in his sixties.

Saturday, 8 December

Snow. Charming letter from Terence Brady and Charlotte Bingham (whom we met at the Keegans), married but collaborating in plays, etc. under their separate names, therefore signed 'B & B', saying what conceited stuff they thought Bernard Levin's piece. This pleased me, as apart from anything else, my relations with Malcolm were no conceivable business of Levin's. The Bradys' letter also revealed the identity of the earlier postcard signed 'B & B', which we attributed to Bruce Hunter and Belinda, his friend, supposing their having another visit in the neighbourhood, to Bruce's mystification, even slight hauteur.

John's Egyptian lodger, Amina Minns, rang to say someone had thrown a brick through ground-floor front window of 137 Kennington Park Road, matter reported by the Rastafarian who lives next door. Luckily John was able to get on to his builder, Jo Page, who will board the window up at once. Annoying, but John is philosophic about it, so many drunks frequenting the neighbourhood.

I reread *Measure for Measure*, a play I never greatly liked, this time much enjoyed. I am struck by how the Duke resembles Prospero, especially in certain rather disagreeable aspects, for instance telling Isabella her brother actually has been executed, when it would have been just as good to say question still hung in the balance. Prospero is usually taken to be The Bard's self-portrait to some extent, so that not for the first time one feels Shakespeare had a slightly sadistic side. Of course an Elizabethan audience may have demanded that sort of situation. Always good on brothel personnel, here Pompey the pimp is funny, as, when being interrogated: ' . . . Now, sir, come on. What was done to Elbow's wife, once more?' *Pompey*:

'Once, sir? There was nothing done to her once.' Shall reread *The Tempest* next to check on Duke/Prospero similarity.

Friday, 14 December

After writing my letter to *The Times* a somewhat pompous personage called Richard Sachs rang to ask I should omit the parenthesis about Levin, saying ('there is time for him to learn, as he is only in his sixties'). I asked objection to this; he said, 'It's rather hitting below the belt.' I replied that it seemed no more below the belt than going out of his way writing a disobliging piece about me, didn't see why I shouldn't pull Levin's leg. He said he would have to consult the Editor. As nothing has gone in, I presume offence was taken.

Why a busybody, who knows nothing whatever of my relations with Malcolm Muggeridge, in any case no imaginable affair of his, should be allowed to be offensive to me, a week or two from my eighty-fifth birthday, why am I not allowed to mention he is in his sixties (an excellent decade), that is hard to understand. I remember when *The Times* did my piece on George Orwell, they put in a drawing of George I thought scarcely at all resembled him. I made some slight demur at this, at which some employee on the paper said: 'It's a very *good* drawing.' The drawing remains for posterity to judge. What employees *The Times* tends to recruit.

On reconsideration, it may be best not to make any public reply to low-grade journalism (all journalism these days). Whatever star governs that sort of thing in any case seems to be afflicting my horoscope at the moment, because in the *Spectator* (always brought down by John), reviewing the Symposium about David Cecil, Tony Lambton (formerly a fan of mine) complains that my contribution is 'snide'. I had thought the piece sailing rather near the wind of sentimentality. Expatriates, especially amateur writers, get very odd, noticeable in several of Lambton's recent letters to the *Spectator,* as we have more than once remarked. In the same number, Allan Massie suggests that now Denis Thatcher has been given a baronetcy, others, including myself, should be made baronets, something I have never had the smallest desire to be. One used to think it might be rather nice to be an earl, but, my God, what a bore that would be these days.

Saturday, 15 December

The oddities of journalists continue. Today I received a letter from Sachs (*The Times*) saying they had not put mine in because it contradicted what

I wrote to the *Observer* (i.e. that 'relations were broken off with Muggeridge' and that 'I received a letter of thanks when I reviewed his Diary'). I pointed out that relations in anything like the former sense *were* broken off, not in the sense Levin suggested, and that the letter of thanks Malcolm wrote for reviewing his Diary was one of quite a few. Anyway, I did not want a tedious affair (only the business of Malcolm and myself) to be continued. One of the reasons why nothing that one reads in the papers is ever wholly correct is that journalists always add something inaccurate of their own to any form of reported information. This latter invariably inept.

Sunday, *16 December*

A nice piece in *Sunday Times* for my eighty-fifth birthday by Penny Perrick. This acceptable in the light of the flak that has been loosed recently. Driven by John, we lunched with Kevin and Rachel Billington at Poyntington. Other guests, Thomas and Valerie Pakenham. Two excellent '70 clarets, missed Châteaux. Valerie is fairly plump these days, nice girl. Thomas all right, if one allows no nonsense. He has to the highest degree the Pakenham habit of contradicting anything anyone else says (e.g. arguing the toss as to date of my own marriage). Rachel still very pretty, indeed perhaps better now a shade older. I brought them a set of American *Dance* paperbacks with incredible covers, which they seemed to like, putting them out on the shelves with the china on the sitting-room shelves.

Rachel described to V Malcolm Muggeridge's obsequies, both RC and C of E in different churches. Frank (Longford) spoke, having made appropriate remarks, added: 'I must say a word to Kitty, I shall never forget her chicken dinners.' Then, remembering Kitty is a shade deaf these days, shouted at the top of his voice: '*I shall never forget her chicken dinners*' (apparently an American expression). He also said to Val on some occasion, talking of going out for dinner, 'It's all right for you, because you sit next to a man, but I have to sit next to a woman.' On return, during night, considerable trouble with my waterworks.

Monday, *17 December*

V drove me to Coleford, where I saw a new doctor, Tim Haggett. Nice young man, who thinks my constant urinating may just be an infection and gave me antibiotics. Contract from Heinemann for *Assorted Estimates*

(?), which I signed and returned to Bruce Hunter. Felt awful, retired to bed, apparently flu.

Tuesday, 18 December

Felt awful. Remained in bed.

Wednesday, 19 December

Haggett got me into the Bath Clinic, where I saw Mr C. U. Moisey. He is lacking in superficial charm on first impact. It is not flu, but a bad bladder infection, with prostate trouble. These will be dealt with in that order, second only after recovery from first in the New Year.

Thursday, 20 December

Bath Clinic. Very low, unable to eat more than mouthful.

Friday, 21 December

My eighty-fifth birthday. Felt like hell all day. V and John looked in.

Saturday, 22 December

Antibiotics seem to be improving the situation a trifle. Moisey (whom I suspect of being North Country) is really perfectly all right, after one has got over his manner, in fact very nice. V and John looked in.

Sunday, 23 December

Somewhat better, V and Tristram looked in. Jonathan Cecil is furious about Tony Lambton's review. Apparently David particularly disliked Lambton, apart from anything else. Jonathan is writing to the *Spectator.*

Monday, 24 December

I came out of the Clinic. Among other troubles, I was dehydrated. While in Clinic I was attached to a metal contraption dripping water into me, which I had to take with me everywhere (even to the loo), like Marley's ghost dragging his past life behind him.

Tuesday, Christmas Day

Lunched at The Stables (Tristram, Virginia, Georgia, Archie). Very enjoyable, tho' still feeling extremely weak. Tristram gave me Pomerol '85; Archie, Château Ramage le Battise '85; Ferdie Mount, Aloxe Corton '84. V smart shirts for birthday and Christmas.

Wednesday, Boxing Day

Stables party lunched here, enjoyable in spite of feeling rather less well than previous day. I have to face that I entered the Clinic a fairly spry octogenarian, emerged having taken a considerable jolt.

Thursday, 27 December

Rather better again. Georgia and Archie to tea. I gave them copies of *Caledonia.*

Monday, 31 December

Last day of not particularly agreeable year. Evangeline very sweetly rang from Washington wishing us a Happy New Year. V answered. Said Evangeline hadn't thought much of a year either.

1991

Tuesday, 1 January

New Year's Day. Feeling better rather than worse, tho' that not saying much.

Wednesday, 2 January

David Piper obit. I always liked him when he was Director of the National Portrait Gallery. All improvements there were due to him, rather than later Director. Mr Moisey rang. I am to see him at 1.45 on Wednesday, 16 January. Card from Polya Bozkova, my little interpreter on Bulgarian Conference twelve or more years ago, perhaps reflecting political changes in the regime. Hilary Spurling rang, V talked to her.

Friday, 4 January

John always brings the *Spectator* with him, in which the Diary, written this week by Frederic Raphael, reverted to Bernard Levin's reference to the row with Malcolm Muggeridge about his review. Rather to my surprise Raphael rebuked Levin for line he took. Neither, of course, had read the review, nor grasped in the smallest degree that the point was Malcolm's sudden stab in the back as a close friend. It seems surprising that people can't find something more interesting to write about. Sent my great-uncle, D. R. Jefferson's, *Eton Atlas*, with graffiti, and the eighteenth-century French Master, Pogny's, book on Heraldry, dedicated to the Eton masters, to Michael Meredith for School Library, with copy of *Caledonia*, latter also dispatched to John Jones for the Balliol Library.

Sunday, 6 January

Read Hazel Holt's *Life of Barbara Pym*, which I enjoyed. Interesting lights on Philip Larkin, who among other things sends account of lunching at The Chantry (not particularly friendly) together with Monica Jones. There are some dots, where presumably he was even brisker. V is going to try and find out what was omitted, as she in any case plans to write to the author. I was not particularly surprised by Philip's tone, still less offended (even if the dots turn out to represent even less flattering comment), but I should have thought Barbara Pym, simply from the sort of person she was, would have liked to hear that there was a lake and grottoes. Anyway, she was quite interested in houses. I never knew Philip at all well, but he is always resentful when he speaks of far closer friends than myself. Some innate sense of inferiority of which fame never took the chill out of his bones.

Tuesday, 8 January

Letter from Helen Fraser, who likes *Under Review* (title she prefers for the new volume of occasional pieces), publication in spring 1992. Will one see it? My Public Lending Right statement (£675) arrived, only about half what sum was last year. Everyone was warned they would probably get less (more people, same sum distributed), but even so this seems rather meagre. However, about 2,000 copies of *Aubrey* taken out, which I always like. Card from Neil Hughes-Onslow deploring Tony Lambton's review of the David Cecil book accusing me of being 'snide' in my contribution.

Mary Lowry-Corry (née Biddulph) obit, in her eighty-fifth year. Will life of Henry Yorke (Green) now appear, presumably held up on account of recounting his affair with Mary ('Miss'), his sister-in-law? One heard latterly Miss and Dig no longer on speaking terms, I don't know with how much truth. Oddly enough also a long obituary notice of Lady Mary Lyon (supposedly née Charteris, in fact daughter of Wilfrid Scawen Blunt). She was ninety-five, also a great figure in Henry's life, as neighbour, *amitié amoureuse*. I doubt if an actual affair (hinted in obit) ever took place. She was ten years older.

I'm still feeling rather grim, but slept all right for the first time last night since first going into the Clinic. Sister Kate Greenfield (now our District Nurse) called to give shot of Vitamin B.

Wednesday, 9 January

Thought it would be a good thing if V had Power of Attorney, as one does not know what one will be feeling like after coming out of the Clinic. This was arranged with Mr Rheinberg of George Creswick's former firm, Faulkner's in Frome. Roy Fuller sent *Spanner and Pen*, fourth volume of his Memoirs.

Tuesday, 15 January

Dr Rawlins looked in, reported on my urine. Unlike Falstaff, not even the urine was all right, the man passing it equally not too good.

Wednesday, 16 January

Went to see Mr C. U. Moisey ('C' is Clifford; what is 'U'?). He said I looked much better. I am to visit the Bath Clinic again tomorrow for a blood test, then on Sunday, 20 January for prostate operation. Tedious to have this blood test in addition, especially for poor V, who drives. Virginia rang to say Howard Sussman had died (probably heart, to which he was subject). This is sad, as the whole family liked him. He was indeed unique among dentists in my experience for general intelligence, liveliness, so that it was even enjoyable to visit him. Max Eilenberg of Heinemann paperbacks (Mandarin and Minerva) rang. He was to have come down here, but that can't be managed in present circumstances, so he is going to send suggested covers for *Dance*.

Thursday, 17 January

The Anthony Powell Society of Toronto sent an excruciatingly funny T-shirt, depicting them all in a group, with titles of a different *Dance* novel on their own T-shirts. V drove us to the Bath Clinic, where they took blood tests, heart tests, X-ray, etc.

Robert L. Selig, Professor based in Chicago, sent work called *Time and Anthony Powell*. The Introduction presents me more or less as a poor boy who made good, which pleased me, otherwise not specially illuminating, though does state that my works represent denial of Freud's theory that novels are merely written to glorify the ego of the author in the hero. It might be added that Freud had very little grasp of the arts, especially novel writing, regarding which he has nothing at all striking to say.

Sunday, 20 January

The Stockwells at The Stables. Tristram has been in touch with Jonathan Cecil, who wrote a furious letter to the *Spectator* about Lambton's comment on my contribution to the David Cecil book, which they have simply not put in. This is the New Journalism, I suppose, which goes out of its way to be insulting, then refuses right of reply. One might have expected something a bit better of the *Spectator.* In the afternoon we drove to the Bath Clinic, arriving at 5 p.m. for operation tomorrow morning.

Monday, 21 January–Sunday, 27 January

Bath Clinic. Operation apparently went off well, quite straightforward. Not suffering from any direct effect at all, but boring side inflictions like itching rash, constipation, etc., a rash being fairly usually concomitant with me of worry, nerves, produced by being in hospital. Felt pretty gloomy. Anaesthetist Dr David Prothero, Welshman. Talked to him about that. He said: 'Disappointing result on Saturday,' fortunately I happened to have seen in papers, discussed with John, England defeated Wales heavily at rugger. Great relief to get home.

Tuesday, 29 January

Denys Sutton obit. I am sad about this. We had become quite friends by letter latterly, chiefly exchange of postcards. Going to Westwood had always been enjoyable, unusual, when the Suttons were there. Denys a man of remarkable intelligence, independent views about pictures, the arts generally, a good Tory. He knew a great deal. I shall miss him. V looking after me quite wonderfully, but I am worried she has so much to do; John also marvellous in all he does in the house and out.

Wednesday, 30 January

Mandy, odd little body from Donna's in Nunney, came to cut my hair, which she did in the bathroom. (£3 + £1 tip.)

Sunday, 3 February

John pointed out that the US Ambassador to St James's designate (subject to approval of Congress), Ray Seitz, was the member of the American

Embassy who (against Fred Morgan's wishes) insisted on speaking at the Hudson Prize luncheon given at the Embassy, then said he had never read any of my books, they might sell better if I did not pronounce my name in such a peculiar manner. He can hardly fail to have dealings with Sir Charles Powell, Mrs Thatcher's great standby, who pronounces his name in the same way.

Reread *The Arrow of Gold*. Remember enjoying it in my day, but really incredible rubbish, although gun-running to the Carlists ought to have made a good subject. The fact is Conrad could not devise a plot, he depends entirely on other aspects of writing a novel. I believe he admits this somewhere.

Wednesday, 6 February

Lawrence Gowing obit. I always got on well with Gowing, in spite of difficulties of speech. He was usually on the right side, if he did not always handle a subject tactfully. I like his painting on the whole.

Neil Hughes-Onslow, who knows Dominic Lawson well, wrote to ask why Jonathan Cecil's letter, protesting about Tony Lambton's review, had not been put in the *Spectator*. That was nice of Neil. He sent Dominic Lawson's reply to me, which was some waffle about the Letter Editor thinking Jonathan's letter too late to appear after Christmas (although Jonathan had faxed it). This seems odd to say the least.

Trevor Powell at last sent the pedigree recognized by the College of Arms, showing link with the Powells of The Travely. It is all written in a minuscule hand, quite illegible, which is tiresome of him. Still feeling decidedly mouldy. Dr Rawlins changed my antibiotics, which I hope will bring improvement. When the Stockwells came here recently Tristram explained that Jonathan Cecil's letter had arrived just before Christmas at the *Spectator*, but that seems a feeble excuse for not putting it in.

Saturday, 16 February

Feeling slightly better. Penny Perrick, known from *Sunday Times* contacts, rang up, most kindly, to ask how I was (possibly there had been talk at the paper of obits), then said she would send some Vitamin E and Primrose Oil tablets, both sovereign, she said, for the sort of ills I am suffering from. The *Radio Times* this week put in puff for Proustian feature by Alan Bennett, announcing with characteristic BBC erudition: 'A bitter-sweet episode from one of Proust's novels *À la recherche du temps perdu*. On the whole the best-known one.'

Friday, 22 February

Margot Fonteyn obit. We used to see a good deal of Margot, apart from at Sadler's Wells, during her affair with Constant Lambert, which was referred to in the notices, tho' never, I think, while she was alive. Charming girl and consummate dancer.

Monday, 25 February

Hitherto V, very sweetly, has been bringing my breakfast in bed since I emerged from the Clinic. Today, feeling I should be confined to bed for the rest of my life unless I made an effort, I rose for breakfast. Bomb scares at the London stations, which are all out of commission, so John is staying on until tomorrow. The war in the Gulf seems to have got off to a good start.

Paul Bailey did a piece about books he had begun, then abandoned. Among these was his biography of Henry Green (Yorke). Bailey said he suddenly felt there was no point in chronicling footling love affairs, drunken episodes, when all that was necessary was to see Henry Yorke's handwriting, which revealed all. It certainly was a strange writing, small, cramped, one sees what Bailey means in it being sinister. Anyway this indicated that Bailey's book was not held up on account of Henry's affair with his sister-in-law, Mary (Miss) Lowry-Corry, recently deceased.

My final judgement on Henry, my oldest intimate friend, who meant a great deal to me when we were both growing up, is that he was really rather a shit. His behaviour to his friends, stinginess, inordinate snobberies, treatment of Dig, vanity about his supreme importance as a writer, combined with no very keen intelligence, all emerge again in rereading the Waugh *Letters*, which I am now doing. In relation to his conceit, Henry once remarked to me in the 1930s, 'I suppose I am generally recognized now as being as good as any novelist can be.' Kingsley Amis once in a review of a reprint of some Green novel (or *Pack My Bag*) said it sounded as if written when the author was drunk; which it well may have been.

Wednesday, 27 February

Reviewed Kingsley Amis's *Memoirs* in the morning, first work attempted
after coming out of hospital, rather a business as *Memoirs* on the whole
not very well written, or put together. Kingsley has taken even less trouble
than usual in this case to make a coherent narrative. After a while book
becomes fragmented, also contains many chestnuts (some quite
implausible), much material about individuals who are of no great interest.
A great deal of rather unnecessary malice. I am one of the few persons
relatively kindly treated, tho' many inaccuracies; anyway he is an old friend,
so do not want to be too critical. There is, in fact, a fair amount of stuff
of interest about Kingsley himself, chiefly his visits to psychiatrists. I had
no idea how neurotic he was from earliest grown-up days. Finished piece,
put it in post, as *Spectator* wanted it as soon as possible.

V drove me to Bath Clinic in afternoon to have post-operation check-
up with Mr Moisey. This went off well. Moisey said return to normal eating,
drinking habits, etc. Did not want to see me again unless something
exceptional happened. He was quite uninterested in my emphasizing how
knocked out I feel, merely saying that was natural enough after a major
operation. Combination of seeing him, doing piece for *Spectator*, caused
utter exhaustion in the evening.

Saturday, 2 March

Tristram and Virginia at The Stables, with Georgia over from Oxford.

In afternoon Dr Nelson D. Lankford rang from Richmond, Virginia. He
is writing life of David Bruce, Ambassador to the Court of St James's,
several other US top diplomatic appointments. Biography for the Virginia
Historical Society. Dr Lankford wanted to know my personal impressions.
I explained that I had met Evangeline first, I think about 1963–4 (Bruces
came over in 1961), we had always know her far the better of the two,
but on occasions when I had met David Bruce he had consistently seemed
to me to have the most perfect social demeanour, charm, of any man of
affairs I could mention. At a private luncheon party he was entirely without
the smallest suggestion of being a figure of considerable political importance, sometimes quiet, sometimes amusing talker; at the same time I
remembered a dinner party where Harold Macmillan was present, then
Prime Minister. Macmillan after dinner taking Bruce aside, talking with
him in a manner that suggested the utmost seriousness. I only met David
Bruce a few times compared with frequent occasions when Evangeline

came here, we to the US Embassy or Albany (tho' there was a period of the Labour Government when we were not asked to the former), but I always had favourable feelings about him.

Monday, 4 March

Tessa Davies to tea after WI. As JP she had to commit an alleged murderer last week. Tristram's film about the deaf-and-dumb boy is to be called *The Count of Solar* (the title he claimed). If it gets off the ground at all, one feels it ought to be a runner-up for international prizes, from Tristram's account of it. He is using deaf boys for actors.

Wednesday, 6 March

Another instance of how anything written gets round to the people concerned, or those involved with them. Had a letter from Claudia Macannock (lives near Wellington, Somerset), who tells me she is daughter of Irene Hodgkins (Hodge), who appears in my Memoirs. Hodge eventually married a successful adman called Varley (father of letter writer); died, Varley then marrying Enid Firminger (whom once I loved), Enid effectively looking after a horde of children after Hodge's death. Mrs Macannock wanted to know if it was indeed Enid Firminger I mentioned in my Memoirs.

Friday, 8 March

Hilary Spurling rang in evening. She had been in Aix-en-Provence 'brushing up her French', preparatory to writing life of Henri Matisse, which she is determined to do. There was the usual Hilary situation of the Matisse family saying Matisse's life had been completely uneventful, not in favour of a biography, then giving in to Spurling pressure. Hilary coming here on Thursday, 11 April. One never knows when one may not move on at my age, so I want to keep in touch. At one moment I feel decease is not going to happen yet; at another, nothing more probable at any moment.

Mark Amory sent a line saying he thought my review of Amis *Memoirs* best that had appeared in taking a new line, which it certainly did. I am inclined to think combination of madness in the family, immense amount of silly publicity about his personality (which, among others, drove Evelyn Waugh, Malcolm Muggeridge, mad), added to a good deal of drink, has disturbed Kingsley rather badly. There has been more publicity about the *Memoirs* than I remember for any book of all similar kind. It is not a good book. Kingsley is more spiteful than I thought and he always adds something himself calculated to spoil any story, e.g. my remark about Auden, which was also clearly not to be repeated in a book.

Sunday, 10 March

Reread Waugh *Letters*, to be followed by *Diaries*. Amongst a good deal that is distasteful or has not worn at all well with passing of time, Evelyn's courting of Laura Herbert remains charming, well expressed, without the least affectation, Evelyn at his best. His behaviour often suggests that he himself had religious mania, something far beyond merely being a devout RC. One cannot, for example, conceive Alick Dru (far more favourably looked on than Evelyn by the Hierarchy) writing such letters as Evelyn did to John Betjeman, Clarissa Eden (Avon), for that matter Daphne Acton (later said to be similarly off balance in regard to religion herself); not to mention Father Caraman, a priest who might be thought to know his own business. They rise to an insufferable pitch with Clarissa for marrying a divorced man, after herself being brought up as an RC. Even Randolph Churchill was outraged at Evelyn's inability to mind his own business; tho' that characteristic persisted in all Evelyn's dealings, important or trivial, even lying at the root of his removal from the Army.

Interesting how little people know themselves. Evelyn, speaking of Swift (whom he had been reading about), says he has a sense of possessing much in common with Swift, but without Swift's 'bossiness', something that did not trouble him at all. Evelyn has claims to having been the most bossy man who ever lived. The best letters from the point of view of being amusing are those to Nancy Mitford, who, in general feebly deferential, had moments of rebellion. In point of fact Evelyn got more from Nancy about upper-class life then he would probably have cared to admit. The supposedly funny ones to the Lygons are dreadful. The letters that display Evelyn's intense interest in all social or worldly matters are on the whole the best.

Then came the shattering blow of changes in RC liturgy, when he speaks of thinking that he will keep his faith, but even that in question. The whole basis of his religion seems very strange, he himself saying it really went back no further than the Council of Trent, the Counter-Reformation. This religiosity must have been a throw-back to Calvinist ancestors, perhaps the Doctor of Divinity who founded the Waugh family at the end of the

eighteenth century. Evelyn's parents seem to have been normal enough C
of E (rather High, anyway Mrs Waugh), Alec, so far as one knows, scarcely
at all interested.

Wednesday, 13 March

V's seventy-ninth birthday. I am to give her shoes which depend on a
catalogue not yet published. Dr Rawlins called, left various prescriptions
(which seem to be working moderately well) for my rash. Caviar for dinner
with Veuve Clicquot Ponsardin '82, quite good.

Saturday, 16 March

Luncheon with Joff and Tessa Davies at Whatley House to celebrate V's/
Tessa's birthday on 13 March. I thought this was to be just the Davieses,
Tristram and Virginia, us. Turned out to be also Lucinda (husband not
present), Lees and Mary Mayall. Pause before luncheon was particularly
trying as I no longer drink before meals. I got down on the floor to
photograph Baxter and Honeybun (neither previously seen). Baxter, of
Burmese extraction, rabbit-coloured, very beautiful; Honeybun his
brother, black and white, with not more than slight Burmese implications
in his figure. Began to feel I would have been wiser to stay at home, found
difficulty in hearing when we arrived in the dining-room. Anyway I am
not good among a lot of people talking and the noise was deafening. I
sat between Tessa and Lucinda. After smoked salmon mousse and chicken
I felt that I would slip under the table. At last I told Tessa I thought we
should have to leave after the pudding (excellent chocolate something)
which we did.

I felt very ashamed at being knocked out at party of this sort. Joff Davies
later said that he thought it a noble effort to come at all after my experiences at the Clinic earlier in the year. We had coffee when we got back
which pulled me together. The New Zealand Chardonnay was pleasantly
drinkable. (Tristram and Virginia stayed till the end of the party and came
up here later.) I hope that my scene did not cause too much disruption.
All the same it is a great bore to have sunk to this state.

Tristram's Michael Palin *American Friends* film is launched next week on
the Big Screen, an exciting prospect. We have been sending a lot of cards
to people about it. I feel somewhat awful most of the time these days. If
it means a graceful exit, one wishes the process could be speeded up,

but it probably doesn't yet. I sit or lie with a rug round me like a character in the background of a Russian novel, the old prince.

Tuesday, 19 March

Dreamt I was in Venice, where they were having a Casanova Festival, everyone dressed in eighteenth-century clothes. Liz (Longford) kindly rang to ask how I was. She had been outraged by Amis *Memoirs*, which I agreed were in the worst possible taste. She seemed surprised that I was not put out about them myself, tho' in fact very mildly treated there in comparison with most, if hopelessly inaccurately. I think the point is that she and Frank accept things like Malcolm Muggeridge 'having lived a licentious life', but when it comes to a crude account of Malcolm, very drunk, trying to have Sonia Orwell in his sixties, not being able to do it, then Kingsley equally failing, they are shocked. Liz also in rather a muddle about when *American Friends* came on. V drove me to Nunney, where I had my hair cut by Mandy at Donna's. Mandy has a face like a putto in a provincial Italian church.

Wednesday, 20 March

Equinoctial gales. Reread Evelyn Waugh's *Diaries*. Did not enjoy this reread as much as expected, in spite of omitting foreign travel, which I always find boring. All the same, the *Diaries* remain an important (perhaps most important) aspect of the Waugh *oeuvre*. They record an extraordinary metamorphosis from being one sort of person (bohemian life, schoolmastering, fitful homosexuality) into a totally different sort of person (White's Club, upper-crust friends, fantasy of himself having become an aristocrat, comparative lack of interest in literature), all done by using, so to speak, the same materials. This quite different in style from a lot of people who 'go up in the world', owing to Evelyn's attitude to himself, for that matter to everyone else. I can think of no parallel among individuals I know, or know of.

To what extent this transformation can be wholly accepted, rather than taken as an actor, who knows his cue without knowledge of the rest of the play, seemed revealed once by an incident at The Chantry. Elizabeth and Christopher Glenconner were staying. Evelyn (I cannot remember why) looked in. The Glenconners are just mentioned in the *Diary* during the war, when Evelyn came across them very casually in Egypt, I think. Elizabeth clearly thought she was meeting Evelyn more or less for the first time. Evelyn rather discomposed by this. Elizabeth was astonished when he said 'Give my love to Christopher' (who was down at the lake fishing) on leaving. She said afterward: 'But he doesn't know Christopher.'

All the same Evelyn did undoubtedly live in a smart world, even if a limited one, together with the perhaps more difficult process of cutting himself off almost entirely from any other. The *Diary* is full of interesting points, not least Evelyn's attitude to his own family. Evelyn also comments that it would have been 'more honourable' for John Betjeman to have earned a living in the family business 'making ornamental ashtrays', than appearing on the BBC. In a way one rather agrees, regretting some of Betjeman's public buffoonery. Could he have written the poems while in the business? It is an interesting question. Of course Betjeman also did an enormous amount of useful and honourable public preservation work, which certainly could not have been achieved had he not led a public life.

An extraordinary aspect of Evelyn revealed by the *Diary* is how soon he began to become an old man, in fact in his late forties, worn out by his sixties. This ageing, like his social transmogrification, seems to some extent to have been brought about by himself taking thought.

Saturday, 23 March

V and John drove to Bristol in the afternoon, where *American Friends* was being shown at the Cannon Cinema. Only about four or five people in the place at a Saturday matinée, but they seemed to be enjoying the film, of which V and John brought back glowing account. It has also received excellent notices up to date. I did not go, feeling that wandering about parking, etc., would be too tiring. Georgia was having a house party at The Stables for Lenka Thynne's (Alexander Weymouth's daughter) dance at Longleat. I went down there about 4 p.m. to photograph them. There were about eight or nine, names not yet established. They were very good (under Georgia's orders) about coming out to sit on the steps of the french windows on the garden side, as it was quite a chilly afternoon. Others arrived later, including Archie with William and Harry Mount. Young people strike one as looking pretty extraordinary these days, but I suppose every older generation has felt that.

Just before V and John returned, Eve Disher rang to thank V for flowers sent her. Eve, now ninety-six, blind, showing indomitable spirit, though said she did not recommend living on into one's nineties, which I can well accept.

Letter from Tom Dardis (who published some of my US paperbacks) saying he was writing a life of American publisher Liveright, who published a lot of goodish stuff in the 1920s, then, I think, went bust. Dardis wanted to know if I could tell him anything about various representatives of Liveright's who worked in London at that period. I knew them all by name, the only one I could give any details about was Donald Friede, who to some extent supplied model for Louis Glober in *Temporary Kings*. Like Glober, an Augustus John drawing was bought when in London by Friede from Cecil Gray, whose wife Tasha brought it to a dinner party Friede gave. She afterwards went to bed with him (tho' not, so far as I know, on the table). Tasha Gray also told the story of the man who collected pubic hair from his mistresses, with which he stuffed a cushion, a character called Edward Heron Allen, who wrote a book on chiromancy, among other works. Friede later became Hollywood figure, had an affair with Jean Harlow, put lilies in her coffin, later attributed to William Powell, her lover *en titre* for the press.

Sunday, 24 March

Reread Kingsley Amis's *Memoirs*. My perforce hurried review correct in judging them badly written, badly put together. All the same containing interesting matter, that chiefly on subject of Kingsley's own neurotic troubles. A good deal of the book is repetition of material used some few years ago, naturally written in rather a different style. For example, the account of Amis family life in Swansea excellently done, while the Larkin stuff is simply from Kingsley's contribution to *Larkin at Sixty*, which inevitably adopts a different tone. The never very continuous narrative breaks into chapters on grumbles about bad behaviour of acquaintances (largely about not paying their round), a good deal better forgotten. Also, as V says, however much you may have disliked your grandparents, it is a mistake to write about them in the manner Kingsley does in the opening chapter, some of which is terribly slipshod. In the same way a futile row about an ATS girl is given at length in Army section (not good). Among chapters devoted to Americans is one on a character called Rosen, man of utter obscurity, who offended Kingsley by making too small Bloody Marys, in general entertained inadequately.

All this shows Kingsley's extreme sensitivity to the way people treat himself, attitude so characteristic of those (e.g. the Sitwells) peculiarly insensitive about the way they treat other people. This sensitivity is possibly allied to Kingsley's fear of going mad, an Amis neurosis hitherto quite unknown to me. Hidden agonies in that direction (fear of flying, account of hospital at end of book where he was being treated for broken leg) seem appalling. The account of my dancing with the black lady when we stayed with the Amises at Cambridge is totally imaginary. True, I did dance with her, kissed her at the end, because the party was closing down, although she was not in the least attractive and, so far from being flirtatious or bawdy, spent all her time talking about how hard it was to be black, rather in the manner of the negro in *Decline and Fall.*

Incidentally, I feel pretty sure that Kingsley was *not* staying with us when Auden died, but Bob Conquest, tho' I admit to making a callous remark about it, because I have never liked Auden's poetry nor what one heard about him as a man. This disregard for the truth on Kingsley's part I find rather shocking, in any case only true things are funny. A hash is made of many stories, which are told at far too great length, often thereby spoiling the point. The fact is the *Memoirs* are on the whole boring, apart from light thrown on the writer.

Evangeline Bruce rang from Washington, as we had sent her the post-card about Tristram's film, which she wanted to hear all about.

Monday, 25 March

Arranged with Cultural Attaché at Finnish Embassy (Frank Hellstén) to take on Finnish translations of *Dance* volumes, which were beginning to pile up here. John conveyed them to the Embassy this morning. Georgia, with three or four guests, remained at The Stables until this afternoon. She said the Longleat Ball was all limited to three rooms on the ground floor, refreshments served in a kind of passage, always filled with people in a state of pandemonium.

Good Friday, 29 March

Read Noel Annan's *Our Age* (recently published), phrase Annan says Maurice Bowra used for anyone functioning roughly between the end of the First War (including some of those who served) and the end of the Second, though I don't think I ever heard him do that. The book begins with some account of people who knew Maurice; then, in a flood of what might be called higher journalism, spreads over almost every subject during the last seventy years or so, ending with the Thatcher adminis-tration. Annan always gets individuals one has known oneself slightly wrong, so that the general effect is fallacious, but one increasingly notices that such is the way history is written. Good passages are, for instance,

description of the Leavises. I suppose it might be possible to write a lively
account of what Annan calls the Oxford Wits, but neither he nor Humphrey Carpenter (*The Brideshead Generation*) has managed to do so.

Also read Thomas Hardy's *A Laodicean* with much skipping, a novel
written when Hardy was already in his forties, unbelievable implausibility,
general silliness.

Monday, 1 April

Tristram, Virginia, Georgia, Archie, together with Toby Coke, Raoul Singh
(Christina Noble's son, now fifteen) at The Stables for Easter. This afternoon Tristram ran off for me tape of *American Friends*, watched again by
V and John, who agreed advantage to see it second time on small screen,
interesting variations. The basically true story of Michael Palin's great-
grandfather – middle-aged don (Ashby) meets American aunt (Caroline)
and niece (Eleanor), both of whom fall in love with him, in Switzerland
on holiday in 1860s, eventually marries niece – very well done, directed,
photographed. To this has been added complicated plot of rival don
(Sime), who is finally voted principal of a college in place of Ashby, seduces
Eleanor whom he leaves pregnant, Ashby marrying her none the less. I
found this not altogether satisfactory as a story, anyway as presented; at
first sight, demurring on conventional grounds that the Victorians did not
behave like that.

On reconsideration I saw that I was arguing against a favourite thesis of
mine that one of the reasons why the prim Victorians were so very prim
was because the rackety Victorians were so very rackety. Once when we
were staying at Felbrigg with Wyndham Ketton-Cremer he showed me the
lawsuit in which 'Mad' Wyndham's relations tried to get him certified
(unsuccessfully). Eton boys gave evidence in which it was said that at Long
Leave so many tarts assembled at Paddington that it was impossible to
leave the station without several of them clinging to you as far as the
street. One also thinks of Wilfrid Scawen Blunt sleeping with absolutely
everyone from Janey Morris to Margot Asquith (then a débutante).

There is a sequence in the film when undergraduates with tarts are
chased by Proctor and Bulldogs, in the course of which Eleanor becomes
involved, thereby somewhat compromising Ashby, but the undergraduates
and tarts did not seem to me sufficiently 'established', so that I failed to
grasp what was happening. This may have been my own fault, as I haven't
seen this sort of film for a long time. I had hoped (on aesthetic grounds)
there would be no bumping about in bed, but the film opens with Sime

and his mistress grunting and groaning, tho' at least they were not naked.
It is as easy to rewrite other people's films as other people's novels, but,
if the film must open on that subject, I should have preferred the mistress
walking across the bedroom in a saucy pair of Victorian knickers, then
she and Sime shown leaving the house separately. Sime seemed to me too
villainous – Bad Sir Jasper – ought to have been smoother. Regency–
Victorian morals, one remembers Surtees novels, while *Verdant Green* hints
at tarts at Oxford in the background. No doubt, as dons were not allowed
to marry, heterosexual ones did find some consolation somewhere. It is
all an interesting question; one would need evidence on this.

Michael Palin himself as his great-grandfather was excellent, looking
genuinely Victorian, not at all overdone, with that odd appearance of
untidiness of daguerreotype portraits of the period. Connie Booth good
too as the aunt, exactly like family photograph of my Jefferson grandmother. I look forward to discussing all this with Tristram. Final judgement
that the film was pretty good, in fact raised so many interesting points that
one hoped for even more than reasonable from it.

Wednesday, 3 April

Graham Greene obit. This was rather a surprise. Thought Graham would
live for ever like Somerset Maugham, even though I knew he had been in
Switzerland (Vevey) unwell for several months. From the word go I had
found his books wholly unreadable, long before there could have been
any question of jealousy, fears of the imputation of which always prevented
me from adversely criticizing them in print later. The plays I found are
even worse. He was good at reportage, a lively journalist, able businessman,
but the novels are vulgarized Conrad, to which tedious Roman Catholic
propaganda is added, the occasional efforts at humour dreadful. In
thinking this I am confronted by overwhelming popular taste for Greene
not only by the public, but almost every writer of eminence, here or
abroad. It seems to me Greene will settle like, say, Henry Seton Merriman,
a novelist by no means without gifts (though he pinched a good deal
from Turgenev in *The Sowers*, V always asserting that Conrad pinched from
Merriman). It is of course true that a writer can reach a stage of general
approbation when literary editors do not like a reviewer to attack him,
reviewers themselves feeling it would be too much of a business to attempt
to undermine a well-known name within a thousand words or so, much
easier to accept in this case the world view.

There was always an element of deviousness, indeed humbug, about all

Graham's public utterances and behaviour. I think he was completely cynical, really only liking sex and money and his own particular form of publicity. I always got on pretty well with him, chiefly just before the war. We had the only colossal row after the war when he was my publisher. He would go white with rage on such occasions, admitting that he had to have rows from time to time for his health. One supposes he was extraordinarily good at assessing people, tho' in my opinion quite incapable of describing individuals with conviction.

He could be good company. I remember especially an evening I spent with him and Malcolm Muggeridge, when Graham described how he had sent a french letter stuffed with hundreds-and-thousands to Wilson Harris, a prim, pompous editor of the *Spectator*, whom Graham greatly disliked and richly deserved to be ragged. During the war I met Graham one evening tearing in a great hurry through St James's Square. He said: 'I've just discovered the Americans in my office [presumably MI6] don't do fire-watching. I'm going to put a stop to that.' It was quite late in the evening. The incident was typical of Graham's whole demeanour, delight in polemics, causing trouble.

The telephone was going all the morning, afternoon, from papers, media, asking for appreciations. I answered these by saying Graham and I were always on good terms, I used to write to him when he received a new decoration, etc., but we neither of us liked the other's books. I took this to be Graham's feeling, as he never mentioned mine, and once reviewing Evelyn Waugh he spoke of him coming under my influence 'with all the Ivos and Ivors'. All the same Graham's death rather unsettling for some reason.

Mr Moss called. Told him to do his usual £100 sort of maintenance on the drive. He said: 'Lovely to see you again.' Much relieved to find I can read Shakespeare in bed again, something I found myself too exhausted to do hitherto after turning in, since my indispositions. I was surprised how much I missed this, tho' it may sound affected.

Saturday, 6 April

Henry Mee rang from the neighbourhood to ask if he could look in. Arrived with his girlfriend, Jane Flynn, for tea. She had just passed her Law exams, will join well-known libel solicitors' firm of Carter-Ruck, where she has up to now been working as clerk. Nice girl, intelligent, attractive, painter's type, perhaps Morland, even Hogarth. Henry very kindly brought me a scarlet shirt of colour he painted me in, which I said no longer procurable at Harvie & Hudson. This came from Pink's in the City. (Unfortunately turned out later to be a size too small, but John says he is pretty sure he will be able to change it.) Henry in great form, hoping soon to get on with his 'World Eminencies', tho' uncertain at present who these are going to be. Curious how few names suggest themselves when one turns one's mind to this.

Henry is selling his house in Jamaica Road because the Bermondsey Underground is to extend beneath it, making too much row for someone who works indoors. He is putting it on the market so as to get an established value, as it will probably be bought eventually by London Transport. Gave him a lot of books, publishers' complimentary copies now sorted out in drawers for distribution.

Wednesday, 10 April

Letter yesterday from Bob Conquest on subject of Amis *Memoirs* in excerpts from newspapers. Another letter today after reading *Memoirs*. These have made Bob very cross in their deliberate disregard for truth, inclusion of matter Kingsley specifically agreed with Bob to omit. I pondered as to curious manner in which people will go out of their way to wreck a friendship, Bob being far closer friend of Kingsley's than I have ever been.

Thursday, 11 April

Hilary Spurling to luncheon, brought with her two small pineapples, which now sit decoratively in small bowls on the dining-room mantelpiece. Hilary wearing a claret-coloured trouser-suit with hat on the back of her head of the same colour, the latter sent from Russia by her daughter Amy, apparently the only thing in the shops. Hilary, looking absurdly young, had air of a character out of fiction, we could not decide who, V suggesting the Artful Dodger. I told Hilary about this *Journal*, asking her to keep quiet on the subject, as it has not been mentioned to anyone else, diaries are apt to make people feel self-conscious, but necessary for her to know about for biographical reasons. She was very funny describing her children, in whom she is intensely interested, but seems surprised to find want lives of their own, a charming side of Hilary's nature, which combines the most subtle *aperçus* with an almost Victorian unawareness, limitations, as to some of the commonplaces of life.

I am reading *Barnaby Rudge* (never properly tackled before), remarked that only Dickens would choose an idiot for a hero, his curiously brutal insensitive side, tho' Barnaby is treated sympathetically, with his raven Grip, without being too outrageously sentimentalized for the period. Hilary at once suggested Dostoevsky. *Barnaby Rudge* rewritten by Dostoevsky (who of course derived a lot from Dickens) is a fascinating thought. I suppose Lord George Gordon would be drastically revised as a kind of Prince Myshkin. Lunch from Flying Casserole: chicken piri piri (with hot sauce, cut up) not too bad, garlic bread (not unqualified success); apple turnover with cream. Château Moulinet, Pomerol '70 (given by Pinters), first-rate (perhaps might have rested upright in dining-room a shade longer).

Friday, 12 April

John unable to change scarlet shirt in larger size, brought elegant salmon-orange one. Finished *Barnaby Rudge*, enjoyable with much skipping. What Dickens really liked doing, superb at, were execution scenes. The Gordon Riots (admirably described) also suited his intensely sadistic strain, illustrated by Mr Tappertit, an essentially absurd figure, losing both his legs in the Riots, then becoming a shoeblack, beating his wife with the brushes, she then taking his wooden legs away, attacking him with them. I am being somewhat plagued with a stiff neck, probably arthritic. Taking cod-liver oil.

Wednesday, 17 April

V talked to Great Elm Literary Group about my works. She found this body quite amusing, intelligent questions. She had run over a pheasant yesterday, which (plucked by Dolly Blacker) we had for luncheon, with a glass of wine, good. My neck seems to be responding to cod-liver oil.

Reread *The Tempest*, which I enjoyed more than usual. What were Miranda's reactions when she first saw a woman, grasped that she had competitors? Did she still think how beauteous was mankind? Did they leave Caliban on the island, more or less in command, or was he taken back and shown at fairs?

Thursday, 18 April

Dr Rawlins looked in with form for donating contributions for roof of Chantry Church. I was surprised to find he knew my middle name, turned out he possessed first volume of Memoirs, had been at school (Christ's Hospital) with John Dymoke, present Queen's Champion. David Rawlins did not possess subsequent three volumes of Memoirs so presented him with these as I happened to have them among the store of sorted books. He said the Dymokes must have been fairly hard-up to be allowed to place a son there, as Means Test fairly drastic. That cannot be so now, anyway for Old Bluecoats, as David Rawlins would do reasonably well, had a son at the school, now teaching somewhere.

Monday, 22 April

The *Spectator* sent for review the new Debrett volume, which is a kind of *Who's Who*, rather than *Peerage & Baronetage*. Apropos of last entry in this journal as John Dymoke included, which he has not been in *Who's Who*. I see the Dymokes now have 3,000 acres at Scrivelsby.

Dreamt last night of Philip Larkin. He and I appeared to be looking over some subterranean mediaeval archaeological excavations.

Tuesday, 23 April

Gerry de Winton obit. Enjoyable memories of staying with him and Pru in their neo-gothick castle at Maesllwch, on the borders of Radnorshire and Brecon, which Gerry had most effectively reduced in size. The best smoked salmon I have ever eaten, recently caught in the Wye. Maesllwch is comparatively near The Travely, occasionally mentioned in the eighteenth-century documents Gerry sent me to look through. He was rather dotty latterly but in a kind of way that made one enjoy his ringing up. Wrote to Pru. This chilly spring makes for stiffness in the joints.

Thursday, 25 April

Tristram's birthday. We rang him. Finished Ann Thwaite's biography of A. A. Milne, which, owing to stupidity of N. Shakespeare, I did not review, although asked for. Fascinating, macabre, well done, though patches of stuff impossible to make particularly interesting. I remember enjoying Milne's play *The Truth about Blayds* as a schoolboy, also vaguely recall Gerald Du Maurier in *To Have the Honour*. By the time the Christopher Robin stuff came along, that sort of thing seemed not worth bothering about (tho' some highbrows raged against it at the time). My parents, especially my father (who had an unhappy childhood), were a classical case of Milne's children's books appealing to older people I have not read *Winnie-the-Pooh* to this day.

Milne seems to have been a capable, fairly awful man. An active pacifist, written a frantic book against war, armaments, etc. immediately before the war, he then saw such things were not on with Hitler in question. Milne was particularly disagreeable when all the trouble blew up about the Wodehouse broadcasts, although Wodehouse was a friend, loving the Milne books. In this incident, Wodehouse very funny ragging Milne (tho' saying he still loved his books) after the attack; one sees Wodehouse's good points, his genuine humour, as opposed to Milne's attempts. Sent a line to Ann Thwaite.

Had a word with David Moore, of The Lodge, yesterday, who was mowing the lawn. He asked had not Henry Mee visited the house recently. On reply affirmative said he and Mr Rolfe, the sweep, had been looking at the Mee catalogue (which we gave The Lodge), Mr Rolfe interested in painting; much admired the Mee pictures. Yesterday, rather less stiff; today slight reversion to former state. This afternoon heard cuckoo for first time, cheering sound after last winter's pains and ruins.

Monday, 29 April

Talking of Milne, I notified Selina Hastings that there was a photograph of Audrey Lucas (Evelyn Waugh's on and off mistress for some years) in the Ann Thwaite biography. Not much information seems available about Audrey Lucas, except that her father, E. V. Lucas, was said to have behaved badly to her. The picture shows a literary cricket team in 1913, in which she sits as the only girl of about fourteen–sixteen. So far as I remember reasonably like, tho' I was only introduced to her for a couple of seconds about twenty years later. The picture shows the world in which Evelyn was brought up. Selina said she had read the second volume of Martin Stannard's EW biography, soon to appear, dripping with Evelyn's awfulness and snobbery. Selina had also read Michael Shelden's *Orwell*, which she will try to get for me. We hope to see her in June. It suddenly struck me that General Colin Powell, black (tho' not very) US Army Chief of Staff, who directed the Gulf War, is obviously Othello. Has he a Desdemona? No doubt we shall hear in future American journalists' muck-raking.

Wednesday, 1 May

Long dream about Alick Dru.

I always used to think *The Awkward Age* and *The Turn of the Screw* the only two Henry James novels I unrestrictedly liked, but on rereading the former found a good deal hard to swallow. One accepts his convention of dialogue as one accepts blank verse, but even in blank verse some variation is made in the manner individuals talk, whereas in James everyone uses the same idiom. Mr Longdon settles substantial sum of money on Nanda Brookenham in order that the impecunious civil servant Vanderbank (apparently having an affair with Nanda's mother, Mrs Brookenham) should marry Nanda, who is desperately in love with Vanderbank. Vanderbank, however, jibs, does not propose.

Accordingly, it is arranged that Nanda should go and live with Mr Longdon as a kind of adopted daughter. At least that is what ostensibly takes place, Mr Longdon is often referred to as the 'old man', tho' only fifty-five; Vanderbank, on the other hand, is called the 'young man', tho' thirty-four. Mr Longdon might perfectly well have taken Nanda as his mistress. One is not certain whether that could not be implied. It may be supposed not, at least as Mr. Longdon to some extent represents James himself, since the frontispiece (one of the awful photographs in the New York Collected Edition), described as 'Mr Longdon's house', appears to be Lamb House, Rye, where James lived. The novel (published 1899) represents James's view of 'modernness', but he seems to have the oddest ideas of upper-class routine social life. Nanda would presumably go to dances, know other young men, hardly be on the shelf at twenty as a notably pretty girl, even if neglected.

Her brother, Harold, however, a fashionable young man, is a splendid picture, sponging on everyone, at the same time evidently popular, asked everywhere, in spite of it. He seems to have no form of livelihood, existing entirely on the borrowed five-pound note. V suggests that Vanderbank has more than a touch of James's supposed boyfriend, the sinister journalist Moreton Fullerton.

When James wants to make a point clear, e.g. when Mr Longdon offers the money to Vanderbank, explaining his scheme, or when Nanda bursts into tears, perfectly plain language is used, which is a great improvement. There is a lot to be said for the story, but it really needs less obliquity, perhaps less length; alternatively, more length fitting the characters into a larger panorama. If Mr Longdon could be shown as definitely being in love with Vanderbank (as he could nowadays), regarding Vanderbank's bisexuality, wanting to settle him as a married man, that would give some motive, but then Mr Longdon would hardly have wanted to be saddled with Nanda.

Thursday, 2 May

V and I voted in Municipal Election at the movable hut, Whatley. After consultation with John Rush, I agreed to contribute to a programme on L. P. Hartley for Edward Storey, Seventh House Films, of Norwich. A shade warmer. Stiffness in left leg somewhat alleviated by change.

Sunday, 5 May

John reported Syndicate at work repairing wall by Stoney Lane Gate, also adding barbed wire.

Monday, 6 May

Reread *The Turn of the Screw*. This holds up pretty well, original in conception, creepy, convincing. So far as one can gather, only the Governess sees the apparitions, tho' this uncertain so far as the two children are concerned, i.e. the Housekeeper definitely does not see Quint and Miss Jessel. At the same time the children are aware of an evil presence when these appear. I usually find James's prefaces uninspiring, but there are two interesting points raised in that portion of the Preface to the collection of short stories in which *The Turn of the Screw* is contained. The first, James's comment that Quint and Miss Jessel are not exactly ghosts, 'but demons as constructed as those of the old trials for witchcraft'. This shows James's acute insight, because the story obviously deals (in one form or another) with what is now called 'child-abuse'. In the recent cases (still simmering) in the Orkneys there has frequently been mention of Black Magic. In fact more than once V and I have talked of the resemblance to former witch trials in Scotland. Now that has also been mentioned in the papers.

The second point (actually the first in James's Preface) deals with a matter much more personal to myself as a writer. Apparently James received more than one complaint that his Governess-narrator in *The Turn of the Screw* was too dim a figure. To this James answers: 'you indulge in that stricture at your ease, and I don't mind confiding to you that – strange as it may appear – one has to choose ever so delicately among one's difficulties, attaching oneself to one's greatest, bearing hard on those and intelligently neglecting the others. If one attempts to tackle them all one is certain to deal competently with none . . .' That is substantially the answer I always give to those who complain that Jenkins (in *Dance*) is a misty figure, tho' that 'reproach' (as James calls it) is made only in England, never in the US or elsewhere.

If Jenkins were described too fully, his parents, affairs, marriage, and so on, the general panorama of individual characters would suffer. More recent critics, as it happens, have taken the line that Jenkins's behaviour displays many clues to his character, but the Jamesian principle holds good, his explanation about the Governess. As a matter of fact the Governess seems perfectly clear. I think she is described as coming from a clergyman's family, one knows perfectly well what the author intends. By the phrase 'at their ease' James also well suggests the manner in which critics, least of all reviewers, never give real thought to the requirements of any given narrative, the complications of writing, tho' it might well be urged that most of those who write for the papers are scarcely qualified at all to do so by lack of all intellectual equipment.

Wednesday, 8 May

Sent letter to Somerset County Council (also signed by V) protesting against increasing demands of Quarries to expand, thereby hoping to close roads used at least since the Middle Ages, construct others to be used only by an individual quarry, generally devastate the countryside.

The University of Vicosa in Brazil made request (for second time) for books in foreign languages taught there, including my own, so sent paperback set of *Dance*. Looking through some book of art reproductions struck by how much Io in Correggio's *Jupiter and Io* (in Venice) (Jupiter in the form of a cloud ravished Io) resembles Mrs Thatcher.

Monday, 13 May

Balliol (James Armstrong) asked for MSS for Exhibition held during week of Gaudy in June. Typescripts of books have been handed over to Tristram and John. Balliol Library already possesses *Caledonia, Poems for Seventieth Birthday of Roy Fuller, Iron Aspidistra*, so suggested (V's idea) Introduction to *Verdant Green*. Letter from Hilary Spurling to V enclosing photographs (goodish) of William Pye's head of me, saying she has written him stern letter about casts. In consequence of this Bill Pye himself rang in course of morning, saying he had received such a ticking off from Hilary that he would like to come here on Tuesday, 28 May, make a few improvements in the head, using special video, might he bring his wife.

Dominic Lawson, Editor of *Spectator*, invitation (via his secretary) to luncheon, replied too stiff in joints. Penny Perrick rang with enquiries, said Hilary on short list for NCR (National Cash Registers) Prize, of which I had never heard, for £25,000 for *Paul Scott*, of which there was a strange review in *The New Yorker*, Penny said would send me, the critic deploring Scott's alcoholism, which might be thought Americans had by now got used to in writers.

Reread *Nostromo* with enjoyment. Years ago I read it only at third attempt. Then I read it again, mildly liked the novel. This time struck me as a most remarkable work, tho' not sure that one wholly believes in Nostromo himself, right-wing foreman of the dockers in capital of this imaginary South American state, Costaguano. The vitality which Conrad manages to infuse into the scene is immense. Nostromo saves a large delivery of silver from the San Tomé mine during a revolution, hiding the silver in one of the islands off the coast. He then becomes disillusioned, begins to steal the silver from the hoard, his self-disgust a typically Conradian emotion. Equally Conradian (tho' I believe to some extent showing Maupassant influence) is character of Decoud, the Parisianized rich young Costaguanian journalist, who aspired to write in the manner of Heredia, then, in spite of his cynicism, becomes involved in Costaguanian politics, conceal-ment of the silver, finally commits suicide. Reading of these goings-on in a Latin-American republic, I feared for the fate of the *Dance* paperback dispatched to Brazil.

Monday, 20 May

Took Rider Haggard's *King Solomon's Mines* (1885) from The Stables to reread (in fact read to me by my mother, I think). Rather a struggle. The best one can say is that the story probably started off a lot of similar ones written by authors less familiar than Haggard with Africa. Extraordinary Haggard should have been spoken of (as he was) in same breath with Kipling, the actual writing appalling. His first cousin, Colonel Mark Haggard, commanded my father's battalion at the beginning of the First War, allegedly responsible for the words: 'Stick it, the Welch!' (inscribed on front of Welch regimental-depot building) tho' my father always denied that, said invented by *Western Mail*. Mark Haggard merely used bad lan-guage when shot in the stomach fatally.

Wednesday, 22 May

Colin Welch, former Deputy Editor of *Daily Telegraph*, never known at all well, nor seen for ages, rang. Said he was reviewing for *Spectator* two books of Quotations (*Modern Oxford* and *Bloomsbury*, I think), taking them to task for not including in section devoted to my works lines composed by me at beginning of the Second War (when making up such things to be repeated with friends, such as Constant Lambert, the Lloyd brothers, at Castano's). A few months later, when I was in the Army, Raymond Mortimer wrote to ask if he could put them in the *New Statesman* (only occasion I ever appeared in that nauseous rag):

> A literary, or Left Wing, erstwhile wellwisher would
> Seek vainly now for Auden, or for Isherwood;
> The Dog beneath the Skin has had the brains
> To save it, Norris-like, by changing trains.

Welch wanted to check wording. He is an odd chap, whose eccentricity probably prevented him from being made Editor of the *Telegraph*. We talked for a time, in fact I thought I should never get away, while Welch rambled on about every sort of thing, but nice of him to remember the quotation.

Took *Dracula* (1897) from The Stables, Tristram's name in it. I last read it as a boy age eleven or twelve, at my prep school, I think, finding the story unexpectedly heavy going. The novel begins all right with Count Dracula's castle in Transylvania on the edge of an abyss, where a young English lawyer, Jonathan Harker, goes to negotiate the buying of some London properties. Story tails off into the diaries of various characters, all written in exactly the same style, also pretty involved. *Dracula* is, in fact, an appalling piece of literary organization, astonishing it should have survived for nearly a century. I indulged in remorseless skipping, noting a few points. There is perhaps a suggestion of homosexuality in the Count warning off three beautiful female vampires from the young man, his special victim, a touch of M. de Charlus in his demeanour. Apart from appearance at meals (tho' not eating himself) Dracula never appears, tho' Harker finds that he cooks, lays the table, makes Harker's bed, presumably does the washing up, as there is no one else in the castle.

Quite how Harker escapes is not clear, rather in the manner of 'with a leap Carruthers freed himself'. Eventually gets back to London, organizes a party of friends to make an expedition to Transylvania, where (ending an existence of several centuries) they reduce Count Dracula to dust by traditional anti-vampire processes, not before he has brought about several

deaths. Bram Stoker, who wrote *Dracula*, was born in Dublin, real name
Abraham (probably Cornish, South Welsh, origins, rather than Jewish),
deriving as a writer from Sheridan Le Fanu, whose *Carmella*, dealing with
vampires, favourite short story of my late brother-in-law Edward Longford.

Thursday, 23 May

Fan letter from Australian Assistant Bishop Ian George, about to become
Archbishop of Adelaide. Sounded reasonably intelligent. Told him I could
already notch up on my gun Robert Runcie. John suggested Archbishop
George was Barry Humphries in another avatar of Sir Les Patterson (Barry
Humphries).

Saturday, 25 May

V's first cousin David Rhys obit, third Dynevor son, lived latterly at house
called Southwick Court not far from Trowbridge with second, younger
wife Sheila. We saw them once in a way. I always liked David. He was about
fifteen months younger than me, so we never came across each other at
Eton, but he was very keen on preserving Dynevor, which V and I also
worked on a bit. He went into catering (scullion to manager of Claridge's),
made a competence on which to retire. Good-looking, charming, great
one with the girls, debs (e.g. Mary Mayall) warned against him. His first
wife, Anne Wellesley, extremely pretty, inherited the Spanish titles (which
go through women) Duchess of Ciudad Rodrigo, etc. This made David a
courtesy Duke, but (rightly, I think) Anne made them over to Gerry
Wellington (who was, to say the least, pressing on the subject).

V, John and I dined at The Stables, where Tristram made excellent
tagliatelle with the pasta machine given him by V as birthday present.
Tristram almost sure to be producing Kingsley Amis's *The Old Devils* on
TV. When reading the book a second time I made list of Welsh names of
characters, with wives, necessary in order to steer through the narrative,
with brief notes on behaviour. This Tristram has copied out.

Interesting letter in *TLS* about hauntings at Lamb House, Rye, where
Henry James lived. Lamb House former residence of the Mayor of Rye,
knighted for giving shelter to George I, when more or less shipwrecked
off Rye on his way to become King of England. Figures of a vaguely
eighteenth-century type were recorded on and off when the writer E. F.
Benson lived there, but the contemporary writer Rumer Godden (enjoyed
by V), who also inhabited Lamb House, writes to say that the poltergeists

Septimius Severus has a man scourged for reminding him that they were at school together

Drawing by AP.

VP and Pamela, Lady Harlech, 28 April 1990.

Anthony Hobson and Lady Naipaul, 28 April 1990.

Belinda Hollyer and Bruce Hunter, 17 June 1990.

Evangeline Bruce and Marcelle Quinton, 24 July 1990.

AP on the terrace, 24 July 1990.

Hilary Spurling and AP with the head by William Pye, who took the
photograph, 18 December 1990.

Snook contemplates life, 1990.

The scene shifters for a Channel 4 programme,
with Henry Mee picture, 1990.

Henry Mee and Jane Finch, 1990.

AP and VP, taken by Lady Antonia Fraser, 11 June 1991.

The curry cook, 5 August 1991.

Lady Antonia Fraser and Tristram Powell at sixtieth anniversary party
for Frank and Elizabeth Longford, 3 November 1991.

AP and Vice-Chancellor Sir Aubrey Trotman-Dickenson, 10 March 1992.

Figs grown on the tree at
The Chantry, summer 1992.

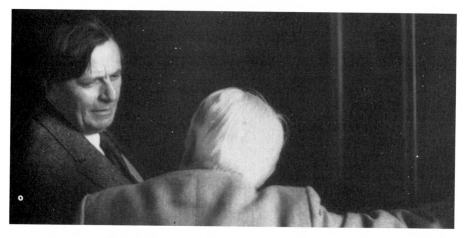

Barry Humphries and AP, 4 December 1992.

AP.

there were so active that she had the place exorcized. Rumer Godden also asserts that she sometimes saw two children in the garden. Latter of note, because James took over Lamb House in 1898, the year in which he published *The Turn of the Screw*, the book in which the two 'abused' children are depicted. This seems to open a new avenue of imposing imagined – rather than real – characters on a given locality, which seems to produce apparitions of which certain individuals, sensitive to such phenomena, are sometimes aware. Also letter in *TLS* from Bob Conquest complaining of many inaccuracies in the Amis *Memoirs* about himself, together with faulty quotation, and attribution, of his limericks.

Tuesday, 28 May

Bill and Sue Pye arrived just after 11 a.m. with video equipment (which she organizes) to do additional work on the head. Sue former-art-student type, also provided to make conversation during photography, which took place in dining-room. Bill said bronze casts should be ready in a few months, but impossible to extract price from him. As one gets older this British inability to discuss money (as opposed to the Americans, refreshingly unembarrassed by it) becomes a shade tedious. I was, however, much amused to hear that the *Daily Telegraph* were said to be 'interested'. When the Pyes were on some do in Japan about two years ago Hugh Casson and his wife also there, introduced to a vast concourse of Japanese as 'Sir Casson and his mistress'.

Bob Conquest rang, he and Liddie to lunch here on 6 June. Bob still seething about Amis *Memoirs*. He and Kingsley are supposed to be lunching together to consider matters. A Cambridge don with American affiliations, Gorley Putt, once met with the Mizeners, who were fairly thick with him, sent typescript of about fifty letters between Arthur Mizener and himself, edited by Putt. Decidedly boring, except that Arthur, whom one always regarded as a cut above average American academic, appears in all the latter's least endearing shapes, e.g. early Communist leanings, hopes of keeping US out of active participation in the war (distinct sense of his own German origins), etc. I recall with some amusement what I said to Arthur about the publisher Max Perkins's sentiments as to keeping out of the war in letters to Scott Fitzgerald. In fact I was staggered by the dissimulations that must have taken place when the Mizeners were here. I did not say anything about this, but V, quite unprompted, said: 'I thought I knew Arthur pretty well, but it's clear I didn't in the least.'

Our Kansas friends on Hellenic cruises, Bill and Virginia Robinson, rang in the evening, on brief visit to London. In great form (Bill having been polished off by V for some little time, as we hadn't heard from them). They are most loyal buyers of my works, although Bill far from literary, having acquired *Verdicts*, which has, however, turned out useful to their grandson, who is doing thesis on Fitzgerald.

Wednesday, 29 May

Reread *Jew Süss* (1926), found at The Stables, by Lion Feuchtwanger, bestseller of the Twenties, then regarded as pretty middlebrow. Middlebrow the book may be, but I read it again with considerable enjoyment. The author has the rare ability in a novelist of keeping up the same tone throughout an exceptionally long narrative, only about once, in a paragraph or two about Hebrew lore, perhaps falling off a shade in this difficult achievement. I should be interested to know how much Süss himself is based on an historical individual, facts, etc.

Thursday, 30 May

John Rush, of Higham, rang, said Edward Storey project for L. P. Hartley programme all right, in principle arranged for Thursday, 5 September. He thought efforts for TV *Dance* might be begun again in October, lots of people interested, but impossible to arrange anything until 'franchise' negotiations at an end. Helen Fraser, of Heinemann, to luncheon. Owing to trains, she arrived about 11.20, quite convenient if business is to be talked, quick get-away in afternoon. In fact nothing much to discuss, but good thing to keep in touch. She said *Under Review* scheduled for May 1992, made no difficulties about advancing that to March. Dark, slight, at moments very pretty. She is really Lady Macbeth, V says, notwithstanding her little-girl voice; in which, after all, Lady Macbeth may well have spoken. I mentioned having reread *Jew Süss* with enjoyment, of which she made a note, as its publisher, Secker, is under Heinemann umbrella. Liked the idea of Henry Mee jacket for *Under Review*, not sure whether first or second portrait better. I shall enquire if Henry has photograph of second.

Helen Fraser had interviewed for a job Sappho Durrell (committed suicide allegedly because her father Lawrence Durrell slept with her), Helen said she was an attractive girl in every way, not taken on because unable to type. Helen said her teenage daughters all devour Jilly Cooper's novels. She returned on 3.30 p.m. train, useful contacts having been made. Luncheon from Flying Casserole: Boeuf Bourguinonne (goodish), meringues with cream, fruit, Helen could not eat her cream, in fact fairly good. Does not drink, tea when she arrived rather than coffee. Selina Hastings rang, asked us to luncheon (probably at Bridge House), on Wednesday, 5 June.

Friday, 31 May

After week's cod-liver oil, right leg no longer stiff, all the same decided not to attend David Rhys's funeral, as inevitably lot of standing about at such functions, tho' I would have liked to be there. All the same, possibly better for V to renew family contacts, which she finds easier on her own. I think that turned out the case, tho' she found the occasion pretty harrowing.

Reread *Hamlet*. Reflecting on the various entries of the Ghost, struck that its appearance took three separate forms, which should be differently portrayed on the stage. Apparitions, as repeatedly recorded, are rarely seen by more than one person at a time, tho' there have been exceptions to this rule. Allowing for that, the guards on the battlements might be shown observing a dim figure in the distance, armour just visible. However, when Hamlet himself takes part in the battlements encounter he actually experiences long conversation with the Ghost. That, by any serious psychical standards, must clearly be some sort of an illusion or day-dream. Should therefore be shown as something different, individual to Hamlet, visually detached from the other characters on the stage. Finally, when Hamlet sees the Ghost, but the Queen does not, a third method should be devised.

Saturday, 1 June

Angus Wilson obit. Met him a few times only, when we got on perfectly well without being types at all sympathetic to each other. He took himself very seriously both as an author and as a queer. I never cared for his novels, short stories, which seemed to me unreal, but many (including Evelyn Waugh) admired them. I thought him a good critic, especially his book on Kipling. Rather an egotistical sour old thing to talk with. We ran into him in Ceylon. One gathers Angus Wilson's demise will be awkward for his long-time boyfriend (said to be nice), who has devoted his life to being a wife, no particular means of livelihood, Angus Wilson royalties diminishing. Will the Royal Literary Fund stump up a pension?

Engagement of Henry Mee and Jane Flynn (girlfriend) announced in

Telegraph. I can congratulate him when he sends reply about photograph of portrait. I had been interviewed in French periodical *Autrement* (quarterly, but appears irregularly) which arrived today, a number devoted to Oxford. As might be expected, often less than accurate. One expects such things as, say, the Hypocrites Club, where '*l'on y jouait au poker des mises très élevés*' (the thought of playing any cards in room packed with drunks, Robert Byron playing the piano, etc.), but I was shocked at Isaiah Berlin represented as saying (if he really said anything of the sort) that Maurice Bowra '*a fasciné Cyril Connolly, John Betjeman, Evelyn Waugh*'. After all, Evelyn himself wrote that Maurice only took any notice of him after he, Waugh, had made some sort of a name for himself. I doubt if they ever even met when Evelyn was up as an undergraduate. Certainly Evelyn was not in the least influenced by Maurice, whose point he never really grasped (as the utterly unresembling, unconvincing Mr Samgrass shows).

Sheila Rhys asked V if she could manage to get something said about David as obituary notice in the *Telegraph*, so much involved in telephoning, ending with Hugh Massingberd ringing, saying he would try to fix something.

Sunday, 2 June

Made curry (reasonably good) from remains of Boeuf Bourguinonne. Finished rereading cycle of Sherlock Holmes stories. While doing this tried to analyse (with complete lack of success), their continuing hold, although, as someone said, if Holmes was not killed after crashing over the Reichenbach Falls in a death grapple with Moriarty, he was never quite the same again. When (*Hound of the Baskervilles*) Holmes took Watson to the Bond Street galleries to rest their minds and later spoke illuminatingly about 'the modern Belgians', one presumes that would probably have been Ensor and/or the Belgian Symbolists, Pointillistes. At some point Watson seems to have exchanged from the RAMC (possibly then AMC) to the Indian Army, because he had *MD, Indian Army* on his old tin trunk, but in the early days had been attached to the Northumberland Fusiliers and Berkshire Regiments. Perhaps medical interposting sometimes took place in those days.

Monday, 3 June

Tessa Davies looked in for tea after the WI. She is going to do a cooking course at Orvieto. Snook showed off to her in a preposterous manner.

Tuesday, 4 June

Alison Lurie to luncheon. Owing to lack of taxis at Westbury arrived rather late, bringing her traditional box of Black Magic chocolates. In spite of having recently broken a leg (still in some form of plastic splint), in excellent shape. She yelled with laughter when told that Arthur Mizener had been somewhat Communistically minded when younger, and isolationist about the war. I was amused at this, had expected her to say that nearly all American academics had been like that at the time, but no. Henry Mee rang during lunch (of which were in the middle owing to Alison being late), so we could not talk. Alison preparing a book of ghost stories. Flying Casserole luncheon: lemon chicken with rice (good), treacle tart, fruit. Alison drank soda water before, glass of Maximio di Trentinto during lunch. Later I rang Henry Mee, got on to his fiancée, Jane Flynn, as Henry out with his mother choosing a wedding present (Sickert etching). They are to be married today week, at St Ethelreda's, Ely Place, oldest Catholic church in London, as she is RC.

Wednesday, 5 June

Turned out Henry Mee has no photograph of portrait on the stairs he gave me, but had painted yet a third to keep in his studio with that of the Queen, Yehudi Menuhin and, I think, someone else, as permanent stock. This is getting like Velázquez and Philip IV of Spain, or Goya and Ferdinand IV. Henry will, if possible, bring down photograph of his third one taken by himself when they call on Saturday, 15 June, as newly married couple. If satisfactory this can be used for *Under Review* jacket.

Selina Hastings arrived about 12.45 to take us to luncheon at the Bridge House, Nunney. This had the air of having rather gone downhill as a restaurant, the antique shop having spread a good deal into the room where one eats (food, however, not bad; avocado, navarin of lamb, or sole, ices, apple crumble). A rather grim-looking lady with the air of a high-powered academic was sitting at our usual table. If she had good hearing she must have been regaled by Selina's latest revelations in connexion with her Evelyn Waugh book.

Enjoyable lunch. Later *Standard* rang to ask me to do a piece about cuts in the Army, traditions of regiments, etc. Replied had been out of touch with such things for too long. Turned out to be speaking to James Hughes-Onslow, nephew of Neil. Had been at Eton with John, whose number and address he asked for.

Thursday, 6 June

Bob and Liddie Conquest to luncheon. They were just back from Russia, food if possible worse, hotel slightly better. When they passed statue of Dzerzhinsky (Chief of what was then called the OGPU, I think) taxi-driver pointed, said: 'Hooligan! Fascist!' Went to the Ballet (*Swan Lake*). Gorbachev in Imperial box, Yeltsin in stalls. They have seen Kingsley Amis once or twice since being in London, but Kingsley always manages that he is never alone with Bob, still wanting to have it out about *Memoirs*. The Conquests drew a somewhat sad picture of the Regent's Park Road household, which now includes Philip Amis. Hilly dreadfully overworked, used to get bit of a rest when Kingsley went to stay with George Gale, but Gale now dcd. Recently Kingsley thought something wrong with his leg, so took to a wheelchair, which Hilly had to trundle every day to the pub. Bob looked a shade tired, I thought, but in excellent form, as was Liddie, who wore a smart pair of limp leather top boots, which the Russians must have loved as suitable for dancing the *gopak*. Flying Casserole: lemon chicken (good), strawberries and cream, almond tart. Bob drank a glass of sherry before, Liddie very small gin and tonic; at luncheon, Bob three-quarter bottle white Antinori, less one glass for me, Liddie and V split bottle red Santa Cristina less a glass left over. Enjoyable party.

Saturday, 8 June

Dreamt I was at large luncheon party, mostly women of fairly mature age, some American. I was sitting next to Princess of Wales (never met), very pretty, easy to get on with. This week's *Spectator* contains Colin Welch's complaint that my lines on Auden and Isherwood are not included in the Books of Quotations he reviews. Welch also objects to remark about the Swiss having never produced anything but the cuckoo-clock, attributing that to Orson Welles in *The Third Man* (I have also seen it attributed to Graham Greene, who wrote the script, but allegedly Welles wanted it inserted). It appears first, of course, in Whistler's 'Ten O'Clock Lectures', included in reprint of *The Gentle Art of Making Enemies* (1888, reprinted 1954), which I pointed out in *Punch*, reprinted in *Verdicts*.

I sent a line to the *Spectator* remarking this, but do not suppose for a moment they will publish it, as people much prefer to go on saying what is known to be wrong: Marie Antoinette's 'Let them eat cake', Queen Victoria's 'We are not amused', etc. Vladislav Gheorghiev, Berkovitza, Bulgaria, appealed for English books for the Dr Ivan Panov School. Says no foreign books available in Bulgaria except Russian, all about good Communists and wicked Capitalists. Sent him paperbacks containing first three volumes of *Dance*. Berkovitza appears as very small place on map, but I suppose one could say the same of Eton.

Tuesday, 11 June

Antonia and Harold Pinter to luncheon. Attending First Night of revival of *The Caretaker* in Bath. Opening last night a success. Donald Pleasance playing the Tramp, which he did at first staging thirty years ago. There is always slight sense of tension with Harold, and when I told him that one of Dracula's hide-outs in England had been at Sidcup (destination of the Tramp), he did not laugh as much as did Antonia. They brought a bottle of Château Lynch Bages '67, which was kind. Flying Casserole (now in rather a parlous state apparently) managed to produce Boeuf Bourguinonne, which was all right, followed up with various cheeses, as neither Pinter eats pudding. Earlier in the morning, when I was about to open something fairly classy in the way of claret for Harold (Antonia likes white), Antonia rang to check the route. I took the opportunity of making sure about their drinking habits; just as well, because turned out Harold does not drink red if he has to drive (like many people he cannot understand that white is, in fact, alcoholically stronger). Consequently I managed to whistle up a couple of bottles of (slightly *pétillant*) Moscato d'Asti, really not at all bad for that kind of wine.

Read R. L. Stevenson's *The Wrecker*, which I don't think ever tried before. The novel (in collaboration with his stepson Lloyd Osbourne) is always within hail of a book for boys, with much practical detail about salvaging wrecks in the South Seas, this one believed to have valuable stores of opium hidden away. Plot quite shapeless, continually going off on new tack. In the end one closes the book with sense of complete pointlessness, at the same time has to admit that it has been read from cover to cover with a certain amount of interest as to what is going to happen. On the way to post letters this afternoon saw what I believe to be a slow-worm on the drive apparently dead. By the time I returned from post-box it had disappeared. At first I supposed it an adder, then remembered Jocelyn Brooke's account of how upset he was as a child when the gardener, making that mistake, killed a slow-worm.

Thursday, 13 June

Remote cousin, Trevor Powell, now in command of establishment at West-bury for selection of officers, came over in morning. He was on the point of promotion to Lieutenant-Colonel, but will now probably not attain this rank owing to Army cuts. Trevor distinctly polished up since last seen, extraordinary thing he looks remarkably like my old cousin Ted Powell (first cousin of my grandfather, who did not resemble him, nor my father), though Trevor's common ancestor died about 1670. V was out shopping. Trevor with car and driver, but had to be back later in the morning. We dished up a certain amount of genealogical matter. Trevor has a house at Beaconsfield, where his wife Elizabeth keen on driving, which she some-times does in Windsor Great Park. I asked if she drove four-in-hands, but that would be only special. Trevor has put *Dance* among the books potential cadets are recommended to read, set in the Westbury establishment's library. I gave him another American paperback set with the comic covers of First War uniforms for himself or other use. He had been in North Wales not long ago, one of the locals referred to him as a 'bloody Englishman', or something of the sort. Trevor replied that he had Welsh blood as a matter of fact. Welshman asked what, Trevor said: 'I'm directly descended from Howel Dda.' Apparently the North Walesian absolutely crawled.

Saturday, 15 June

Dull weather. V and I watched Trooping the Colour. Henry and Jane Mee, married last Wednesday, arrived for late tea, Henry immensely cleaned up by three days' matrimony. They seemed very happy, showed an album of photographs of the wedding, including Henry's detective brother, who gave them as wedding present number plate MEE1, which John says must have cost a matter of thousands. It resulted in Henry being at once stopped by a policeman as a potential cocaine baron. Jane's solicitor boss, Peter Carter-Ruck, libel lawyer of some notoriety, apparently a Dickensian figure. We gave them the two last *Oxford Dictionaries of Quotations*. At first we were just going to give the *Modern* one, then that seemed so full of rubbish, politicians' speeches, and so forth, that the previous one was added. Henry had not had time to photograph third portrait, but will try to do so in near future. Dreamt that Alan Pryce-Jones was showing a tourist party round a ruined (seemed to have been bombed) town, perhaps Spanish. As we were picking our way across it, he said: 'I must go off now, because I have to get a horse for the rest of today's tour.'

Tuesday, 18 June

V and I lunched with Lees and Mary Mayall at Sturford, now so greatly overgrown that entrance to drive scarcely visible from road, like entering the palace of the Sleeping Beauty. The house itself gone rather a beautiful yellow, façade covered with roses. Lees said his legs increasingly stiff, otherwise not feeling too bad. Lees suffered further losses on Lloyd's, like so many others. I did not realize that once in, impossible to get out, unless your particular syndicate happens to work to an end, re-form. Their daughter Alex recently broke rib in car smash, but nothing serious. Son Robert now working in Richard Booth second-hand book conflation at Hay-on-Wye, where Robert fills place as antiquarian expert, which they did not possess. Pay not munificent, but Lees thinks place will suit him better, London not his scene. Robert has a flat at Hay, a pretty town. Main features of luncheon from Marks & Spencer in Warminster: smoked trout; blanquette de veau (épinards à la crème by Mary); pastry, all not at all bad. V drank claret; I glass of Loire white, called, I think, Jurançon. Pleasant party.

Wednesday, 19 June

A character from the *Standard*'s 'Londoner's Diary', Marcus Scriven, who has rung me once or twice about odds and ends, asked if I would lunch, which was arranged for today at Ston Easton Park (one of Scriven's suggestions), country house about ten miles from here, now hotel-restaurant. I was quite glad to see this place, which belonged to a family called Hippisley-Cox (Hippisleys there since Dissolution), sold up a few years after we came here. We went to the sale. Everything was in the utmost disorder, grounds like a jungle. This was about time when Evelyn Waugh decided to leave Stinchcombe, a moment when he was very taken with Ston Easton (megalomania not the word), but wiser counsels prevailed. The place eventually became the property of William Rees-Mogg, Editor of *The Times*, whose family have been in this part of the world for some centuries. Rees-Mogg no doubt found it too big to handle, resulting in Ston Easton's present state. All now immensely tidied up, grandiose, the house (later eighteenth century, one would guess), with rather the air of an official residence.

Marcus Scriven, of whom I have had not the slightest earlier conception, turned out an eminently presentable young man (Radley, Christ Church, regular Captain Welsh Guards), whom V thought almost embarrassingly good-looking when I brought him back to tea. While talking to him on the telephone he had mumbled something about having been in Belsen for three years, turned out to have been when serving with NATO force that included German and Netherlands troops. Belsen now called Hohne, Scriven lived in former Nazi officer quarters, where further remains were excavated during building additions.

One of Scriven's brother officers in the Welsh Guards had been Philip Dymoke, second son of John Dymoke, whom he described as taut, good soldier, about to go to Staff College. Remarkable how the Dymoke family seems at last to have recovered itself. Scriven left the army about three years ago, during which time he has been reporter (on *Daily Mail*, I think), then *Telegraph*, now edits 'Londoner's Diary' on *Standard*, with helpers, but not unknown to write whole page. He struck me by describing various papers he had been on by groups of people who played chief part in his work there, something I had never before heard a journalist do, as usually too self-regarding to take in other human beings, except so far as they provide formalized 'stories' for copy.

We were the sole lunchers at Ston Easton (no doubt more lively in the evening), the waiter looked rather like a stable-boy by Stubbs (*Brushing down Gimcrack*). General atmosphere of the place, staff well turned out, luncheon eatable in rather la-di-da way, not without traces of *nouvelle cuisine*, at £25 a head. I had sliced-up melon with decoration of fruit and ice cream; hot salmon (goodish) with rather awful salad; some form of chocolate pudding; better coffee than usual, with chocolates. I asked for hock, got rather fiery Johannisberger of unknown date (if any), of which I had one glass, Scriven consuming the rest after a Buck's Fizz. He came back to tea. More enjoyable experience than expected.

Friday, 21 June

Haircut at Donna's (Mandy) in afternoon. About 7.30 p.m., when in my bath, V reported French journalist, Pierre Assouline, of *Lire*, ringing from Paris for interview next week, piece to appear in September with publication of next two volumes of *Dance* translation (*At Lady Molly's, Casanova's Chinese Restaurant*, should, in fact, also be *The Kindly Ones*, I think, but thankful for small mercies with French publishers). Wrapped in a towel, feeling rather like Marat, I discussed arrangements, including conversation with Mme Assouline, who is English. In the end was arranged that Assouline and a photographer should come on Thursday morning, afterwards V and I lunch with them.

As I had expressed a wish to V that she should see Ston Easton in its new embodiment, this seemed like an immediate wish granted by a genie. I therefore suggested Ston Easton Park as the place Assouline should stay, at the same time indicating to his wife that it was not likely to be cheap. To this she replied: 'No problem. The paper pays.' Accordingly Ston Easton was agreed, whether ever accomplished, another matter.

Reread Z. Najda's (Polish) biography of Joseph Conrad, the only life of Conrad that is any good, being extremely good, though I emerge from the book with a less romantic view of Conrad than hitherto held. He was a very tricky character indeed. One sees why Henry James thought Conrad so 'rum'. He was punctilious about many things, but telling the truth was not one of them, while at least part of his 'rumness' seems to have been inability to come to terms with his own identity. On the one hand, anyway in early days, he took the line that he was not a professional writer, might easily go back to the sea, even take up some other job. Later, on the other hand, he used to be irritated by critics always mentioning his nautical past, referring to him as a writer about the sea.

True, many of Conrad's books are not about the sea, but he himself had always plugged that 'image'. At the same time he showed the greatest integrity as an artist from the start, only falling off a bit when hard up (which he was perpetually, however much he earned) towards the end of his career. His abilities and failings are of great interest. He was not at all scrupulous about borrowing money, Najda pointing out that Conrad always lived in the traditional manner of a Polish gentleman (about ten per cent of the country regarding itself as such, cf. Wales, where an even higher percentage did), regarding a certain amount of dash, debt, as a necessity. His friends thought Jessie awful, no doubt with reason, but the marriage obviously worked well. One would be interested to know who took Conrad (at a fairly mature age) to the Forty-Three (as reported in her Memoirs by its proprietress Mrs Meyrick), a London night-club of notable squalor.

Thursday, 27 June

French interview all worked according to plan, Assouline previously sending me two copies of *Lire*, one containing his interview with Graham Greene. He and the photographer, Pierre-Olivier Deschamps, arrived on the tick of 10 a.m., having reached Ston Easton the previous day. Assouline rather old-fashioned type of Frenchman, squat, wearing a suit, small moustache, specs, probably late forties (two children, five and eight). French *nil admirari* well developed, but reasonably intelligent. Said he was third generation in Morocco, thought his grandfather possibly of Spanish extraction, a *pied noir* in fact. One wondered whether the surname might once have Hassan included, or combination of. He had written several biographies, one on Georges Simenon to appear here (Chatto) next year. Deschamps, Picasso-Harlequin type, younger, much more the sort of Frenchman one has become used to. Blue open shirt, jeans, Italian girlfriend in Bologna, could not speak much English, but quite jolly. Had spent three years studying medicine, then gave it up, journalist for a short time, present ambition to be a movie photographer.

Assouline said circulation of *Lire* about 150,000. Sort of illustrated literary periodical we don't run to here, not in the least highbrow, at the same time demanding a certain amount of knowledge of books. We set to right away, Deschamps photographing all the time, including some outside shots when the interview ended about 12.30. Assouline (who asked for one of my book-plates) did the interviewing quite well in a conversational manner, not at all formal. He will edit all that later. Heaven knows what I shall be reported as saying. Snook forced his way in, left after being photographed.

We then, including V, set off for Ston Easton, Deschamps driving, which he did well (for a Frenchman, Assouline said). Bearing out the impression that the whole occasion was arranged by a genie, a kind of dream or mirage, the whole staff there had changed. Instead of the Stubbs stable-boy waiter, there were two waitresses, equally eighteenth century, remarkable looking, one a dream of beauty, the other perhaps more interesting, V thought possibly Goya. This time the place was not deserted, a couple drinking a bottle of wine with their luncheon, a quartet, two British, two American, all bores in a fairly high category. At one moment the male Briton remarked: 'Edith Wharton said there were only two places to live, Paris or Santa Barbara.' This seemed to convey nothing to anyone else at the table. One would have thought improbable that Edith Wharton had ever even heard of Santa Barbara, much less supposed it, or anywhere else in California, a desirable place to live.

Assouline swept everybody in to lunch without the chance of a drink (unless that had been insisted on), which for once these days I should have been quite glad of after a stiff morning. I suspect Deschamps would not have minded one either, certainly not V. However, Assouline ordered a bottle of Beaujolais. V and I opened with some sort of lobster and prawn affair, just eatable; V then vegetarian dish of tagliatelle type, she reported as excellent; I had guinea fowl done in some exotic manner, good, tho' I could not manage it all: rather awful little *nouvelle cuisine* salads (deplored also by the Frenchmen), followed by ices, Deschamps having bread-butter-pudding (enjoyed by Verlaine when in England), in which there seemed to be no bread, but eatable. After lunch photographed me in the grounds of Ston Easton, which will no doubt appear as our property. We then returned to The Chantry, where further interrogation, photography took place. They left about 3.45 to catch a plane back to Paris from Bristol. By that time pretty exhausted, but we agreed a not unamusing day.

Saturday, 29 June

The Bulgarian to whom I sent the first three-in-one volume of *Dance* wrote to thank, so I was glad to have forwarded the next three three-in-ones. Still rather stiff in the legs from all the standing about on Thursday. Balliol sent catalogue of their MSS Exhibition during Gaudy Week. Interested to see the copy of *Caledonia* not that I presented recently to Balliol Library, but one, quite forgotten, given to Kenneth Bell, I suppose at the time it was produced. John Heygate had given them a First Edition of *Decent Fellows* in 1974, the year he did himself in.

Reread *Measure for Measure*, at each rereading the awfulness of Duke becoming more than ever apparent; for example, not the smallest indication that Isabella wanted to marry him at the end. She was obviously a beautiful girl of the highest principles, who could undoubtedly have married had she so wished, in fact decided to become a nun of the strictest order. 'These poor informal women.' The play is put together with great economy. Lucio, always interrupting, maligning everybody, one feels might be a portrait.

Wednesday, 3 July

The calves broke out of the Park Field into the garden causing some mess. Georgia has job with obit department of the *Telegraph*. Mary Mayall sent a French postcard (to thank for information about gadgets for opening wine bottles), which set out Capricorn characteristics (including 21 December, my birthday, the cusp, usually put in Sagittarius), one of which frivolity at intimate moments, illustrated by a couple fornicating in facetious manner, its tone more German than French, perhaps influence of EC. Riposted with a large very serious fornicating Japanese couple, found in a stationery shop among the Christmas cards.

Sunday, 7 July

V brought Charles Pickthorn back for glass of sherry after church. We talked of his Surtees Society publishing Kipling. Pickthorn spoke of reprinting *Uncle Remus.* I encouraged that. He seemed in rather shaky state, but open to any ideas about reprints.

Tuesday, 9 July

Selina Hastings arrived about 3 p.m., ostensibly to discuss Evelyn Gardner, of whom she wants to compose an obituary tribute in *Harpers & Queen,* notwithstanding no sign whatever of Evelyn packing it in; in fact likely to see us all out. Conversation covered a wide ground while doing this. Apparently Jennifer Ross had some sort of fall not long ago, now complete write-off, which is sad. Selina had been in touch with Alan Ross some weeks ago, when he seemed all right. The Amis–Kilmarnock household sounds stranger than ever. Apparently the Kilmarnocks have to leave their bedroom door ajar at night, as does Kingsley himself, a night-light in both rooms, because Kingsley so afraid of the dark. I am rereading *The Old Devils,* to be *au fait* with Tristram's TV adaptation, in which one of the characters (Charlie Norris) has a breakdown because he is left alone in the dark, unable to find his way back to where several of them are staying at a seaside place. This seemed exaggerated, but apparently not at all.

Saturday, 13 July

Hilary Spurling rang saying she had seen Bill Pye head, most impressed. There had apparently been moment when he had decided to destroy head as unsatisfactory, then a camera crew came to the studio, one asked if head represented AP, so Pye made various alterations, now considers it put right. Apparently at least twice life size, nearer three times. He is going to France for a week, hopes to finish by end of this month. Hilary at her most forceful, rather what one imagines Mrs Thatcher ringing one of her Cabinet. Told her I was rereading her Compton-Burnett with great pleasure. Had forgotten that Ivy 'identifies' herself as Charlotte in *The Real Charlotte,* which in fact she told V in first instance.

Monday, 15 July

John Monagan rang from Washington, asking how I was. Told him I began to feel quite recovered about a month or more ago. In good form. He sounded a bit frail himself, I thought. Evangeline Bruce, now in London (visiting us with Quintons on 1 August), asked if *The Fisher King* had been filmed, as film of that name now on in New York. It is, in fact, by one of the Monty Python gang called Terry Gilliam (I think) described as (sent by Evangeline): 'A story about one man's attempt to redeem himself from a life of fatal cynicism by his unlikely alliance with a visionary street person.' This seems a little different from my novel. After all, the novel might be filmed one of these days when I am dead and gone. Odder things have happened.

Tuesday, 16 July

Georgia to lunch. Not for the first time one grasps how much one belongs to the age of Caxton when she describes computer life in an open office, where everyone is, so to speak, in the same room. Archie and William Mount are off to the US in about ten days, where they hope to find fame in rock, starting in Los Angeles, then travelling all over the place. Flying Casserole lunch, lemon chicken.

Friday, 19 July

Dreamt I was waiting in hall of biggish house in North London (after something like doctor's or dentist's business visit), when man came down the stairs with two boys of about fourteen–fifteen, one looking rather ill. He was Malcolm Muggeridge. He was wearing a hat, something he very rarely did. When he saw me he said: 'Tony...', then took me by the shoulders, kissed me on the forehead, went out through the open door.

Saturday, 20 July

Whenever I see a page advertising assorted paperbacks at a special price with illustrated covers, I always feel like a well-brought-up child gazing out of the window at rough children playing noisily in the street, secretly rather longing to join them. Today, to my intense surprise, I found the first three volumes of *Dance* advertised at the top of just such a glaring page in the *DT Colour*. This is the result of recent paperback deals I had forgotten about, as firm referred to as Paperback Book Club, apparently called QPD (Quality Paperbacks Direct). This caused satisfaction.

Sunday, 21 July

Tristram, Virginia, Archie, at The Stables. Archie sets off on Wednesday for US; New York, then meeting William Mount at Memphis, whence to Washington, Los Angeles, etc., on some sort of musical tour. Virginia and Tristram had seen new wing of National Gallery, of which they greatly approved. Tristram has been in Cardiff preparing *The Old Devils* film. There was a review in today's *Sunday Telegraph* of volume of translated erotic mediaeval Welsh poetry by some of the most famous bards (Dafydd ap Gwillim, *et al*), never published before, indeed efforts apparently made to suppress during nineteenth century. Occurred to me a pity this not known by Kingsley Amis when describing Malcolm Cennan-Davies, character in *The Old Devils*, retired businessman who translates early Welsh poetry as hobby. Mentioned this to Tristram, giving him cutting, who says he will try to bring this into film.

Tuesday, 23 July

Reread Ivy Compton-Burnett's *A House and its Head* and *A Heritage and its History*, which led me on again to Hilary Spurling's two-volume biography. This is brilliantly done, an extraordinarily vivid picture not only of Ivy and her companion Margaret Jourdain, but of the Compton-Burnett and Jourdain families, all achieved in a completely unlaboured manner. It is in its way an extremely tough story. I had forgotten that Ivy was quite such a *madonne des tantes*, anyway that her queer circle was so extensive, so much foundation of her daily life. I then tried *Pastors and Masters* (first of the Compton-Burnett revised style after *Dolores*, also first to be read by me), but found my former difficulties with Compton-Burnett novels, remembering who was who, in which she seems to me unnecessarily unhelpful to the reader. I am accordingly rereading V's Compton-Burnett *Handbook*.

   Also tried to read *The Spoils of Poynton*, but found it dreadful rubbish. The fact is that Henry James never grasped the machinery of English social life. If Mrs Gareth, her son, the two girls, Fleda Vetch and Mona Brigstock, really lived the lives they are represented as living at the various incomes indicated, much more explanation is needed as to why they behaved in such an unusual manner. It is similar trouble in *The Awkward*

Age (a much better book), the fact James could not take in the iron laws of an English upper-class girl 'coming out'. His proper names are also dreadful. Why should a perfectly ordinary girl be called Fleda Vetch, or a country house Waterbath, names that would be perfectly acceptable in P. G. Wodehouse, not in a James type of novel?

Friday, 26 July

We lunched with Selina Hastings at The Barn, Hinton Field, done up by Pamela Harlech for her daughter Pandora, let to Selina from time to time. The Barn is far from a barn, more like a New York duplex or Long Island cottage, done up regardless. Guests: Jim and Alvilde Lees-Milne, Geoffrey and Sally Wheatcroft. We brought *Julia Fortescue and Her Circle*, which gives account of background of the Gardner family, Selina wanting to borrow it for projected work on Evelyn Nightingale. I sat on Selina's right with Alvilde on my right. Selina described being in local hairdresser's in Primrose Hill area, when Marilyn Quennell brought in Peter (almost handcuffed to her), saying, 'Will you cut its [*sic*] hair. Get rid of those whiskers and those disgusting hairs in the nostrils.' She then left. Peter settled in chair, attended by new, somewhat unpolished assistant, who said: ''Allo, Peter, 'aven't seen you for some time. 'Ow've you been?' No reply. 'Seen anything of Kingsley lately?' No reply. 'You write books too, don't you?' No reply. 'What are they about?' 'I'd rather have my hair cut without conversation.' It so happens that Sally Wheatcroft (daughter of TV 'personality' Frank Muir) runs a gift shop in Regent's Park Road. She, rather fascinating looks, only married fairly recently. They live near Bath. He, heavily built, whitish hair, middle-forties, general-purposes journalist, seemed reasonably agreeable. I asked what the particular job on the *Telegraph* (chiefly *Sunday*), found he had just been sacked, since regarded as henchman of Perry Worthsthorne, also just sacked. Perry apparently wrote to Max Hastings saying he was taking three months off to write his Memoirs, receiving answer to the effect that he need not come back. Hugh Massingberd said to be hanging on by his eyebrows. I can't remember how exactly Wheatcroft was fired, but it partook of the traditional journalist sacking on Christmas Eve. Perry talks of starting a Quarterly, which should be a quick way of going bankrupt.

Both Jim and Alvilde pretty deaf these days, tho' V thought Jim looked better than when we last saw him over here. He seemed to me rather frail. He is oddly uninterested in his own life, which I noticed when he lunched with us. I have just finished reread of Hilary Spurling's (splendid) two volumes on Ivy Compton-Burnett, in which Jim occurs quite often. He first came to Braemar Mansions (the Braemar Gatherings, as Roger Hinks called them) through knowing Margaret Jourdain over houses and furniture. I asked him why one had never heard of a great friend of theirs, Hermann Shriever, interior decorator. Jim could offer no explanation, vague about Shriever, but said Margaret Jourdain's last words were: 'Don't give Shriever any meringues.'

Alvilde in goodish form, has now transferred herself into a 1920s dowager. Smoked cold chicken, excellent potato salad, really super raspberry *brulé* made by Selina, white burgundy. Enjoyable party. I was extremely tired after, I must admit.

Saturday, 27 July

V and John drove to wedding of Benjie Fraser and Lucy Roper-Curzon in Salisbury Cathedral. Good music, Harold Pinter in grey tailcoat, Salisbury teeming with tourists in shorts, the Close packed with them, one of the curses of modern times.

Reread *All's Well that Ends Well*. Not a favourite. Resembles *Measure for Measure* in nice girl wanting to marry horrible man, tho' in latter Mariana of the Moated Grange actually saves Angelo's life, which might have some effect on his feelings, as he at least wants to be a man of high principles, certain that Diana might not stick to her determination to marry but Bertram's promise that he will love Helena is quite unconvincing, especially in the light of his behaviour to Diana, the girl he was in love with and wanted to seduce. In both plays the substitution of one girl for another takes place. A condition being she should be silent and stay only an hour. One wonders how this would work in practice. The comedienne Maud Lorraine used to say: 'Well, it's always strange the first time', so possible the man, dealing with a virgin, could be deceived, but not very likely. Robert Graves actually wrote a poem on former subject called 'A Slice of Wedding Cake':

> Why have such scores of lovely, gifted girls
>   Married impossible men?
> Simple self-sacrifice may be ruled out,
>   And missionary endeavour, nine times out of ten, etc.

It should be added that in the case of substitution, the seducer might be surprised at being received with open arms instead of unwillingly. Parolles is treated more lightly than most of Shakespeare's villains. One cannot help wondering whether an autobiographical note might be stuck in: 'War is no strife / To a dark house and a detested wife.'

Sunday, 28 July

John says the Syndicate (Paul Lewis) reports that during the night the Stoney Lane gate-lock broken, barbed wire also torn down, evidence of lorry wheels at Lilly Pond. They suspect attempt to net fish by poachers. Paul Lewis produced new key, which V will have copied this morning. Inform police.

Tuesday, 30 July

Wrote review for *Harpers & Queen* (Selina Hastings Literary Editor) on Michael Shelden's *Orwell*. Good biography, I think best, anyway most readable, up-to-date, tho' Shelden sometimes finds himself not altogether at ease with some British surroundings. He has a good deal of new material about various things, especially some rather dubious friends of George's during the Spanish Civil War, for instance Georges Kopp, supposedly Belgian, in fact apparently Russian, with more than one concealed family. Looks as if Eileen Orwell had an affair with Kopp in Spain. I never found Eileen at all easy to get on with. Both she and George, as quoted here, stepped out occasionally, George admitting to me he did. Malcolm Muggeridge put round that George had Stevie Smith in the Park, but that was a misunderstanding. George tried to have her, but unable to bring it off (too well endowed). So far as I know, that was anyway not in the Park.

Shelden does not get Sonia Brownell, George's second wife, at all right. Sonia certainly did not marry him because she thought he would make a lot of money. There was no evidence that he would. In any case Sonia was not in the least like that. In some ways Shelden gets the hang of how she behaved when George was dying, anyway at moments, but V says the reason why Sonia was not there at the last was because she had a cold, which would have been fatal for George and no one knew death was about to happen. There is, however, a slightly blood-chilling story about Sonia when she was seventeen holding boy who could not swim under water to save herself from his clinging. I think her chief reason for marrying George was because Cyril Connolly told her to.

Girl from the *Spectator* rang to ask if Debrett's *People of Today* might reproduce my (by no means rave) review of their book of reference. She added she was a fan. I asked her name. She had clearly escaped from a Betjeman poem as it was Isobel Brotherton-Brackley.

Thursday, 1 August

Day of traditional Bruce–Quinton picnic. They arrived about 1.40, having been held up by traffic, also Tony insisting on going through Nunney. Food good, somewhat Teutonic in tone: roll-mops (white salt fish enclosing onion), roulade (salmon and rice pie), various salads, fruit flan. Marcelle drank water throughout, Evangeline only beer at luncheon, Tony Quinton gin and tonic before, Château Bernard Raymond '79 (drinkable if not particularly exciting), which V and I shared. Quintons in good form, Tony talks more since retirement, no doubt lack of lecturing. Marcelle wearing skirt in broad stripes, green, yellow, white, like flag of an African state, but pretty blouse.

Evangeline at first a trifle piano, tho' beautiful, cheered up as things progressed. Beardsley being mentioned, she said she had never seen any of his pornographic drawings. I said I had the *Lysistrata*, which, rather to my surprise, she twice asked to see, so I produced it. Gave them some of my books. Good party, tho' fairly exhausted after they left about 4 p.m. for London. Dreamt I was at some sort of large reception sitting on sofa, with someone else, perhaps V. The Princess of Wales came and sat down between us. She was rather flirtatious, putting her head downwards towards me, as if she expected to be kissed on the ear. I said: 'I'm sorry, ma'am, but I can't hear very well what you're saying.' She replied: 'That's because I'm wearing a kilt.' She was, in fact, in ordinary evening dress.

Monday, 5 August

Grey, windy day. This weather added to apprehensions about my French publisher, Christian Bourgois, and wife coming to luncheon; whether they would ever arrive, if we should be mutually comprehensible. In the event they turned up on the tick of one o'clock, having spent the night in Bath. Bourgois was tall, heavily bespectacled, with a touch of Arthur Mizener, V thought. For some reason he reminded me a little of my wartime opposite number, (Captain) Jean Keraudrin, tho' I imagine from a higher social bracket. Bourgois and I were dressed almost identically in pink shirts, fawn trousers, he wearing a dark-blue blazer instead of linen coat. He was quiet, agreeable, unlike the French journalists I have been dealing with lately, kissed V's hand. Mme Bourgois (Dominique) small, plumpish, Titian-red hair, slightly flat Slav-like face, attractive, good at seeing jokes. At first things showed signs of being a shade sticky, then all cleared up, as if they were relieved at our turning out better than expected.

Dominique Bourgois, who talks excellent English, alleged she had met Tristram some years ago over some film, we could not make out which. Bourgois talks a bit of English too, so, with one's own French, no serious language difficulties. Mentioned I had been rereading Philippe Jullian's *Montesquiou* and *d'Annunzio* (which they did not know about), also books on Symbolist painters, thought him good writer. I knew he died quite young a few years ago, did not know it was suicide, his house with all pictures, collection, burnt down about same time boyfriend died. Sad story. I met Jullian once or twice, but only for a moment, in London. He illustrated Proust, drawings a bit on the feeble side.

The Bourgois recently moved to apartment in Rue de Grenelle, Faubourg St Germain, place of residence of various Proust characters, if I remember rightly. They had taken a cottage at Sissinghurst for a fortnight (possibly one in which Nigel Nicolson lives), where they were to be followed by John and Iris Bayley. The Bourgois were driving there (a good four hours) after leaving here before 3 o'clock.

Enjoyable, interesting party. If a bit exhausting, a lot of ground covered. Bourgois, sherry as aperitif, came in on bottle of Château Bernard Raymond '79 at luncheon, Dominique, soft drink, water. I offered Bourgois any available books upstairs. He took paperback Memoirs, which I inscribed to them both. To unwind, made curry after they left in preparation for the Naipauls on Thursday. Vidia also published by Bourgois, who talked of great Naipaul success on Paris radio, so hope to hear more.

Tuesday, 6 August

Helen Fraser rang to check subtitle for *Under Review*, said Heinemann now publishing in February (rather than March), which I prefer. Told her I thought they had a winner in Shelden's *Orwell*. Heinemann have just signed him up for book on Graham Greene. In the Orwell connexion, V pointed out that Sonia Orwell's affair with Merleau-Ponty (more or less during George's last days) had resemblances to Pamela Flitton's involvement with Ferrand-Sénéschal. That, or similar, name (at least possibly a double-barrelled one) suggested to me by Frenchman at the Embassy, with whom I discussed a suitable surname for French intellectual on extreme Left. Sonia also not without her necrophilic side, e.g. story of drowning boy in Shelden's book, presiding over deathbeds of George, W. H. Auden,

Joe Ackerley, Ivy Compton-Burnett (I think), perhaps others. Sonia never occurred to me as contributing to Pamela Flitton at time of writing.

Thursday, 8 August

Fine day for Vidia and Pat Naipaul coming to luncheon. I made a curry, so was not present when they arrived. On coming into the library greeted Vidia, for a moment not seeing he had grown a beard. Beard of naval type, speckled with grey, perhaps Conrad figure. Said his agent (Gillon Aitken) would be furious. Whether because of personal taste, or supposed detrimental effect on sales not clear. Vidia gave good account of Christian Bourgois, thought him nice, enthusiastic about his publications, got very tired by the end of a day's work. They have two grown-up children. Asked what Bourgois had been wearing, said he was very keen on clothes (as indeed is Vidia), paid a great deal for them. Pat, looking less harassed than sometimes, brought box of chocolates. Vidia not writing anything at the moment except odds and ends of journalism. Enjoyable party.

Evangeline rang. She is off to Italy tomorrow (shares house with Marietta Tree), where Roy Jenkins is staying. We talked about Roy's autobiography, *Life at the Centre*, which publishers sent me, am half-way through. Evangeline had heard it was good, which it is, tho' on the whole I don't find the politics interesting. How the Labour Party loathed each other, as one supposes all politicians do their colleagues. Vegetable curry, of which Vidia had three helpings, almond tart, the Pommard '85 Tristram gave me for birthday, light, smooth. Pat had only a drop, nothing before, Vidia glass of sherry.

Sunday, 11 August

The Brazilian university to which I sent set of *Dance* (as they were requesting books) wrote to thank. Finished Roy Jenkins's autobiography, *Life at the Centre*. Enjoyable. Roy is one of the few politicians who can read and write. The early age at which his unavoidable pursuit of the smart life became plain is interesting, e.g. conscripted to the Army in the normal manner, drafted to Royal Artillery, at once posted to series of increasingly chic Yeomanry units (West Somerset Hussars, Leicestershire Hussars) transformed to Gunners.

Wednesday, 14 August

Hazel Holt to tea. She (b. 1928) worked in an anthropological society with Barbara Pym, whose life Hazel Holt wrote. V corresponded with her. Grey-haired, large specs, photographs suggest *jolie laide* when younger. Agreeable, lively, married, living near Porlock, does miscellaneous journalism, writes detective stories. Met her husband at Cambridge after the war, when, also up, he had come out of RAF. Said Dadie Rylands had been Oedipus in *Oedipus Rex*, Dr Sheppard (famous Cambridge figure, Provost of King's, I think), speaking at end of performance, said Rylands (in VIth form when I was a lower boy) had acted in the 'original production'. Hazel Holt thought Barbara Pym had not had a sad life; on the contrary, unproductive love affairs all part of her normal existence. Gave her some books. She is great cat fan; Snook gracious.

Monday, 19 August

Gorbachev pushed out. Only solution seems provisional dictatorship under Bob Conquest. Found that Van Gogh during his period in England once preached a sermon at Richmond Wesleyan Methodist Chapel. This would appear to be the place where the Q2 Amateur Dramatic Society gave a performance of *The Garden God*.

Thursday, 22 August

Gorbachev back in Russia. Reread *Julius Caesar*, favourite, full of good things. One notes presentation of Antony's character as knuckling under when Caesar's assassination has taken place, then affecting well-conceived sentimental stirring up of public sympathy with Caesar. Later being tough in getting rid of Lepidus from the Triumvirate shared with himself and Octavius.

Monday, 26 August

Obit in *DT* (written by Georgia) of Innes Lloyd, TV producer, who was to have done last aborted *Dance* BBC project. Nice man, only sixty-five. Had worked with Tristram on *East of Ipswich, No. 27*, and others.

Tuesday, 27 August

Bookseller George Ramsden (Stone Trough Books) sent catalogue of A. J. A. Symons items, with notes by Julian Symons. In this found H. Montgomery Hyde's *Christopher Millard* (New York & Amsterdam, limited to 500 copies), which I supposed had not been finished by the time Montgomery Hyde died. Hyde had promised to send me a copy, as it contains Millard's letters to me, but may have died before that could be arranged. Rang Ramsden at once, with whom I had long talk. He was complimentary about my Memoirs, is sending book (£19.95).

Thursday, 29 August

Diana Beaufort-Palmer sent framed Beardsley prospectus for *The Savoy*, which I was glad to have, although glass broken (V got mended at once in Frome). Diana suffering from heart, etc., clearing the decks preparatory to living somewhere to be looked after. Heinemann rang to say proofs of *Under Review*, to have been received by them yesterday, delayed, giving me melancholy satisfaction of having foretold that if they arrived on time it would be the first occasion when a printer had ever been punctual.

Reading Montgomery Hyde's Christopher Millard book, which (as bookseller said) leans heavily on A. J. A. Symons, also Millard's letters to me, does, however, contain certain interesting facts, such as circumstances of Millard's convictions for homosexual offences. I never thought Mr Deacon very like him (Millard more of a gent), but suppose I could not have written just as I did about Deacon had Millard still been alive. In spite of that, as usual nature copies art. I had no idea that Millard was active member of Labour Party. During the General Strike (with two male companions) he used to sell the *Workers' Gazette* (the strikers' parallel to the Government's *British Gazette*) in pubs etc., just as Mr Deacon and Gipsy Jones sold *War Never Pays*.

Sunday, 1 September

Georgia at The Stables with Toby Coke. Her job at *Telegraph* obits coming to an end.

Tuesday, 3 September

Turns out Christian Bourgois did do next three of *Dance: Chez Lady Molly,*
Cazenova's (sic) *Chinese Restaurant, Les Braves Gens,* which arrived this
morning. Much relieved at this, as only two would have held up continuity.
Bourgois spoke of *two* all the time and wrote of two. French publishers
really are inimitable. Letter in today's *DT* from Georgia on subject of
single-sex schools (of which she is in favour). Later in the day *Evening
Standard* rang to ask if I had any reactions to it, but could think of nothing
dazzling to say so probably nothing will appear.

Wednesday, 4 September

Proofs of *Under Review* arrived. Hilary Spurling rang, asking what Hugh
Kingsmill looked like. She is very old friend of Michael Holroyd (unique
in having read his novel, which no one else knows about), wants to
celebrate publication of his life of G. B. Shaw by giving him Russian dolls
painted by herself: Shaw, inside whom Augustus John, inside whom Lytton
Strachey, inside whom Hugh Kingsmill, representing Holroyd's biographies. I was once in same division at school with Holroyd's father, red-
faced, hearty, one would say boring, did not know him at all, apparently
greatly disliked by son.

Thursday, 5 September

Seventh House Films doing programme on L. P. Hartley, arrived
(creditably in time as road was up) about 3 p.m. Edward Storey, Clive
Dunn, co-director/producer; Richard Crafter, cameraman; David Smith,
apparently assistant cameraman; John Rowe, electrician, wife June who
drove him. Storey, actor/ecclesiastical type, with shock of white wool hair,
whom V thought slightly like less emaciated Roland Gant. Dunn, scrubby
beard, both agreeable. Leslie's younger sister Norah gave them interview
at Fletton Towers, near Peterborough, Victorian pile built by tycoon, who
owned neighbouring brickfield, went bankrupt. Leslie's solicitor father
saved him from absolute disaster by taking over house and brickfield.

Norah Hartley breeds wolfhounds of enormous size. Peterborough
Cathedral was celebrating some historical event about the Danes, wished
one item to be a deer hunt. Storey, who lives at Peterborough, apparently
an important figure there, asked to arrange this. They dressed a man up
as a deer, borrowed Norah Hartley's wolfhounds. I thought he was going

to say three actors were torn to pieces before they achieved a successful act. In fact, Norah Hartley had to stand further side of the stagman (shades of the Horned Dance, etc.), and call her hounds, to achieve desired effect.

Mary Wellesley, V's cousin and old friend of Leslie's, now exists as complete hermit, curtains drawn all the time, only candle-light, so would not give interview, but sent helpful letter. I told a few stories. V gave them tea. They were off soon after 5 p.m., crew going to Norwich, as Anglia Television. Film probably will not be shown till next summer, but promised to send a video. Somewhat exhausted. Copy of *Lire* arrived with interview. Inevitably fairly grotesque, good photography, giving somewhat inflated idea of size of our *gentilhommière*, as some of Ston Easton Park included. Next article in paper on Sade.

Sunday, 8 September

Tristram, Virginia, Archie, at The Stables, the last just back from US, where he seems to have enjoyed himself. Tristram continues to give funny accounts of shooting *The Old Devils*, Kingsley Amis attended scene at Swansea railway station, in general the film becoming increasingly like real life all around into which author, producer, actors are being swept, like one of those books in which someone is writing a novel which they are also involuntarily living.

John saw Dr Jacobi last week, who is a fan, also fisherman, not long ago himself devised a fly he named the Louis Glober, whether literally constructed from the elements of Glober's hobby, John did not have the courage to ask. However, on this last visit, Dr Jacobi reported that he had actually caught a fish with the Louis Glober fly.

Tuesday, 10 September

My review of John Wells's London Library book appeared in the *Spectator*, in which I spoke with feeling of the awfulness of Mr Cox, the famous old monster at the issue desk, who was always unfailingly grumpy, unless you happened to be one of his nobs, to whom he was loathsomely obsequious. Received an extremely funny letter from Hugh Dacre (Trevor-Roper) on this subject, expressing appreciation, his own dislike for Mr Cox.

Finished Robert Byron's Letters to his mother. I had not bothered to get this from the Library at first, because travellers' tales tend to bore me, but reviews suggested it might have interest. On the contrary, found them fascinating, especially earlier part about Oxford, which, so far as *Brideshead* might be held to have any validity, gives a good picture of that Oxford world, such as it was. I think Robert scarcely knew anybody there, or throughout his life, he did not think would ultimately be of use to him. I had not grasped that he was the Mum's Boy to end all Mum's Boys, tho' a very tough one, whose travels showed the greatest energy and endurance imaginable, especially as he seems to have been feeling ill almost all the time. He was, I think, a trifle mad, not very nice, but a most remarkable figure.

The always implied relationship with the Poet was not, as I had supposed, through the Byron brother who went to Ireland, but an interesting pedigree traced back to Lancashire, from which the first three generations of Lord Byron's family came in the Middle Ages. One would imagine that really energetic research would almost certainly reveal them as the same family, as Byron is a place in Lancashire.

I was amused to find John Heygate spoken of as nice by Robert before the Waugh divorce, indeed commented upon to his mother as the guest at the house she liked so much in contrast to Evelyn Waugh. Robert was, of course, queer, but (apart from obviously liking good-looking friends of his own class) I don't know what form this took. He saw a good deal of (the essentially hetero) Gerald Reitlinger in various places to which they both travelled. The Squire told me that on a train with Robert in the Far East somewhere he found Robert was having an affair with the Japanese *wagon-lit* man.

Thursday, 12 September

Finished *Under Review* proofs, which John will take up on Monday. V went through her reading with me. Don't think I have ever seen a worse mess made by printer, literals, lines omitted, wrong headlines, pagination getting out of step. Peter Mumford looked in about three trees I am planting to replace those brought down by hurricane, probably three limes along the wall. He also had general look round, on subject of which he will report. I forgot to mention pruning of fig-tree, will do so when I reply to his letter. Dreamt last night we went to reception given by Princess Margaret in a smallish palace. She was lying on a *chaise-longue* à la Mme Récamier. I went to say something to her. She indicated she could not hear, I was to come closer. I put my head down quite near her face, repeating what I had said. She gave me a sort of kiss, then leant back, closed her eyes, went to sleep. Later someone said, 'You will have to get a taxi to take you home, it's rather a rough journey.' This we did, at one point driving down a short, very steep slope.

Sunday, 15 September

Driven by John, we lunched with Anthony Hobson at The Glebe House, Whitsbury. Elizabeth Jane Howard, Rodney Milnes, staying. Jane wearing a loose white garment suggesting heavily pregnant woman, V thought might be what is called a Mother Hubbard. Jane has moved to Bungay, Suffolk, which she likes, revealed no details. Milnes, music critic, edits paper called *Opera*. Seemed nice, very quiet. Food excellent: home-grown small melons, chicken pie (chicken in white sauce), iced raspberry pudding. I had small glass of Pomerol with nice tannin taste. Anthony's son William (First in Greats) in Australia, working five days a week in restaurant. Apparently went there chasing a girl. No doubt will snap out of this sooner or later as obviously able. Charlotte at Russian university, as learning Russian, offered chance of course. Anthony had finished his *DNB* piece on Maclaren-Ross, but left him my letters, which he said he would like to read.

Monday, 16 September

V took John to Westbury station as usual, car damaged on way out of station. Repairs estimated two weeks. Mr Edwards of CU informed.

Tuesday, 17 September

Bob Conquest rang, just back from Russia, with Liddie, in this country only two days. Much fêted, but food-poisoned, ate unboiled egg, regarded as madness by Russians. Saw on TV Yeltsin with Cabinet standing to attention while old Russian National Anthem played. Lunched with Kingsley Amis, with whom matter of *Memoirs* now made up, Kingsley having given some sort of an apology for his behaviour. Bob says (I would agree) Kingsley went through state of semi-madness from which now emerged. Upset, it appears, by cuts from people, lack of invitations to parties. Roy Fuller, as I feared, in very rocky state, unable to take telephone calls. Bob spoke of utter philistinism of general landscape (which, as it happens, V and I had been discussing yesterday). If *London Magazine* shuts down, nothing else whatever of that sort will ever take its place.

I really don't think this is just one's age. Younger people agree, US as bad, if not worse. Conquests probably over here again in October, when they will try to come down.

Wednesday, 18 September

As car out of commission, hired Mr Withers of Mells to take us both to Nunney for V's hair-do, haircut for me (£6, Mrs Lloyd says is insulted by tip). He used to be second chauffeur at Ammerdown, and drives in that indefinable manner of chauffeurs in private service, including driving into our gatepost on the way home.

Friday, 20 September

Helen Fraser, of Heinemann, knowing my addiction to that sort of book, sent typescript of *The Sign and the Seal*, by Graham Hancock, describing his search for the Ark of the Covenant, which in the event he did not manage to see, but does show convincing reasons to suppose still exists at Axum in Abyssinia. I found it fascinating, in spite of author's horrible style. He does not come to any definite conclusions regarding the Ark's undoubtedly dangerous character (cf. George Sassoon in *The Manna Machine*), suggesting it contains radioactive meteorites, which bring up the cancerous tumours referred to in the Bible. The book contains all sorts of interesting points, not all far-reached, noted in the course of Hancock's researches, not least his discovery in Abyssinia of the Knights Templars' *croix patté* carved in several obscure places. He thinks the Templars got on to the disappearance of the Ark early on. They associated with architecture, and that their descendants were the Freemasons. Also that the Grail was the Ark. I also read through volumes four, five and six of *Dance* in French. These seem to be reasonably well done. *Les Braves Gens* (*The Kindly Ones*) the best. In fact, found myself unexpectedly cheered by having half the sequence in French.

Monday, 23 September

Mildav began painting window frames in spite of signs of equinoctial gales. Fan letter from Frenchman about translation of *Dance*, student, working in a library (Bruno Lopat). V pointed out he lives at Allée Joachim du Bellay, sixteenth-century French poet she likes, who wrote poem about his cat. Mentioned this in my reply. Virginia, down to tend The Stables garden, dined. Smoked Breton chicken, V's new baked beetroot, chives, yoghurt

salad, good. Drank Aloxe Corton '84 Ferdie Mount gave me at Christmas.
All right, but unexciting. Archie, earning an honest penny during the vac
by conducting round the House of Lords, saw Frank, accosted him,
explained who he was. Frank asked: 'Do you make a living wage?'

Thursday, 26 September

Evangeline Bruce sent David Bruce's War Diary (Kent State University
Press), which I much enjoyed. He more or less founded the OSS
(American MI5), went all over the place, having an extremely exciting
time, always telling you what he is reading, eating and drinking, an excellent habit in diarists. I thought him an exceptionally nice chap whenever
I met him, a characteristic which comes out in the Diary. Wrote to Evangeline. Satisfactory and surprising news from Bruce Hunter this morning
that University of Chicago Press want to do *Miscellaneous Verdicts*. For some
reason Chicago has always been particularly well disposed towards me.
Helen Fraser rang later to discuss jackets for the five pre-war novels, which
Heinemann are doing in paperback next year. I have no very brilliant
idea. V suggested their original jackets, certainly worth considering. Helen
delighted about University of Chicago news, as Heinemann will almost
certainly dispose of plates of *Verdicts* to them, or whatever they do
nowadays.

Saturday, 28 September

Bob Conquest's ominous view of Roy Fuller's state confirmed by Roy's
death. This is a considerable blow. He was one of the people I greatly
liked. We had not met for some years, but kept in touch, usually when he
or I produced a book. One always felt his intelligence, grasp of literary
issues, as something near and sympathetic. Roy was aware latterly that he
had made abysmal mistakes politically, treating them with amused laughter
at himself, but he must have been surprised by recent demolishing of
Lenin's statues, etc., while no doubt remaining in his heart committed to
some sort of romantic Leftishness. I thought he was a good, essentially
personal, poet, who will 'live', tho' never sure his best things get into the
anthologies. I suspect his home life may sometimes have been a bit difficult, as is hinted in the poems. When he and Kate stayed here one
of those curious photographic phenomena took place (no doubt easily
explicable by something having happened to the film), showing Roy with
the dim vision of a youngish girl in the sky above him (see album).

Monday, 30 September

Spoke with Helen Fraser about covers for reissue of five pre-war novels, suggesting perhaps Nicholas Garland, in principle political cartoonist, but does amusing small drawings for *Spectator.* Helen liked this idea very much, knows Garland slightly, will proceed with negotiations to that end. Also mentioned a few corrections in *Verdicts*, if University of Chicago to come to Heinemann. Asked if Roland Gant's corrected set still exists. She thought this might be in Heinemann's library, will look, as recent three-in-one paperbacks still contain mistakes. Told her about film called *The Fisher King* (of which the Congressman sent review). Helen did not know about this. I remember years ago seeing small bit of a film called *The Lost Lady.* Found there was a book with that title, got hold of it as the film seemed rather good. Book by Willa Cather (writer I do not find exciting) nothing whatever to do with film I saw. Hope people will buy copies of my *Fisher King* for same mistaken reason.

We had smoked salmon, bottle of fizz (De Courcy '85, light, not bad, given by Heinemann for my last birthday, does not figure in now the late Cyril Ray's book). I suppose '*Krug je ne suis, Mumm je ne daigne, je suis Brut de Courcy*'. During dinner we listened to tape of Carreras, Domingo and Pavarotti singing items, varying from 'E lucevan le stelle' to 'Wien, Wien', in Caracalla's baths. Enjoyable celebration of our engagement.

Tuesday, 1 October

I am getting the Aubrey book from the *Spectator.* Tylden-Wright was on *TLS* at end of time I was editing novel reviews there soon after the war. Just met him. About twenty or more years ago he wrote a biography of Anatole France, which I reviewed for the *DT,* perfectly respectable, so far as I remember, but far from exciting. Can't imagine that he will have much to add to what I myself said about Aubrey, unless on the academic side, Aubrey's views on Science, Education, etc., but a chap has already written on those things. We have had only two figs up to date this year, those large juicy ones certainly.

Wednesday, 2 October

V had check-up with Mr Umpleby. All well. Reread *Antony and Cleopatra.* 'To the vales, and hold our best advantage.' 'No more a soldier; bruised pieces, go, / You have been nobly borne.' 'All strange and terrible events

are welcome.' 'The quick comedians / Extemporally will stage us.' North's
Plutarch comments: 'Some say also, that they found two little pretie bytings
in her arme, scant to be discerned: the which it seemeth Caesar himselfe
gave credit unto, because in his triumphe he caried Cleopatra's image, with
an Aspicke [asp] byting her arme.' Sent *Verdicts* corrections to Heinemann,
already in touch with University of Chicago Press. They have sent corrected
proofs of *Under Review* for Index.

Monday, 7 October

Hilary Spurling rang about the Pye head. Hilary at her most forceful, had
gone with John, taking Bruce Hunter, to see finished version in Bill Pye's
studio at Wandsworth. All agreed head was superb; as Hilary said, 'More
like you than you are yourself.' The head's fate is now dependent on the
Telegraph wanting to buy it, which Max Hastings is said to desire (he is a
great fan). He would have to persuade the proprietor, Conrad Black, to
agree. I see no objection. The making of bronze casts would be contingent
on this sale to pay foundry costs.

However, Hilary, with her usual assurance, says she feels certain of being
able to dispose of the head even if the *Telegraph* did not come up to scratch
with the sum, £4,500. If casts are made, these (as I understand) would be
limited to three at £2,000. I should be equal to this, Hilary appears to
want one herself, I'm not sure what would happen to the third. If all this
comes off, it will be yet another monument to Hilary's iron will. She says
the head is huge, more than life size. I said I really could not travel
to London for an official presentation (than which, quite apart from
administration difficulties on getting there with one's stiff joints, I can
think of nothing more appalling), but would be prepared to lay on
luncheon here for a stated few. It is planned to do this simultaneously
with publication of *Under Review*, certainly appropriate, tho' February not
the most clement of months. It remains to be seen what will happen,
including my own continued presence on the face of the globe.

Reread Larkin's *Oxford Book of Twentieth Century Verse*. Not sure that Philip
really a very good anthologist, or in choosing gives poet's best poems.

Wednesday, 9 October

Rather upset inside, which, combined with doing Index for *Under Review*,
produced reception less than welcoming to a tall, grey-haired, distin-
guished-looking military figure, who announced himself as Stephen

Phillips. He is interested mainly in Brecon, pins really enormous sheets of pedigree together, and is not nearly keen enough on verifying his references. I suppose I deserve this, but do not care for even closest friends to call without warning, unless in exceptional circumstances, let alone a total stranger (tho' latterly he has taken to using the opening 'Dear Anthony', a habit I dislike if used unmet) in the middle of the morning.

I explained that I could not possibly talk to him there and then, but, as he was interested in a Vaughan 'Challenge' pedigree I had told him about, gave him (rather caddishly) Michael Fariday's address, who discovered it, being himself a brilliant genealogist. Stephen Phillips looked a shade surprised at being hustled out so soon, though I tried to be as agreeable as possible in the circumstances. I asked him his regiment, which turned out to be the XXIVth, South Wales Borderers, now Royal Regiment of Wales with The Welch. If he'd only rung he might have come to tea some time, but as Ronnie Knox used to say, 'a man's first duty is to his plans'.

Friday, 11 October

Stomach upset recovered. Peter Mumford's merry men planting three trees (limes in Paddock Field), cutting down others including dead yew by front door, which will make things look rather different.

Tuesday, 15 October

Snook caught a bat last night. It was in the library, so we turned off the light there and in the hall, opened the door, also front door, put on outside light. There was sudden violent scuffle. In the dark I felt Snook leap into the air, then rush out with bat in his mouth.

Bob Conquest rang, much jet-lagged from return from Russia, then sitting up till 3 a.m., talking, drinking, with Mrs Thatcher at Stapleford Park, Leicestershire, where some sort of a conference was taking place, including Henry Kissinger. Bob shocked by complete disregard in US of Roy Fuller's death. Told him I thought obits most inadequate here too, *TLS, Spectator,* Sunday papers, nothing up till now, tho' long obits in *DT* and *Times* (latter written by Bob himself, tho' much altered). Roy undoubtedly, we agreed, country's best poet. Reflects growing division between American, British, poetry, for that matter literature in general. Bob said there are 15,000 card-holding poets in US. He had travelled in Concorde.

Wednesday, 16 October

Reviewed book for *Spectator* on John Aubrey by David Tylden-Wright, just met years ago when he reviewed French subjects occasionally for *TLS*, thought him dull. This confirmed by Aubrey book, mostly abstracted from my *John Aubrey and His Friends*, minimum acknowledgement, written in muddled tedious manner, repeats Lawson Dick howler of supposing Aubrey had estate in Kent, other mistakes, on top of which uses jacket identical with my own Hogarth Press paperback. Have complained about this in review.

Read Francis Steegmuller's *Jean Cocteau* (sent by publishers, I think, not read previously as not much interested in Cocteau). Quite enjoyable picture of period, people Cocteau knew, as Steegmuller goodish writer. This led me to reread Maurice Sachs's *Le Sabbat* (in American translation, fuller than British one), which I quite enjoyed tho' tails off at end. Sachs, as described by John Russell, in tradition of French literary scallywags deriving from Villon, amusing account of early home life, getting to know figures like Gide and Cocteau, their better points, bogusness, etc., well delineated. Sachs eventually shot by Gestapo. Quite by chance also read Jocelyn Brooke's *Orchid Trilogy*. Fascinating contrast: Sachs (b. 1906), Brooke (b. 1909), both homosexual, literary ambitions intensely solipsistic, Jewish, dishonest, very bright, Brooke dyed-in-wool English bourgeois. All the same one sees odd similarities, which I'm sure would have amused both, as both intelligent. Brooke modest to the point of having really no ambitions at all: Sachs aiming to be perhaps a kind of Stendhal.

Sunday, 20 October

Georgia, at The Stables with Toby Coke, came with him to morning drinks. Coke nice boy.

Thursday, 24 October

Lees and Mary Mayall to luncheon. V had a word with Mary about Lees's health, not good, but treatment may improve. He didn't seem too bad outwardly. Bats had set off burglar alarm in their house the other night. Luncheon cooked by (Mrs) Moura Dillon Malone, from Whatley Cookery School at The Grange (the Witts), to which apparently people come for month's course from all over the world. Pâté (eatable, not exciting), rice dish (excellent saffron rice), which turned out more or less mild curry (meat good), excellent lemon tart. Not enough dressing on salad. Two bottles of Sangre Agarena (Valencia), not bad in circumstance, half bottle remained. Mayalls both had two fairly stiff gin and Cinzanos before. V a shade queasy later, but not necessarily applicable to food.

Friday, 25 October

Kate gave me Vitamin B injection as usual, to which she added flu injection at her own suggestion, said to be advisable with increasing years. She turns out to be interested in wine, about which we had a discussion. Virginia to dinner, when we ate remains of Moura Malone's lunch, drank Léoville-Barton '84, which I found a bit thin, but V and Virginia liked.

Saturday, 26 October

Letter from Kenneth Rose (who writes 'Albany' in *Sunday Telegraph*) enclosing offpull of Desmond Seward's *Brooks's: A Social History*, in which the section dealing with the St James' Club (now combined with Brooks's) states categorically that Widmerpool 'is' Denis Capel-Dunn, the passage in *Lady Molly* quoted, which also identifies the fat man in the St James' as Lord Castlerosse, something that never crossed my mind. Anyway doubt if Castlerosse ever paid for a meal for himself. I am interested to learn that Capel-Dunn was son of consular clerk in Leipzig called Dunn, and known in St James' bar as 'Mr Bloody'. Sent a tempered answer to Rose's request for confirmation, saying Desmond Seward was an amusing fellow, I should not be surprised were he on to something. Added regrets that so little had been said about death of Roy Fuller, but don't expect anything will come of that.

Reread *Timon of Athens*. Unsatisfactory play. In Hollywood terms: man has money and friends; man loses money; man loses friends; man infinitely fed up at this; man dies. In short, there is no development. One sees Shakespeare's thesis, Timon irretrievably disillusioned with the human race, but really no action in that, only a condition (as General Hackett would say). Plenty of violent vituperation, though nothing really memorable.

Tuesday, 29 October

Yesterday arrived *Anthony Powell*, in Macmillan series Modern Novelists, by Neil McEwen (Professor, Okayama University, Japan). This seems satisfac-

torily done, tho' author rather upset by planchette occultism. I am glad a
bare-essentials handbook of this sort now available, as all other similar
works beyond words bad. When I write to McEwen shall suggest that he
and Macmillan try to persuade Twayne publications, American firm which
produces similar series, to replace drivelling volume by Neil (as it also
happens) Brennan, an ass unspeakable who produced a volume about me
in 1974, which in any case needs revision even had it been properly done.
Yesterday Mr Moss appeared. Told him he could do £200 worth of
repairing drive, which he carried out.

Wednesday, 30 October

Hilary Spurling rang in the evening, saying she had letter from Max
Hastings saying *Telegraph* would buy cast of Bill Pye's head. This is funny
beyond words, from at least a dozen angles, while being a truly extraordinary example of Hilary's enterprise and will-power. The Spurlings
had been in Rome (for the first time), restricting themselves to classical
monuments. Hilary said they looked at over four hundred busts, to which
she thought the Pye head (apparently enormous) compares very favourably. Casting is taking place at this moment, the finished product to be
expected at Christmas or New Year. The presentation promises yet further
hilarity. Really a fantastic achievement on Hilary's part.

Speaking of Rome, I have been indolently looking through four volumes
(Nonesuch, bought by my father) of North's translation of Plutarch's
Lives, chiefly reading the marginal headings. When Sulla was in Greece
(Thessaly, I think) his troops found a satyr asleep, ascribed as in every
respect as represented in sculpture, etc. They brought him before Sulla,
but the satyr could only make neighing noises, and whinnyings like a goat.
Sulla 'abhorred him', so he was 'carried away'.

Thursday, 31 October

Gales. Rain. At about 6.15 p.m. lights went off (apparently widely), on
again rather less than two hours later. Graham Lord, Literary Editor of
Sunday Express (always tending to be disobliging about my works), wrote
to say he was doing biography of Jeffrey Bernard, professional drunk who
contributes usually amusing weekly pieces to the *Spectator.* In one of them
Bernard said he was at the New Beacon, my private school, so sent him
paperback of Memoirs. Lord asked if I could tell him anything about the
place. Replied he should refer to *To Keep the Ball Rolling.* Read *The Mirror*

of the Sea (unread before, I think). Contains early sketch for *The Arrow of Gold*, not one of Conrad's best novels. Much poor, turgid stuff in these reflections too.

Tuesday, 5 November

Read new Kingsley Amis novel *We Are All Guilty*, kind of fable, only 92 pages. A seventeen-year-old boy, Clive, for no particular reason, breaks into a warehouse, watchman chases him, falls, sustains no serious injury. Clive arrested. Everyone (vicar, social worker, etc.) at pains to explain to him the crime not his fault, due to having stepfather with whom he does not get on. Book ends with Clive wandering off, aware he has committed a crime, should be punished, but unable to explain this to anyone, including man he injured. One sees the point, but a bit thin. This sort of book typical for novelists of increasing age, cf. *Old Man and the Sea*. I don't feel convinced Kingsley's dialogue is accurate, let alone psychology of very cardboard characters. If Clive could work all this out for himself, surely he would not have broken into the warehouse in first instance? It is the old cowboy heresy, that if cowboys could behave as represented in books, films, they would not be cowboys. Anyway, if you're going to write a book of this sort, surely there ought to be a girl in it too, having parallel experiences?

At 2 p.m. arrived photographer Erik Russell to take Evelyn Gardner photographed on my small camera, one of a group of twelve snaps, in oldest album, not much larger than a big stamp. This for Selina Hastings's projected obit of Evelyn in *Harpers & Queen*, tho' I assured Selina, Evelyn will outlive all of us. Erik Russell, tall, pig-tail, black sweater, black trousers. Had enough gear to set up small studio in Hollywood. After an hour and a half went in to see how things were going. A low-flying plane prompted him to say he had joined the RAF at seventeen, then left because they would only make him a navigator. Said he did not want to be a bus conductor. That was twenty years ago. Great talker. Father gynaecologist, also genealogist. Russells come from Scotland, but alleged to go back to Conquest. Agreed name really meant red, but had some French word/ place from which they supposedly derived. Asked if he could take some of me, which he did. Evelyn Gardner cropping up in this way follows on death of George Heygate, day or two ago, John's eldest son, whom he disinherited for some reason, a solicitor.

Friday, 8 November

Yesterday a female secretary from ARC rang in the middle of lunch to ask if they could photograph Finger Farm (which they hope to demolish) from Stanley Mead. This was on behalf of a character called Mr Dutson. Told her they certainly could not, that it was a great piece of impertinence for them to have used secretary to ask, which she could tell Dutson. He rang this morning. Repeated that to him. He said Planning Authority has requested ARC to let them have a photograph from there (which is quite a long way off). Gave him a stiff talking-to about quarries thinking they could bully everybody, they must learn they could not. Said if the Planning Authority wrote to me in detail I would certainly consider it. I thought this gave opportunity for repeating objections to what ARC want to do. Dutson said there was a suggestion that they should put a ladder in Mells Lane to do it. Told him he must be quick as another quarry (in fact, ARC too) was trying to close Mells Lane.

Postcard this morning from Selina Hastings asking for information about Eleanor Watts (now Lady Campbell-Orde), friend of John Heygate and Evelyn Waugh. I remember some question of Heygate marrying her but did not, I think, have affair. She had noisy fat brother named James, one imagined queer, who turned up once at The Squire's about 1938. Eleanor (known as 'the Lancashire lass'), reasonably pretty without being particularly attractive (b. 1908). Selina says she now alleges that Heygate did propose to her. First she turned him down. Then he ran away with Evelyn Gardner. During period when Evelyn Gardner was sent to Venice by her family, hoping she would recover from Heygate, he proposed to Eleanor again, that is to say if Evelyn Gardner turned out not wanting to marry him.

The fascinating thing about all this is that James Watts, who always appeared as Eleanor's brother, seems to have been illegitimate, as no sign of him in *Burke's LG* where the rest of the family are to be found. Apparently when the two Evelyns were still married, they were going to stay with Eleanor at her father's house in Cheshire (the Wattses were what Jim Lees-Milne would call 'rather *nouveau*'), Heygate coming too. All the running-away then took place, so only Evelyn Waugh went up there. At first Eleanor's father had not yet arrived, so Evelyn Waugh had to sleep in the butler's house to avoid an imputation of impropriety. Eleanor was a trifle cagey with Selina as to what she told her, as she was writing her own Memoirs. The interesting thing about all this is Evelyn Waugh, then on the upward climb, happy to be asked to the country house of a North

Midland *parvenu* family, something he would have run a mile from a year or two later.

Remembrance Sunday, 10 November

I (V in church) watched the Cenotaph service for a few minutes. Rather impressed by appearance of Mr Major, whom I had not seen before, tall, good figure, dignified movement, distinctly aristocratic, one would have thought. Tristram and Virginia at The Stables. Shooting of *The Old Devils* now finished. Tristram had to sit on jury judging three or four Welsh films for some prize. He had been promised captions in English, but these failed to materialize. Other members of panel talked a bit of Welsh. Asked one of them what they were all about (comic football teams, etc.), told basically rows between South and North Walians.

Tuesday, 12 November

Amusing letter from my former publisher Tom Wallace (Norton's), become agent, complaining about American publishers nowadays using 'midlist' as pejorative for books that sell 2,000–3,000, as he says only wanting something that will appeal to the 223,000,000 people who watched on TV the Judge Clarence Thomas case. President Bush describing Thomas as 'the best man for the job, also very good' (sic), referring to the Supreme Court.

Candida Lycett Green in afternoon, driving through the foulest weather, to collect letters we have from her father, John Betjeman. She is fifty, still very pretty, slight look of her mother, father only in her laugh. Jolly, lively, perhaps not great humour, married to Rupert Lycett Green, John said he thought a bit of a loner, former Second Lieutenant RAs (presumably National Service), then proprietor tailors Blades, in Burlington Gardens. They have about 250 acres near Marlborough, where they breed horses. She has let herself in for appalling job as Betjeman received about 200 letters a week, I believe, which he was keen on answering. He sold letters to him to Victoria University, Canada, where they are still uncatalogued. Candida wants to make some money, which well she might with five children, three girls, two boys. Girls sound all rather bright, one married, one boy at Eton, one at prep school. She took all letters not routine thanks, etc. She is having trouble with agents, also to some extent with Jock Murray, who Betjeman said could never make his mind up whether he was a 'gentleman or a stationer'. Interesting visit.

Candida about twelve last time the Betjeman family came here. Said she regarded her father as her guru, went to him for everything. When he died rang up Philip Larkin, whom she had never met, to ask advice. Her mother was still alive; also Elizabeth Cavendish. They may to some extent have neutralized each other. Said she had no idea what hymns ought to be sung, Larkin, of course, well-known atheist. Possibly Candida left as literary executor. One can well believe it was an awful muddle.

Having recently reread *The Orchid Trilogy*, reread *The Dog at Clambercrown*, probably Jocelyn Brooke's best. There are moments when one becomes a shade weary of his chronic self-absorption, well expressed as much of that is, because Jocelyn Brooke was like Cyril Connolly in having a personal myth which was a perpetual fascination to himself, the source of their best writing. Jocelyn also an excellent critic, nothing like as well-read as Cyril but entirely uncorrupted by Cyril's desire to impress, snobbish wish to be in the fashion. Jocelyn particularly good on Joyce, D. H. Lawrence, Aldous Huxley, the last always holding him slightly in thrall.

Friday, 15 November

Letter from Higham saying Chatto want to remainder *John Aubrey and His Friends* (680 left). This is a particularly idiotic moment to choose, with Tylden-Wright's book about Aubrey still being reviewed, every one of which mentions my book. Also matter of his having identical jacket might have caused people to buy mine, thinking it cheaper paperback edition of his. Rang Higham on subject (Kate Lyall Grant).

Monday, 18 November

Duckworth sent Hugh Lloyd-Jones's collection of reviews, etc., *Greek in a Cold Climate*, which I enjoyed greatly. Wrote to Hugh.

Tuesday, 19 November

Candida Lycett Green returned Betjeman letters, together with her own book on small houses, inscribed to 'the perfect couple in the perfect house'. The book looks interesting, well illustrated.

Letter from American, Jonathan Kooperstein, with whom I have corresponded earlier, saying (apropos of reading my review of *Night and Day* selection in *Miscellaneous Verdicts*, referring to Shirley Temple libel case with Graham Greene) that he has come across Shirley Temple feature film of fifteen minutes, *c.* 1932–3, called *War Babies*, in which children impersonate bar not far behind Front Line in First War, showing typical characters in Allied uniforms, etc., Shirley Temple herself playing a French tart, who exchanges hugs and kisses for lollipops. Mr Kooperstein reflects on what would have happened if shown at the trial by the Defence. Shirley Temple mentions *War Babies* in her Memoirs. It was shown on a very obscure TV network, no doubt never came to England.

Thursday, 28 November

V one of 500 in IEC Wine Society to receive magnum of sparkling Loire Crémant for ordering early. Cheering symbol of good luck. Letter from fan (Denis Church, Walberton, Sussex) who had lost his sight in the army, read *Dance* in braille over period of thirty years. Fascinating to me as performing, so to speak, in another medium. Robert Mayall, engaged to satisfaction of Lees and Mary.

Reread my old favourite Stendhal's *Henry Brulard*, enjoyable as ever, even if author does go on rather long about awfulness of his father and Aunt Seraphie. When he joined the 6th Dragoons, Stendhal rode from Lausanne to Milan in September, having been on a horse only two or three times before. Was immediately run away with. Then crossed the Alps by the St Bernard. All still under seventeen. Tried further Stendhal readings but became stuck.

Reread *Macbeth*, another favourite. How did Lady Macbeth rub her hands together while carrying a taper, which so far as I know could not be put down. I suppose it could be done rather lightly. The famous line 'Time and the hour run through the roughest day' reminded me of my Platoon Corporal saying of the Brigadier's inspection, 'It will pass, sir, like other days in the army.'

Friday, 29 November

After we had been in Mexico and Guatemala close on twenty years ago an archaeologist called Norman Hammond, authority on those parts, now a Cambridge don, came to see us, quite why I can't remember, corrected names under photographs, etc. He was also a fan. I had a letter from him asking if he could look in for an hour or so this morning, I can't imagine why. He was going to see a godson at Marlborough. He had grown a small beard in the interim, has son at Eton, daughter at King's School, Cambridge. We talked about archaeology. Hammond also a genealogist. I had been rather bored at idea of having the morning broken up, as had various things to do, in the end quite enjoyed the talk. That sort of thing shakes one up, I suppose.

Monday, 2 December

Yesterday anniversary of our wedding day. V gave me very sweetly collected John Glashan, the surrealism of which one can take only in small doses, but very funny. Celebrated this evening with smoked salmon and Laurent Perrier '83, rather medium fizz. Hilary rang. The head is finished, will be brought down on Wednesday, 18 December by Spurlings and Pyes, who will lunch.

Saturday, 7 December

Pleased at being offered D. Litt. at University of Wales. They say this is not as rule given *in absentia*, but hope to plead age. I should much like to go to the conferment at Cardiff, as I think it would be entertaining, Prince of Wales their Chancellor. In any case regard it as triumph their getting over obsession with Welsh speakers, all that stuff. Hilary Spurling rang. Pye head now finished, has been arranged that Spurlings and Pyes should bring head down for luncheon on Wednesday, 18 December. Dreamt I was at luncheon party of eight or ten in rather gothicky country house, mostly men, Kipling sitting opposite me. We talked about this and that. I said: 'Do you think manners are worse now than when you were young.' Before he could answer a rather strange-looking man I did not know, black moustache, said: 'Are you asking that for *Queen*.' I said: 'It's typical of what I mean by my question being at once assumed to be for an interview for a paper.' Woke up.

Friday, 13 December

A trifle under the weather for a couple of days, so V, going to the surgery anyway, asked Dr Irish, our new GP, to look in. Anyway good thing to meet him, rather than first in an emergency. As V said, Irish has a touch of Archie, tall, young, at Clare, Cambridge, family came from North Wiltshire, married with son of three months. They are going to live in Nunney, which is convenient. Irish checked all the usual things, which seemed satisfactory. Mrs Irish also doctor. Good impression.

When in 1903 a group of Serbian (then Servian) officers broke into the royal bedroom, murdered King Alexander I and Queen Draga (who was more or less a tart, very unpopular), a copy of Stendhal's *De l'Amour* was later found there, annotated in the Queen's hand. This puts the final Stroheim touch to the prototypically Balkan act of violence of the period. The bodies were left in front of the palace in Belgrade, a building which when in the 1920s I saw it looked like a large Edwardian shop in Leicester Square.

Wednesday, 18 December

An Homeric day, fortunately also a fine one. Bill and Sue Pye arrived a bit before 1 o'clock with the head, which he brought into the dining-room without letting anyone see it, Hilary and John Spurling about five minutes later. We had prepared a place on the Brodie table. Artemis (as she is now thought to be) to go on the mantelpiece under the Richard Wilson, Apollo probably under Commander Philip Lewis Powell in the library. Bill Pye, who was very pleased with the position, took some little time to arrange the head, then Hilary unveiled it. It must be agreed to be a great success, large (about three times life) in grey-green bronze. Luncheon cooked by Moura Dillon Malone, we drank the Crémant litre magnum, which was absolutely suitable, the right sort of amount. Noise at luncheon was deafening. Both the Pyes have strong voices, talk a lot (Sue is a painter, what sort unknown). She talks, as does he. Bill Pye has a thing about being kept out of the Tate etc. by 'the Establishment', which may well be true. They all left about 3.30, the Pyes to go to East Knoyle, where he has a godmother, then back to London; the Spurlings, so far as I know, back to London. We were both extremely exhausted. I had slept rather badly the night before, did not feel too good that morning. All the same, enjoyable day, the head, I think, very good.

Thursday, 19 December

V heard from Margaret Elton that Eve Disher had died. She must have been well into her nineties (ninety-seven), longing for it. Eve was in a way a great friend of V's, with whom at one moment she used to draw. Eve was an artist of some talent, who never quite had her dues owing to her own modesty. She was tiny in size, a friend of various queers, in consequence of which Paul Cross left her some really valuable modern picture with an income which kept her going in old age. Geoffrey Gorer left Eve a case of wine a month for life. She rescued Arthur Elton from being queer so that he married the beautiful Canadian Margaret, had a family, who looked after Eve at the end. They were very good about that. Advance copy of *Under Review* arrived, Henry Mee jacket looks excellent.

Saturday, 21 December

My eighty-sixth birthday. Felt a good deal better than I did last year. V gave me shirt well chosen by John, who gave me handkerchiefs, Tristram and family sent telegram, also he and Archie rang in evening. Cable from Robert Macnamara, retired American publisher who once came here to luncheon. I had to redo my Insurance document, always a boring process looking for a paper in a file while I managed to scorch a hole in pocket of the jacket I wear every day, kneeling beside the electric fire. Peculiarly annoying. Evangeline Bruce rang from Washington with birthday greetings, love to us all, very sweet of her. Told her about the bust. John Monagan had sent V a book about Colorado by John Wesley Powell for me on the day. I think he half believes I am related to all Powells in America. The AP Society of Toronto sent a printed postcard of Mark Boxer-style drawing (perhaps by him) inviting to a sherry party to celebrate my birth, caption: 'However did you become one of this set', dissipated-looking man and girl in bar. Good day on balance.

Sunday, 22 December

Marcelle and Tony Quinton rang in evening, Marcelle saying she thought line would be jammed previous day. Tony's leg better.

Monday, 23 December

George Lilley, my bibliographer, rang from Llanbedr, where he is librarian at St David's University College. It appears it was he who put my name forward for an Hon. D. Litt. at the University of Wales. Said there would be no difficulty about my being too groggy to go to Cardiff, just question of deciding what form conferment should take as an alternative. Sent him a copy of *Caledonia*, of which I found a few.

Tuesday, 24 December, Christmas Eve

Helen Fraser rang on subject of covers for non-*Dance* novels. Looks as if Nicholas Garland is going to be no good. Am consulting Georgia to know if she can suggest any young artists. There seems real difficulty at the moment to get someone suitable, Posy Simmonds if not ideal for my purpose very good in her own line, no longer doing book covers. Helen Fraser tentatively suggests Susan Macartney-Snape but still vague about her.

Wednesday, 25 December, Christmas Day

Slept rather badly. Warm, windy. V gave me shirt (thin brownish-mauve stripes), John mints. Brought his own dark suit from me down to show. Gave V Chardin (Italian) catalogue. Lunched at The Stables where Virginia laid on really superb classical Christmas dinner, last year's pudding she made, excellent sauces, stuffing, etc. Tristram gave me Moldavian wine, Virginia Cantemerle '84, Georgia tin caviar. Half-bottle Heidsieck Dry Monopole, Archie Italian '87, Tristram new album for postcards, kilo of cheese (Jereboam). Toby Coke staying, to whom I gave four paperback volumes of *Dance*. Conversation with the young people about cartoonists makes me think that there is a broad alternative between *Private Eye*-ish (which includes *Spectator*), which I don't want, or book illustrator type (under which Posy Simmonds might be said to come). Enjoyable day. Less tired than lately.

Thursday, 26 December, Boxing Day

Charlotte Lennox-Boyd and her young man Charles Mitchell came in for a drink before lunching at The Stables. He looks a bit as if just struck by lightning. They are getting married in April, will, as I understand it, live in Battersea. They declared themselves fans so I gave them the four paperback volumes.

Monday, 30 December

Yesterday Kenneth Rose's 'Albany' column in the *Sunday Telegraph* was headed 'Widmerpool Identified'. This in consequence of Desmond Seward having included the St James' Club in his history of Brooks's (which absorbed the former), where he says the model for Anthony Powell's Widmerpool could be found at the bar there, a loudmouth barrister, son of a consular clerk in Leipzig, called Denis Capel-Dunn. Rose rang me about this, to which I gave an evasive reply, saying Seward was a bright fellow, might well be on the right track. As a result of the 'Albany' piece (with Marc drawing of Widmerpool in uniform), Susanna Herbert (I think granddaughter of A. P. Herbert) rang. I was yet more evasive, but that morning another piece appeared at the bottom of the front page in today's *DT.* John was so surprised at breakfast he dropped an egg. A character called John Colvin, former Ambassador in Mongolia, now contributes, saying he thought Capel-Dunn was the most awful man in the world, exactly like Widmerpool. I do not know Colvin, who started life in the Navy. Later in the day a character called Jasper Humphries, from the 'Londoner's Diary' in the *Standard,* rang on this same subject, but asking about the public's general interest in individuals who appear in novels. After waffling for some time about this, he asked if there had been any talk of my being given the OM. I said only on the part of friends, so far as I knew.

In Kenneth Rose's piece he said the Capel-Dunn information released Manningham-Buller (Lord Dilhorne) from suspicion of being Widmerpool, except that 'Manningham-Buller had got a boy sacked from Eton for making indecent advances to him'. Manningham-Buller did indeed get a boy sacked (Dick Dauncey, to a small extent model for Duport, tho' I never really knew Dauncey, a friend of John Spencer's), but not for making a pass at himself, Manningham-Buller, always enormous, bespectacled, hideous, no one could conceivably have sent a note to him, waved from a window, or anything of the sort.

Tuesday, 31 December

Last day of the Old Year, rather a mixed bag, certainly better than last one. Peter Quennell knighted in the New Year's Honours, hilarious for all sorts of reasons, not least for adding to the Primrose Hill Knightage, Sir Victor, Sir Kingsley, now Sir Peter to swell the pubs. Sent a congratulatory postcard (photograph of Ruskin *c.* 1884). We ate the tin of caviar Georgia gave me at dinner, drank the half-bottle Heidsieck Monopole Brut Archie gave V, both good.

'Another pint, Sir Kingsley?'

'Thank you, Sir Victor, but I think it is Sir Peter's round . . .'

'On the contrary, Sir Kingsley, I believe . . .' etc. etc.

1992

Wednesday, 1 January

New Year's Day. Feeling better than this time last year.

Thursday, 2 January

Hilary Spurling asked me to send a line to Max Hastings expressing appreciation of the *DT* buying the head, as entirely Max's doing, so I wrote.

Friday, 3 January

Mrs C. Haddon (Churt) wrote to the *Telegraph* saying her husband had been in the Cabinet Office under Capel-Dunn and they had greatly liked him 'in spite of his bizarre personality'. Such was no doubt inevitable. However, the letter was headed 'Another view of Widmerpool', not 'Another view of Capel-Dunn'.

Sunday, 5 January

The Widmerpool theme was picked up by Simon Hoggart in the *Observer* (a column I do not usually read), but the whole family missed it and the paper was not preserved. Shall wait until its arrival as a cutting. Hoggart said it was disappointing to find Widmerpool, a character to rank with Mr Micawber and Falstaff, just a high Civil Servant, thereby in true journalist fashion getting the story a little further wrong. All the same, nice to express these feelings about W.

Friday, 10 January

Selina Hastings writes to enquire about a letter signed 'Clare' to Evelyn Waugh (apparently dug out by Mark Amory, who edited Waugh *Letters*), why at this late stage not clear, probably of 1930s date, complaining of Evelyn's behaviour after staying at the Easton Court Hotel, Chagford, at the same time (in what circumstances also not clear), where Evelyn (Alec Waugh before him) used to go to write. Evelyn had apparently left Clare cold, with an unpleasant letter. Selina is trying to discover who Clare was. The tone seems to me curiously similar to the previous lady who Selina ran to earth, I should suspect like the latter, from Alec Waugh's world. V suggests trying the Easton Court's guest-book. Even as it stands this seems to begin to show an interesting pattern.

Tristram rang asking for Christian Bourgois's address, telephone, in Paris, as Tristram has some TV project involving Dominique Bourgois. Helen Fraser rang on the subject of design of cover for non-*Dance* novels reprint. The artist we agreed to try, Sue Macartney-Snape, not available, meanwhile Bruce Hunter (or rather his friend, Belinda) suggests Emma Chichester-Clark, who seems possible. Helen is going to try. The Chichester-Clarks are a North of Ireland family involved in the government, Emma about thirty-five.

Saturday, 11 January

John's forty-sixth birthday. We had pheasant for luncheon, V and I drank half the bottle of Château Cantemerle '84 (John does not drink) that Virginia gave me for my birthday, good vineyard, but three-out-of-seven year, which was in fact not at all bad. We finished it at dinner. I gave John pair of black shoes chosen by himself.

Wednesday, 15 January

To my surprise and satisfaction, the University of Wales press release announcing their conferment of degrees arrived this morning including my name for an Hon. D. Litt. Among fellow recipients were Neil Kinnock and Lord Jakobovits (also unable to be present). Kinnock will either be Prime Minister or out on his ear by then. Later the *Western Mail* (Rachel Clark) rang to enquire into my Welshness, of which I tried to convince her.

Hilary Spurling rang. The Pye head has now been officially installed at the *Telegraph* at a ceremony Hilary attended. Also there were David Holloway, Hugh Massingberd, others, all this Hilary described as a tremendous success, indeed was very excited about, as she has a right to be as all her doing.

Then Helen Fraser rang, saying that one of the artists considered for doing the non-*Dance* novels, Sue Macartney-Snape, had rung in an excited state saying her dream was to do my covers. Her agent had replied on her behalf that she was taking on no work until about six months from now, as she is having a show, but she is so great a fan, she much wants to do the books. Helen is going to see her and report back. The *Telegraph* magazine is doing an interview when these arrangements are made. Hugh Massingberd also doing an interview for the *Spectator* for which he is taking us to luncheon at the Bridge House, Nunney, today week. Mrs Edgeley rang to make sure of the date, so warned her that Hugh had a considerable reputation as a trencherman.

Friday, 17 January

Sister Kate Greenfiel came for last time to give me Vitamin B. I shall miss her as very nice, good about advice regarding one's health. She is going as District Nurse at Frome, as she does not want to get stuck in her job. She will introduce the new nurse next week, inevitably arriving on the Tuesday or Wednesday interview, which I forgot to mention.

Saturday, 18 January

V to London to see her sister Pansy, over from Rome, at luncheon with Henrietta Phipps (Lamb); later she saw Elizabeth Glenconner. Sheila Rhys rang, she wanted to talk about her son George's marriage in April. V returned after successful day. John cooked an excellent luncheon. We drank a half-bottle of fizz at dinner (of obscure origins), given me for my birthday by Georgia. I was slightly aware of this in the night; V not.

Monday, 20 January

Letter from Professor Geraint Gruffydd, former Librarian of the National Library of Wales, now head of Celtic studies in the University, congratulations on the Hon. D. Litt., saying in the most complimentary terms it should have been given before, adding that he had nearly asked that I might leave my 'archive' to the National Library, but heard I had left it to

Eton. I have, in fact, more than once thought of leaving my genealogical material to the National Library, but one never knows what one's heirs may want to do. There is certainly no commitment to Eton. On the whole I think I should like anything they do not want to keep or sell to go to the Bodleian, if possible not to leave Great Britain, unless money is very tight. I should not myself have liked genealogical stuff to be disposed of and not passed on to me. People sometimes feel differently, anyway more decided, about that sort of thing after a death has taken place. Peter Mumford came to put the limes in the Paddock Field. We gave him a cup of coffee as we were about to drink coffee.

Tuesday, 21 January

Tim Richmond, with assistant William Teakle (?), came to take photographs of the Pye head with me sitting beside it for *Weekend Telegraph Colour*, arriving sharp on 2 p.m. They had a great deal of photographic bric-à-brac, large white screens, etc., so that the dining-room looked like a studio by the time they had finished setting the stage. The actual posing was equally elaborate, but did not take more than about an hour. Richmond, in his late thirties, thick-set, hair in modern fashion looking as if he had cut it as short as he could by himself with nail-scissors, black sweater, black trousers. He turned out an interesting chap. With two generations between doing other things, he was descended from three generations of Richmonds who were painters, the best, George Richmond, influenced by Blake. His son painted Lady Ida Sitwell, who is represented when young with a zither. She was in fact unable to play a musical instrument of any kind.

I learn from the *DNB* that Thomas Richmond, the first, was a miniaturist, who married the daughter of Engleheart, another miniaturist. This one was son of the Yeoman of the Stables of the Duke of Clarence, he was born in 1771, of an old Yorkshire family at Bawtry. I have an idea I have some forebears from Bawtry in the Waterhouse–Hawksmore branches. Tim Richmond said he had lived with a girl for nine years and they were thinking of getting married. He was impressed with the house and intelligent. I noticed when he held up his hand to indicate the direction I was to look how typical an artist's hands his were. Teakle, if that was his name, was tall, dark red-haired, romantic-looking young man, married, a vet's son from the Taunton part of the world. He too was quite bright. They were out of the house by about 4.30 or before, less tiring than some such visits.

At Whitfield the shooting is largely supported by syndicates who pay. Last week one of the syndicate's members was Max Hastings. What a coincidence for a novel. Pansy Lamb, staying there, apparently lectured him on hunting, which Max does in Northamptonshire and Northumberland. We hope to hear what she said. Possibly on Surtees, whose books I believe Henry Lamb liked.

Wednesday, 22 January

Kate arrived to introduce the new Sister, Bobby Huish, who takes over. Hugh Massingberd dropped in at 1 o'clock. We had a glass of sherry. He is to do the caption for the Richmond photograph of the Pye head in the coloured *Telegraph*, a notice of *Under Review* in *Sunday Telegraph* and write some sort of 'Profile' in *Spectator*. He most kindly brought a bottle of Perrier-Jouet '85 and some smoked salmon, then took us to luncheon at the Bridge House, Nunney, which was not too bad. The Edgeleys are still rather convalescent from bad flu. Hugh was full of ideas; for instance that *The Garden God* would make a musical for Andrew Lloyd Webber. I have written to John Rush asking if he thinks that worth putting up.

Another of Hugh's ideas was that Jonathan Cecil should do a one-man show, on the lines of Patrick Garland's John Aubrey performance, about Jim Lees-Milne's *Diaries* of his visits on a bicycle during the war to preserve country houses. This apparently shocked Jim himself, which is immensely funny. In fact, Garland could not have put on his show had I not written my book on Aubrey, who was not in the least like the Garland Aubrey (Aubrey was essentially a gent, which Garland did not depict), but it helped a lot to introduce Aubrey to the public, which one always welcomes. The thought of Jonathan performing with Jim is hilarious.

Hugh also had a lot of *DT* gossip. It was generally agreed Max Hastings was ruining the paper, increasingly down-market. We came back to the house, where I dug out a copy of *Caledonia* for Hugh, and he took some of the books upstairs, including a lot of paperbacks, leaving about 4 p.m. Enjoyable, but extremely exhausting day. I think, in fact, the photography session of the previous day had been more tiring than I thought at the time. Heinemann are being tiresome about not ringing back to say what is happening about my complimentary copies being sent out. A day of fiendish cold, fog and frost.

Saturday, 25 January

I rang Helen Fraser yesterday to find out the situation about the artist doing non-*Dance* novels. This remains uncertain. Dealing with the mix-up about complimentary copies of *Under Review*, on which there is an obvious hoodoo, broke out again by V accidentally sending them to Sparey's with the waste paper. However, that was cleared up this morning by Mr Sparey (greengrocer) seeing a mistake had been made, and rescuing them. All going well, John will get them, subsequently take them to Heinemann on Monday.

Sunday, 26 January

John Sparrow obit. I first met him in Sligger's rooms, possibly Sparrow was still at Winchester. I always liked him tho' never knew him at all well. I can claim that I, too, had noticed the buggery in *Lady Chatterley* before Sparrow pointed it out publicly.

This afternoon V and John separately saw three or four Land-Rovers coming up the valley towards Orr Farm and leave by the gate between Bullen Mead and the Farm, making a great mess of the fields and subsequently the road. V and John did not reach them before they had moved on. It is not clear whether they were having some sort of a car scramble or poaching, evidently on some sinister purpose. V summoned the police, who took details.

Monday, 27 January

Last week Chatto sent *Surviving: The Uncollected Writings of Henry Green (Henry Yorke)*, which I have been reading. Henry's works always make me feel uneasy, because he was such an old friend, while I always liked his writing so little. Some people admire his books enormously. Henry himself used to refer to 'my hated friends', so perhaps one should not worry. On the whole his writing seems to me affected, his peculiarities of style pointless, but this collection would give anyone who did not know them a good idea of the scope. If you knew Henry and his family, they give some interesting autobiographical glimpses.

The book has a really excellent Memoir of Henry at the end by his son Sebastian, with Introductions by his grandson Matthew, described as 'the novelist', and John Updike. Matthew, horribly, uses 'fortuitous' as 'fortunate'. Updike refers to Rose Macaulay as Rosemary Macaulay, a strange personality at once invoked. Sebastian's piece contains dialogue by Henry describing conversation at Forthampton between his parents, which is very funny indeed, if you knew them, and exactly right. There are also occasional flashes of his wife Dig. Otherwise I found little of interest.

Cyril Connolly used to complain that Henry was inordinately conceited. There is no doubt that was largely at the root of the trouble. He was far too pleased with himself and, like so many from upper-class families, he was also immensely narcissistic and obsessed with his own family. The account of the Fire Service, in which Henry served during the war, is good, though occasional apparently pointless phrases. Sometimes (as in all his writing) appears an out-and-out cliché. Undoubtedly there was something there, but it never seems to me to find a satisfactory way out, as said before, frustrated poet does seem the answer, not outstandingly intelligent, not really very 'nice'.

I have been suffering from a slight feeling of nausea for the last four or five days, usually coming on towards tea-time, so V called in Dr Irish, who inevitably arrived during the middle of lunch. He is a nice, sensible chap, but could suggest nothing. We agreed better not pills, if that could be avoided. He thought mostly this damp cold caused it, which is just what I have felt myself. The *DT* rang. Isabel Lambert obit. Could I add anything to what I said in my Memoirs. V suggested what a splendid figure Isabel made when dressed up to attend the Ballet, for someone who usually met her in the fish queue in Albany Street. Isabel did provide some sort of an answer for Constant Lambert at the close of his life, tho' one was never sure she did not add even worse habits to heavy drinking, which gave him the horrors at the very end. I dreamt that I was being shown round a very well-appointed bookshop, in which the bookseller emphasized how many were Welsh translations, including Kipling's *Puck of Pook's Hill* stories.

Tuesday, 28 January

A letter from Dr Alan Kemp, Registrar of University of Wales, giving proposed arrangement for conferring the Honorary Degree here, attended by the Vice-Chancellor, Sir Aubrey Trotman-Dickenson, Dr Kemp himself and George Lilley. Valerie Rawlings reports that La Bisalta in Frome, former Haligan's premises Vicarage Street, is good, so I am going to suggest this for luncheon after the ceremony.

Thursday, 30 January

Helen Fraser rang. She has seen Sue Macartney-Snape, now commissioned
to do my covers. Macartney-Snape has a sister who lives in this neighbourhood and would like to call some time when staying with her. That would
be an excellent thing.

Sunday, 2 February

Tristram's film, *The Count of Solar.* As a boy the Count was kept out of his
inheritance by his family, because he was deaf. This was just before the
French Revolution. An abbé who trained deaf and dumb boys managed
to reinstate him. Tristram gave a talk in the morning, about the problems
of deaf persons used as actors, the film in the evening. It was done in a
first-rate manner, colours specially good, also costumes. I did not see it
all, but Tristram is going to bring down a tape. Altogether original, what
is so rare, really about something.

Tuesday, 4 February

Bob Conquest's *Stalin* arrived. Candida Lycett Green sent a copy of her
book of houses, which we thought she had forgotten about. Tessa Davies
to tea to see the head, with which she appeared very impressed. After
pressure from Hugh Massingberd, I sent a letter to the *DT* (in fact written
by Georgia, who has returned there) telling correct story of the punt full
of ladies passing through Parsons' Pleasure at Oxford when a party of
dons were bathing naked, one of whom tied his towel round his head
rather than his waist. This was said to be Maurice Bowra. It was a chestnut
when Maurice was born, as usual journalists losing all point, especially as
they were all Balliol dons. As it was, just as the punt was disappearing, a
lady was heard to say: 'I think that must have been Mr Paravicini. He is
the only *red-haired* don in Balliol.'

Wednesday, 5 February

We watched rather a macabre programme on Henry Green (Yorke). This
bore no resemblance to Henry's background, completely mystifying
picture of what he was like, by stating a lot of generalities about his
character. In point of fact I should have said he got on extremely well
with his father (who was half Dutch, much point being made of Henry's

Englishness), though greatly obsessed by both his parents, of neither of whom was a picture shown. Henry's narcissism, and self-pity, cold-fish side, about as great as possible for a human being to possess. A good deal presented by his son Sebastian, which was done well. I was interested to see Sebastian. There was a photograph of Dig as a deb, about 1918–19. Various old girlfriends, a barmaid who had served Henry, secretaries in Pontifex, all talked about him. It was allowed he drank excessively. True, he is a difficult figure to attempt a description of because so much is obscure.

I reread *Henry IV.1*, an old favourite. One increasingly feels the unpleasantness of Falstaff and Hotspur. The former might easily have been unreal if less well presented; 'To pluck bright honour from the pale-faced moon.'

Friday, 7 February

A photographer was supposed to come at 11 a.m. for a picture in the *Independent Colour.* He rang up announcing himself as Herbie Knott, saying he was running three-quarters of an hour late. Asked whether he knew the way to the house, replied yes, had been here before in 1984 for the *Sunday Times*, would arrive 11.45. Arrived 12.25. He spent literally three-quarters of an hour arranging junk and did not start actual photographing until well past one o'clock. By this time I was slightly put out, having particularly emphasized to the paper that I didn't want a lot of time wasted and, as Edith Sitwell once remarked to me, 'I only have one lunch a day.'

In the end, after about half an hour's photographing, told him he had to go. I left him packing up his ironmongery. He drove off well through our luncheon. He was quite a nice chap, I was sorry to be so irritated by him, but all quite inexcusable. He tried to photograph Snook, but really the stupidity of photographers, flashing some kind of range-finder several times in the face of an already restless animal, then taking hours to put in a new film. Knott said rather bitterly: 'I hope you have a nice lunch,' rather as if the occasion was me letting him down, after bothering him to photograph me.

Monday, 10 February

An American fan letter from James Weaver, a Member of the House of Representatives, enthusiastic, saying *Dance* read forty or fifty times. Modest fan mail received about the Parsons' Pleasure letter in *DT,* including David

Twiston Davies, expressing pleasure to see my name again in the paper, which was nice of him.

Tuesday, 11 February

Paul Bailey, with BBC girl and engineer (Ian Hunter), came in the afternoon about 3.30 p.m. to do an interview for *Third Ear*, the book programme on Radio 3 (7.05 next Tuesday). The fascinating thing was that the BBC girl was called Sally Marmion, a name I thought had died out. She was quite interested in her family, which came, so far as I could gather, from Manchester a generation or so ago, but also having some Irish connexions. The suggestion on the whole would be she was of the Tamworth Castle branch of the Marmion family. Paul Bailey had last come here about twelve years ago to talk about writing a biography of Henry Yorke, which he gave up fairly recently saying it was just a list of pointless love affairs and drunken bouts.

He had some very funny stories about his visits to the Yorkes. On one occasion, lunching with Dig at Wilton Place, they had some carrots on their plates. Dig said: 'Don't you think carrots somehow awfully common.' On another occasion Michael Holroyd went there to talk to Henry about Lady Ottoline Morrell, regarding whom he was writing something. Dig let him in. They went upstairs. There was what Holroyd thought was an old tramp on the stairs snoring. Dig said nothing. They stepped over him. Went into the drawing-room. After a bit Dig asked if Holroyd would like some tea. Holroyd said yes. Dig stepped over the tramp again, went downstairs, brought in the tea. Holroyd wondered whether he would ever see Henry. After a while the tramp came in. Dig said: 'Oh, there you are, Henry.' Henry shook hands with Holroyd. Said: 'I'll be with you in a moment.' Went out of the room, washed, shaved, came back, gave a perfectly coherent series of answers about Lady Ottoline. Really a great relief to be interviewed by an intelligent man like Bailey, who asked (with apologies) most of the usual questions, chiefly about *Dance*, but in a bright way. I see from *Who's Who* that he began life as an actor. I rather think he said somewhere that his father was a dustman.

Wednesday, 12 February

Hilary Spurling rang, to warn me head would be in the *DT Colour* this Saturday. It will be on view from Monday in Heywood Hill's bookshop.

Thursday, 13 February

Frank (Longford) fell down the stairs in the night at Bernhurst, colliding at the bottom with a grandfather clock, which was wrecked, Frank had to go into hospital, where he had his spleen removed.

Monday, 17 February

Tim Richmond photograph in *DT Colour* showing the Pye head was excellent. Tristram said I looked like a retired football manager. Henry Mee rang. He was delighted with copy of *Under Review* with his (studio) portrait on the jacket. Also pleased that five of his portraits (the Queen, Alec Douglas-Home, Mrs Thatcher, Harold Wilson, Denis Healey) are going in the new Parliament Building in due course. He says the building itself is awful. The obvious thing would have been to have used the vacant County Hall, but nobody seems to have had the wits to think of that. Instead an architecturally Victorian, badly adapted building. Mee is moving in near future to a charming corner house in Lloyd Square, if they are not done out of it before then.

I read David Cecil's biography of Max Beerbohm, which V got from the library. It came out twenty-five years ago. Somehow I never felt David had quite what was needed for the job, but I did him an injustice. It is perhaps a shade too good-mannered but does draw attention to Max's faults and, all in all, there is not a great deal to say. It is an odd story, and Max's literary abilities are hard to assess. His best caricatures are undoubtedly first-rate, also some of the stories in *Seven Men*.

David does not pinpoint the letter Max wrote to his first wife Florence, apparently making sure that she did not expect any physical relations. Rupert Hart-Davis, in his *Max Beerbohm Letters*, with surer instinct for that sort of thing, does so by juxtaposition, the next letter, undated, beginning 'darling'. Max's two marriages seem an odd piece of luck. Also odd that his second wife reported him saying (apropos of Ruskin) that it was extraordinary for a man to marry if he knew he was impotent. David's biography shows the utter absurdity of suggesting that Max was homosexual, tho' certainly oddly geared. He could play what seem to one unpleasant practical jokes, e.g. when he and friends in an hotel went into a chauffeur's room when he was asleep, put his watch back two hours and left a pile of champagne bottles by the bed. Like so many biographies this is lacking in dates and one would like more details about money.

Tuesday, 18 February

I listened to my BBC talk with Paul Bailey about writing on Radio 3. I was not very clear (reception not good here), nor towards the end was Paul. Probably better nearer London. There was a moment when Paul (who did it well) laughed a lot when I said that I had always supposed that the book *I Stopped at a Chemist* was to buy a contraceptive. I could not catch what Paul had thought.

Wednesday, 19 February

Letter from the great-niece of the Balliol don Paravicini (Mrs Helen Tabner, née de Paravicini), who was delighted at the Parsons' Pleasure story being corrected by me in *DT*, as she is compiling a history of the family. Apparently the Paravicinis are usually fair-haired, but when her father, ill in bed, grew a beard it was bright red, which seems to confirm the Parsons' Pleasure anecdote. I sent her the verse about Paravicini in *Balliol Rhymes*, telling her that *Under Review* (available on Monday) reproduced it.

We watched a TV programme about Barbara Pym. V found this just tolerable. I always think someone acting a figure who died only the other day is likely to be unsatisfactory, in this case (although a decent actress) making Barbara Pym infinitely dreary, unprepossessing. I never met her, but, although not a beauty, she was obviously rather elegant, not at all unattractive.

I read Kate Fleming's book about her mother, Celia Johnson, which I found mildly interesting, theatrical life, the Fleming marriage. What a pompous ass poor old Peter was, tho' I liked him; how utterly appalling his mother. Celia Johnson played far the best Nurse in *Romeo and Juliet* that I have ever seen, in fact the only one that made any sense of the part.

Monday, 24 February

Publication of *Under Review.* No notices yesterday as might have been hoped, nor, as it happens, any letters today for me of any kind. V attended a meeting of fifty or sixty in the Church this evening protesting against ARC's efforts to close Mells Lane.

Thursday, 27 February

Mr Joyce, of Cooper & Tanner, came in the afternoon to talk about the property, rents, etc. He had walked it, found all in reasonably good state, some thorn growing in places, which he would refer to the tenant. He also found signs of poaching, which was the trespassing souped-up Land-Rovers noted some weeks ago as 'scrambling'. This is known to the police. The situation little different from the last time. Question of rents came up, bad agricultural situation, but need for them not to be too low for sudden very large increase to take place. Michael Joyce is a reassuring person to act as agent.

I read Nigel Jones's life of Patrick Hamilton, which V got from the library, followed by a reread of *Hangover Square.* Hamilton was an odd chap with an equally odd uncomfortable upper-class background, which included his father getting through £100,000. Hamilton himself was at Westminster and almost at once began to earn a living on the stage. Then he briefly went into the City, but did not like it and returned to writing plays with great success. In fact his plays and novels kept him comfortably off all his life, especially *Rope* (which Arthur Waley took me to). I'm not sure that I ever saw *Gaslight.*

Hangover Square, generally regarded as Hamilton's best novel, holds up pretty well of its kind. The description of the hero's passionate, hopeless love for this beautiful, worthless girl is extremely well done, his fits of derangement in which he ultimately kills her and her lover, commits suicide, less interesting. For a long time Hamilton was an obsessive Marxist, eventually giving up. This added a sentimental side to most of his novels and prevents him from being a pretty good writer by always restricting him to a particular genre of abnormality. His own sex life seems to have been fairly odd. He never really writes about that in what might be called a straightforward way.

Sunday, 1 March, St David's Day

Notices of *Under Review* coming in, most satisfactory, *Evening Standard* (Kate Wharton, former wife of Peter Simple) excellent, *Spectator* (Stephen Spender, what might be expected, all right in old Spender's innately stick-in-the-mud way), *Sunday Telegraph* (Hugh Massingberd, loyal and true), *Sunday Times,* the surprise of the bunch, a really glowing encomium from John Bayley, to whom I sent a line. Naturally one is always pleased at an ecstatic review, but cannot help being struck by the fact that John is one of the very few critics that exist these days who really gets the point of things.

Tuesday, 3 March

Haircut (Chérie) at Debbie's. Obit Ruth Pitter, age ninety-four. I have never done more than thought of her as a sympathetic poet and a great one for cats. There was an interesting note about her by Elizabeth Jennings. Jennings said one would expect John Betjeman to be a warm admirer of Pitter, with her Anglican enthusiasms in common. He did like her, but Pitter's real fan was Roy Fuller. I found much to ponder in this, possibly Roy's innate niceness, with lack of the faintest jealousy or perhaps envy, quality less immediately evident in Betjeman.

Wednesday, 4 March

John Mackenzie of the *Sunday Express* rang to ask for information about Henry Mee chiefly with reference to Henry's picture of Mrs Thatcher. Mackenzie seemed to think very highly of Henry. Delighted and surprised when I offered to give him Henry's address, telephone number. Said I must be pleased with reception *Under Review* was receiving. One continues to be struck by Henry's remarkable capacity for effortlessly attracting publicity.

Friday, 6 March

Virginia, having gardening day at The Stables, came to dinner. She is on her way to the Clives at Whitfield. She had been in Cardiff, where Tristram laid on for viewing the first two episodes of *The Old Devils*. Kingsley Amis, who had been in Swansea with various pals of former times like his nice solicitor friend Stuart Thomas, was seeing these film run-offs. The Swansea lot, including Hilly Kilmarnock (not Ali), were all fairly well tanked-up, and came over to Cardiff in a minibus.

Kingsley took his drink about with him wherever he went, as when watching the film. Kingsley suffers from a terrible neurotic fear of being bored for a second, which of course means he is in a state of nervous boredom most of the time. Tristram reported that Kingsley was enjoying *Under Review*. The book is dedicated to him. This is the first notification that he had received it. Cold Breton smoked chicken, salami, one of John's super salads. We drank the other bottle of unknown provenance, Château

La Lagune '83, excellent. Possibly given by Virginia herself, tho' she thought not; possibly Archie.

Tuesday, 10 March

The day of conferment of the Welsh University Hon. D. Litt. The weather was a mixture of sunshine and torrential rain. The Faculty (as V calls them) due at 11.45, arrived at 12.15, about which nothing was said. This was somewhat nerve-racking for us waiting. The Vice-Chancellor, Sir Aubrey Trotman-Dickenson; the Registrar, Dr Alan Kemp; my presenter (also my bibliographer) George Lilley. Sir Aubrey, in his late sixties, was rather lame, with a very slight stutter. A Wykehamist, Balliol man and scientist, he was also obviously a fair genealogist, with some background of a large house, possessed by I'm not sure which bit of his family. His Welsh connexions seemed a bit thin as such, except an intensely Welsh great-aunt of whom he spoke. Dr Kemp was not, I think, Welsh on his father's side, but born and brought up in Barry Dock. His mother was from North Wales. He spoke with a strong Cardiff accent. We had drinks, then got into our robes in the hall, George Lilley having some of his own, institution unknown, certainly not mere MA Oxon. George got me into mine with the extraordinary sleight of hand he possesses in such things, and we processed into the dining-room where the young man from Chantry Television was already almost invisibly installed with a video. V followed with a camera.

The ceremony took place. All seemed to go very well. We then journeyed to La Bisalta in Vicarage Street, Frome, which was quite good, nice dining-room looking out on to trees, garden, good food. There were, however, terrible delays. I really was extremely hungry by the time my Parma ham and melon came. These were followed by spaghetti (in fact some other form of pasta, perhaps fettucini), all quite good, and really excellent Chianti. I could have done with a drop more of the latter, but probably better without these days. We were then taken home. A successful if immensely tiring day. This business of it all being a dream was the strongest impression. V agreed entirely about the dreamlike, unsubstantial quality of the whole experience. She was an immense help in carrying the whole thing off.

Friday, 13 March

V's eightieth birthday. Sister Bobby, who gave me my Vitamin B yesterday, nearly had a fit when told this. She said she thought V was sixty, which indeed she looks, if that. I gave her some shoes and a birthday card of kittens for the soppiness of which I apologized. This proved quite unnecessary, for if in that particular quality mine perhaps came first, she received no less than thirty-one pictures of cats in all, some competing with my own. In the afternoon she, John and I watched video of the D. Litt. enrobement. This was well done by the chap from Chantry TV, immensely funny. I felt rather ashamed of grumbling at Kingsley Amis not having acknowledged receipt of *Under Review*, because he wrote a really charming letter about the book, having read it twice. He also made several excellent points.

Saturday, 14 March

Sue Macartney-Snape came soon after three o'clock to talk about the non-*Dance* covers. She was staying with her sister at Coleford. I always imagine any woman who comes to do this sort of job will be a Helen of Troy, and am usually disappointed, this time she turned out an extremely attractive blonde, late thirties, tho' looking decidedly less. She not only likes all sorts of artists one likes, Beardsley, etc., but was keen on Ed Burra. In fact we got on a treat, and I have great hopes of her covers. Tristram and Virginia gave a birthday dinner for V at The Stables. Guests: Archie, Georgia, Henrietta (Lamb) Phipps, Mary Clive, George Clive, Lees and Mary Mayall, Robert Mayall, with Robert's fiancée, Maria White-Spunner (*jolie laide*, marriage imminent, both lots of parents pleased, White-Spunner looked rather jolly, I thought, tho' I did not manage to speak to her), Joff and Tessa Davies (looking very pretty), ourselves, John, sixteen in all. Smoked salmon, chicken risotto, birthday cake, champagne, red wine. I had a couple of glasses of fizz. I was ferried from and back to the house by Archie very kindly. Unusually good party.

Sunday, 15 March

Georgia and Henrietta came over to say goodbye, as they had to go back to London. They were both looking fairly battered after party. Tristram and Archie came in later for drinks (Virginia had too severe a hangover). Tristram made one of his perceptive remarks discussing the party, saying that Lees Mayall, contrary to appearances, was really rather shy. Sue Macartney-Snape and her sister Debbie Royds (big, less delicate version of Sue), with Poppy Royds, two, came over. I showed Sue ancient photographs to give background for the period.

Hilary Spurling rang in the evening saying she had only just got hold of *Under Review* from Heinemann's brilliant dispatch department and was enormously enjoying it. I am very pleased at that.

Tuesday, 17 March

A friend of Virginia's told her that an extremely distinguished scientist, Dr Steve Jones, had chosen *Dance* for his *Desert Island Discs* book, so I sent Dr Jones a line of thanks c/o BBC. His address turned out to be Genetics & Biometry, Galtonian Laboratory, London University. He sent me a tape of the programme in return. Dr Jones said: 'There is a series of books by Anthony Powell called *A Dance to the Music of Time*, which is a lovely way of describing evolution. If I could take one of these it would be *The Valley of Bones*.' Good smack in the eyes of reviewers who drivel on about *Dance* being only of interest to a small upper-crust group, also those who don't like the war volumes, tho' some like these best.

Wednesday, 18 March

I accompanied V to Frome to see the dentist, as I thought my lower plate had again become a trifle too loose. This was Mr Richard Joy, whom I had not met (Lister having left the practice). Richard Joy, son of a Frome doctor, is contemporary of Tristram. They used occasionally to meet at local children's parties. Agreeable personality, dark, heavy spectacles, V thought a touch of Max Hastings. Like somebody I know but not quite Max, I feel. In the end we decided to leave well alone as regards plate.

I reread *Henry IV.2*, one of the most enjoyable, except the odious behaviour of Prince Hal at the end, although I concede Falstaff, who could be a sinister bore too, had to be disposed of. Shallow is perhaps my favourite character in Shakespeare, a very interesting figure. In the end he is swept in as apparently equally blameworthy with Falstaff, Mistress Quickly, Doll Tearsheet *et al.* When Shallow talks to his man Davy, was that played in a camp manner? Shallow's wife is never referred to, nor children. One always feels, as so often, that he is one of those Shakespearian characters who conveyed more to an Elizabethan audience than one knows.

Thursday, 19 March

V had a tedious day with the dentist, another area of her teeth having
gone wrong in the night. *The Old Devils* is receiving rather unfriendly
notices, one suspects because the sort of hack who does TV criticism is
shocked at a bogus Welsh TV personality being made fun of, and that very
well. Too near the knuckle for some of them.

Tuesday, 24 March

We watched Part II *The Old Devils* last night, mostly introducing the women.
Not bad, if a trifle confused. Then so is the novel. V commented that it
was not so much Alun Weaver in search of Wales, as Kingsley Amis in
search of his youth as a young don there. Later notices of *Old Devils* are
better.

Wednesday, 25 March

The sweep, Mr Rolf, who has a wonderfully elaborate hair-do, came. In
spite of the fact that Mr Rolf now employs a machine (shades of Mr
Grimes in *The Water Babies*), not leaving a speck of soot, Mrs Lloyd still
traditionally puts sheets over everything. Friedrich Hayek, the political
philosopher, demolisher of Socialism, died age ninety-two. Alick Dru introduced me to Hayek's *The Road to Serfdom*, when it appeared in 1944. A
good book. Tristram rang to say he and Virginia are off to Washington to
show *The Count of Solar* to a Deaf Institution. They will be back on Monday.

Tuesday, 31 March

I read William Empson's *Seven Types of Ambiguity*, never done before, also
reread John Meade Falkner's *Moonfleet*, not looked at for very long time,
a good couple of books to help each other along. Empson is always
enjoyable, although, as with all professional literary critics, one cannot
share the excessive hair-splitting of meaning, although Empson's knockabout humour is always immensely enjoyable. When he makes quotations,
Shakespeare to Omar Khayyám, he always has something both funny and
apposite to say (for instance, Proust's novel being like a description of a
novel that unfortunately had been lost). Wish I had known Empson beyond
meeting him once (perhaps a couple of times), when I was able to tell

him how pleased I was when he referred to something Templer səid, as if everyone ought to know who Templer was.

Moonfleet I read in John's private school copy (J. Powell in front). It is prototype of a thousand boys' stories of smuggling, Dorset, etc., the beginning better than the latter part, which becomes too grotesque, also too painful (JMF had extremely sadistic strain), the hero and Elzevir Block, his father-figure (unless looked on pederastically), being imprisoned in the Netherlands for ten years, and branded on the cheek with a Y, the arms of the Mohuns (Moons). There is a Y-shaped charge in heraldry which this could be. They are on their way to the Dutch East Indies to suffer further horrors for the rest of their lives, when shipwrecked off Moonfleet, where Block is drowned, but John Trenchard comes into a somewhat improbable fortune, and gets his girl, the wicked Squire's daughter. We celebrated V's birthday at long last with caviar, a bottle of Veuve Clicquot Ponsardin '80, both good.

Saturday, 4 April

Nice day for V to attend the wedding of Charlotte Lennox-Boyd and Charles Mitchell at St Germans, Cornwall, driven by Tristram and Virginia, Archie and Georgia, plus Toby Coke, arriving by train. John cooked an excellent luncheon here (chicken, veg), then we had an unsuccessful attempt to run off the Welsh Hon. D. Litt. tape at The Stables, something essential missing for tape, as we got ordinary TV successfully. V returned having had excellent day. Reception at Ince, where she sat between John Wells and General Sir Frank Kitson. General Kitson (whom she found easy to talk to) had been much impressed by Henry Mee having given us one of my portraits. Poor Virginia had Brian Moyne to sit next to.

Monday, 6 April

Having perforce got my American fan mail into some sort of order (nowadays reduced to three or four a year) owing to upsetting the box, I have been doing the same to other than American and Canadian. For roughly the last thirty years British fan mail seems to have worked out at about a letter a week, that is to say fifty plus/minus a year of which about twenty are relatively serious letters of appreciation, thirty autograph seekers, institutions asking one to lecture, etc., readers wanting books to be signed. Latterly, I have refused to do this, unless meeting people in the flesh, saving a good deal of trouble, but brought on by finding a bookseller (presumably) sending (literally) crates of books under different names from an accommodation address (one discovered by Roland Gant). Among these last refusals I include even obviously serious letters so far as not preserving is concerned. Over the weekend Tristram ran me through the routine for doing the video, which I successfully worked on my own with Hon. D. Litt. tape this afternoon, though still not certain I did rewind correctly. I shall try again.

Tuesday, 7 April

V attended the Inquiry about ARC. Ninety-three written objections from local people as to proposed closure of Mells Lane. I tried the tape on the video again. It worked, but apparently in quite a different manner.

Thursday, 9 April

V and I voted at 9 a.m. The former small movable hut in which municipal official sat has been replaced by a truly extraordinary double-decker bus painted light blue with pictures of animals all over its exterior. Michael Legge was telling, being relieved by Patricia Lomer, to be relieved in her turn by V at 11 a.m. Apparently it was a school bus, so that's why so painted.

Friday, 10 April

The Tories elected with a majority of twenty-one. The BBC is feeling it dreadfully. One takes great pleasure in the incompetence of the opinion polls. Sister Bobby has gone to Carlisle to look after her ill mother so Vitamin B was given by her stand-in, Sister Angela.

Monday, 13 April

Charming letter from Vidia Naipaul describing how much he is enjoying *Under Review.* He said he had been gripped by the election much more than usually. He met John Major last October; and found him 'quick and dazzling'. This is not the sort of praise Vidia gives to everyone. I said Mr Major should be subjected to the traditional ordeal of Prime Ministers (Mrs Thatcher) of sitting between both of us (Vidia and me) at dinner.

Tuesday, 14 April

Second day of cold and wet after some show of spring. The magnolia at its best ever. V attended some of the Inquiry in the morning, and heard put the hydrologist's evidence for ARC. Anti-arguments heard in May. Lees and Mary Mayall to tea, both in reasonably good form, tho' Lees rather lame. A good deal of gossip, the two recent weddings being dished up.

Friday, 17 April

A Canadian fan sent a cutting of figures from the *NYT* of colossal losses of a firm called Digital, with comment: 'Confusion to your enemies.' Rather good joke, as Digital had used my comment about Michelangelo's snowman (that it must have been the best snowman ever).

I read Kingsley Amis's *The Russian Girl*. Not good. The figure obviously based on Bob Conquest. Russian expert, also tremendous womanizer (not, in fact, in the least like Bob), falls for a Russian female poet, who comes to England to organize protest against her brother being held in prison. Complication is that she is a bad poet and her brother a real criminal. Is the hero to sacrifice his integrity by supporting her cause? This, I suppose, a just possible situation, tho' in any circumstances always hard to lay down dogmatically who is a good poet. In any case, would a protest for such a cause be quite so easy to get up these days?

Any seriousness the book can claim is destroyed by the hero's farcically awful rich wife (why he married her never explained), who had apparently burnt down the theatre in which her previous husband was to produce a play, destroys all the papers and clothes of present husband; on hearing he is leaving her, causes his car to have serious accident which nearly kills a man.

Kingsley has no idea whatever what Russians are like, makes the story unnecessarily improbable by introducing some Czech brothers called Radetzsky (famous Austrian eighteenth–nineteenth-century Field Marshal), saying their grandfather had been in the Imperial Lancers when he would be much more likely to be a Pole, if a Lancer, a Czech likely to be in Dragoons and, if really a Pole, only technically a Czech, why stress his behaviour as being very Czech. Kingsley knows nothing whatever about Eastern Europe. The novel's end is both improbable and abjectly sentimental. This all regrettable after the admirable film of *The Old Devils* (I am rereading the novel).

Saturday, 18 April

Sue Macartney-Snape has produced good rough for *Afternoon Men* cover
(Susan Nunnery). With *From a View, Waring,* that means three all right,
but *Venusberg, Agents and Patients,* might be tricky.

I read (as it turns out reread, because a note made towards the end)
Lucan's *Pharsalia,* Civil Wars (Pompey, Caesar, Cato, *et al*), selection translated by Robert Graves. Not madly exciting, but lively odds and ends like
long account of the powers of witches, how they are more powerful than
the gods, can alter the height of mountains or divert rivers, this all apropos
of Pompey's son, Sextus Pompey, consulting a famous witch, who lived in
Thessaly. Amusing to read a work that is anti Julius Caesar.

Sunday, 19 April, Easter Day

The Stables party, Tristram, Virginia, Archie, Georgia, Toby Coke, for
drinks in the morning (all bringing Easter gifts, which makes me rather
ashamed as I never produce anything at Easter). Martin Stannard's Vol.
II, *Evelyn Waugh: No Abiding City,* widely reviewed. I had rather hoped to
be sent a copy, but did not think worth making serious effort to effect
that. The general view is that Evelyn was a pretty awful man, but a genius
whom Stannard has been too hard on. I think Evelyn shade overrated
these days (compared to the big shots), and don't find him such an
enigma, given his colossal egotism, will-power, lack of interest in what
other people were like, the last which he himself admitted. Those, with
his gifts, all led fairly logically to the end result. Paul Johnson caught my
attention by describing Christopher Sykes (all three RCs) as 'jealous' in
his EW biography. An interesting view. It remains inexplicable why Stannard, who has little if any humour, nor grasp of the sort of world Evelyn
aspired to, wanted to write about him. Stannard seems to have dug out
some financial details that might be of interest. Putting the book down at
the library.

Monday, 20 April

Arthur Calder-Marshall obit, age eighty-three. He was regarded in his
youth as a promising novelist. I never thought him much good at novels,
but he wrote a respectable biography of Havelock Ellis who needed a
biography, also enjoyable boyhood memoirs of knowing, when Arthur was
a boy, infinitely minor poet, Neuburg (Vickybird), and Neuburg's friend

Aleister Crowley. Arthur was not a bad old thing, if inevitably rather depressing figure latterly (he would ring up occasionally). He gave V a somewhat unfriendly notice for *A Substantial Ghost,* which one can only attribute at that stage to envy of anyone writing a book at all.

Archie's twenty-second birthday, luncheon party at The Stables, the house party plus William Mount, who drove from Pembrokeshire on way to London. This took four and a half hours owing to traffic. Tristram himself going into a question of a film about the Russian Futurist poet Vladimir Mayakovsky (1895–1930).

Reread *Troilus and Cressida,* usually a favourite, for some reason did not enjoy so much as usual. The plot seemed to take a long time to get going, anyway never quite clear. Pandarus, Cressida's uncle, is anxious for her to link up with Troilus, in spite of her early protests that she finds his brothers, and others, more attractive. It is not at all obvious what advantage as a 'pander' Pandarus is getting from this. Was Troilus actually paying him? Cressida then says she has been protesting she does not like Troilus 'in the way women do when in love with a man', goes to bed with him, but when she has to return to the Greek lines (being only a hostage with the Trojans) she immediately starts up affair with Diomedes. It might well be argued that is just the way women do behave, but such hardly seems the argument of the play. Did it express something clearer to an Elizabethan audience, as one feels so much of Shakespeare did, or was the play just a pot-boiler as has been suggested?

Tuesday, 21 April

Virginia to dinner, who talked of her father, whom she can only remember as rather strict. Cold meats, drank Mouton Rothschild '76, given me by Roy Jenkins for the bet about the American election. In spite of fairly considerable age, four-out-of-seven year, absolutely superb.

Wednesday, 22 April

The Eton Annual Report mentioned the Shelley Centenary celebrations, so I sent a line to Eric Anderson, the Head Master, saying I hoped they would not forget Gronow having been a friend of Shelley at Eton, talking about Shelley's chemical experiments that nearly blew the school up, adding that to write about Shelley rather presumptuous, as Eric Anderson probably came across Gronow's *Memoirs* when editing Walter Scott's *Diary.*

This morning at 9.45 a.m. Eric rang to ask if I would come over on

Saturday to the celebrations (VI Form doing various recitations) if he sent a car. This was very kind, but I could not face the physical exertions required. Great bore that these things are on offer when one is past them, also rather disturbing to oneself. Eric Anderson is a nice, sensible chap. One imagines very good for Eton, well up to dispersing the myth that Shelley was desperately unhappy there. Apart from anything else, Shelley (not a particular favourite figure of mine) was extremely tough (all that sailing with Byron). V has gone off to get an early reconnoitre of the Inquiry.

Saturday, 25 April

Tristram's fifty-second birthday. We rang to wish Many Happy Returns. He and Virginia are going to lunch in Peterborough to celebrate, where Johnny Noble has opened an oyster bar.

Wednesday, 29 April

Francis Bacon obit. Can't say I greatly like his painting in spite of obvious ability, often agreeable colour, something a bit *voulu*, feeling I have about Daumier, Van Gogh. I met him twice; I think once certainly with Sonia Orwell, both times possibly. The second time I may have sat next to Bacon at dinner, not particularly easy, at the same time not at all disagreeable. We talked at one moment about Conrad, whose books he liked. Incidentally, I learn from Martin Stannard's Vol. II *Evelyn Waugh* that a criminal friend of Francis Bacon's was responsible for removing Evelyn's gold watch from a drawer at Stephen Spender's, who was giving a party. It was eventually recovered (glass broken) through the good offices of Frank Norman, naturally after a colossal fuss involving most of the Underworld.

Pam Berry had invited Evelyn and Spender to meet at luncheon, hoping they would have a row, but Spender was immensely obsequious. Evelyn took out his gold watch, which had stopped, or something wrong, remarked: 'I must take this to Cartier.' Pam gave very funny imitation of Spender saying: 'Oh, sir, if you will entrust your beautiful watch to me, I will take it to Cartier, as I am passing,' etc. Spender then gave a party for rough trade that evening; in the morning the watch had disappeared. Frank Norman was staying with Bill and Annie Davis in Spain when we were there, also gave funny account. Pam said most squalid aspect of whole *histoire* was that when Spender told her about it, he began: 'When I went down to the kitchen to shave . . .'

Friday, 1 May

Selina Hastings, as thanks for a few scraps of information, very sweetly
sent me *No Abiding City*, Martin Stannard's Vol. II of his biography of
Evelyn Waugh. Rather to my surprise I thought it pretty well done so far
as covering the ground, tho' at times horrible phraseology ('lover' for
'mistress', often worse than that), a few howlers. Interesting fact I did not
know (Auberon Herbert crying on the way to the wedding, where he was
giving Laura away, Stannard calling him 'Best Man').

I never quite took in before that EW had regarded Cyril Connolly,
literally, as what he himself would have been like had he not been an RC.
This a fascinating subject to ponder. Cyril was much 'cleverer' than Evelyn
in many senses, far better read, but not at all 'creative', except, if you
count that, in parody, introductions, small effects. For elegant writing not
much between them. Cyril in general cautious where Evelyn a bull in a
china shop. One funny thing is that Evelyn's views on Tito are now turning
out not so silly as once supposed, Churchill nowadays being often charged
with making a mistake in backing Tito. As I had been unenthusiastic about
Vol. I, I sent Stannard a line expressing enjoyment of Vol. II.

Saturday, 2 May

Snook's fourth birthday (on or about). Ferdie and Julia Mount gave V a
life of E. F. Benson, the novelist, not particularly interesting except that it
said Benson had been much in love with Vincent Yorke, father of Henry
Yorke/Green, at Cambridge. The author added that it was uncertain
whether the love was mutual. I can imagine nothing that would have
annoyed the Yorke family more than suggesting this possibility, but I
remembered that once when I was staying at Forthampton (probably age
about sixteen) *Dodo*, Benson's first novel, a bestseller, had been mentioned,
Mrs Yorke had said to me, I think, perhaps speaking generally: 'Of course
Vincent was Dodo.' Having hitherto supposed (rightly) that Dodo was a
woman, I wondered if I had got the sex wrong, but did not think much
more about it. V now tells me that Dodo was generally taken to be Margot
(Tennant) Asquith, Margot probably the cause of mention of the book at
Forthampton.

In the light of Benson's Cambridge love for Mr Yorke we took *Dodo* out
of the library. It is the most abject rubbish. Dodo, a wilful, beautiful, witty
society girl, was recently married to the good but boring Marquess of
Chesterford, whom she doesn't love, having just refused the Marquess's

cousin Jack Broxton, who hasn't enough money, tho' she does (anyway to some extent) love him. Her baby dies. She asks Broxton to run away with her; he nobly refuses; the Marquess dies. He has seen Broxton kiss her hand, but believes Broxton that nothing wrong had taken place; on his deathbed begging Broxton to marry Dodo. The reader has not been prepared for Broxton being the Marquess's heir, so Dodo will retain her position. When married she had rows with her husband about seeing a rackety Austrian Prince, to whom her fiancé, the new Marquess, equally objects. This Dodo will not stand, eloping with the Prince on the last page and becoming a Serene Highness. The above are the only men of consequence in the story. I cannot think Vincent Yorke would have taken part in any drama such as this. Was he simply jilted by Margot Tennant?

David Cheshire rang. V bore the brunt. David was a shade incoherent, she said. He had just seen *The Album* and very pleased about last picture being a photograph taken by himself.

Sunday, 3 May

With great brilliance V has, I think, solved the Yorke/Dodo problem by pure reflection. Towards the end of the book Dodo goes to a family of baronets called Grantham as a bolt-hole. The son of the house is mildly taken with her. The Granthams think a great deal of themselves, but son and father are always explaining Lady Grantham's gaffes by pointing out that she is a foreigner (Spanish). This could have been Vincent Yorke's mother (Dutch, de Tuyl). The house, very rambling, might even have been Forthampton before modernization.

To continue with a somewhat similar subject, Stannard's *Waugh* II quotes a letter of Henry Yorke/Green (one of several somewhat arse-creeping ones to EW) about *Work Suspended*; 'Plante is a tremendous character . . . he made me think of Tony Powell.' This interested me, so reread *Work Suspended*. Plante, chief character, is an immensely systematic writer, who lives on his detective novels, works in Morocco, signs of his having an affair with a married woman when the book ends. Incidentally, in the compendium of recently published writings of Henry Green, Henry says he cannot read Evelyn's book. I cannot see the least resemblance to myself in Plante, nor can V, tho' Henry may have thought me a systematic writer (compared with himself) and, like most writers supposing other writers make much more money than they do, believed that of me.

John down at the lake supervising the Syndicate cutting up trees that

have fallen in the big grotto. Tristram and Virginia down. Tristram came
to the house. We had a talk while V and John played snooker.

Monday, 4 May

Tristram and Virginia came to morning drinks. They had lunched the
previous day with Vidia and Pat Naipaul. Vidia has to have an operation
on his spine. Something a bit wrong. One suspects all these exercises,
standing on his head, and so on. Nevertheless, he was in excellent form.
Pat looked a bit frail.

Thursday, 7 May

Marlene Dietrich obit. She (with Stroheim) was the only film star for
whom I ever felt the least fascination. We saw her in Hollywood at the bar
all the stars then frequented (called the Cock & Bull, I think), not at all
disappointing, very small, perhaps even smaller than most stars. V attended
the Inquiry.

Saturday, 9 May

I greatly enjoyed John Bayley's book on A. E. Housman, which he sent us,
and wrote a line about it. A letter from Miss Tracey who conducted one
of our Swan Hellenic Italian tours (on land) about twenty years ago, saying
I was 'the only nice person' on the worst collection of people she had
ever taken round, including still doing it. I couldn't remember any of
them except a woman V and I thought a secret drinker; another from one
Jeremy Blakiston of Reading, asking if Widmerpool was to some extent
modelled on Tom Driberg. True, the latter was keen on the arts, but he
was at the same time insatiate homosexual, but Labour MP who became
a peer, sinister relations with the Russians, self-proclaimed promoter of
Youth. Interesting parallel, less the homosexuality, in some ways.

Monday, 11 May

I read, with considerable skipping, the Koran (tr. N. J. Dashwood). Repeti-
tive, lacking in narrative powers, in short not a patch on the Bible.

Wednesday, 13 May

Bruce Hunter sent the printed covers for *Afternoon Men, From a View to a Death,* and *What's Become of Waring,* by Sue Macartney-Snape. These he thought splendid. I agree. The background of *Afternoon Men* is perhaps a shade crowded. I was not shown this, only the large head of the girl. It is a point that should always be kept in mind with covers, the bit that is seen when standing in a bookshop. *From a View* superb. Extraordinary that it should have taken fifty years to depict Major Fosdick in drag, instead of a man falling off a horse. V continues daily at the quarry Inquiry. Today the Inspector came to look at Mells Lane and various other places, like Finger Farm, a nice farmhouse ARC want to demolish. This was all on TV tonight, including V, excellent programme, improved by a beautiful day showing off the countryside to best advantage.

Friday, 15 May

In the afternoon V contrived to see the Inspector taken to the English China Clay tunnels, which more or less closes the Inquiry; anyway so far as V is concerned. Virginia, down for gardening, came to dinner (us and John). This supplied by Select Suppers. Started with cheese and egg tartlets (tasteless but eatable), then chicken with cucumber sauce, rice (poor), carrots with sesame. I thought it all not much less than filthy, but everyone else seemed to find it quite good. Château Lynch Bages '78, getting sweetish, perhaps a shade old, but good, plenty of body.

Saturday, 16 May

Sheila Rhys, second wife and widow of V's first cousin David (Dynevor) Rhys, brought Joan Colville, née Villiers, another (Jersey) first cousin, to tea, also Joan's son Robin (fiftyish). V says one must see Sheila on a horse judging show-jumping to appreciate her at her best. At present she is still not recovered from David's death (he was indeed a charming chap) and her son George's recent marriage, leaving her on her own, no doubt lonely. Joan, identical age with V (looking neat but years older). I used to think her rather chilly. Now she treats me rather as if she were an old girlfriend. Robin, who has had various kidney transplants so has never been able to do much, looked exactly like his late father, showing every sign of being like him in character. V took them down to The Stables to see Virginia.

Tuesday, 19 May

Hot. V took me to Frome, then on to Nunney, for routine eye check, then haircut. Eyes only faint deterioration to be expected in eighteen months, no change in specs, can still read smallest print used in test. This time done by rather motherly woman of about thirty with Somerset accent. Haircut by Chérie (Sherry), wearing shorts, black and white stripe blazer (C. M. Wells's house colours). I am conscious of doddering in Frome. John Bayley's book about A. E. Housman was enjoyable, presenting new aspects of Housman (notably that he often wrote humorously). That had not occurred to me. He is a poet I like at his best but he is often embarrassing at his worst. John B shows how that can sometimes be shown to be a joke. We have been corresponding. I am going to send him and Iris some works of mine he is missing: V will send the life of her grandmother.

Wednesday, 20 May

Peter Mumford and his Merry Men doing things for Tristram on The Stables trees. Bob Conquest rang, he and Liddie are embarking on their Baltic cruise, during which Bob will lecture. They return early in June, when they hope to come here. An American academic (Bloomington), Michael Shelden (who did goodish book on Cyril Connolly, less good on George Orwell), rang. He is writing now on Graham Greene. I told him what little I know. He makes on the whole a good impression.

Saturday, 23 May–Tuesday, 26 May

Georgia and Toby Coke at The Stables. On Tuesday (Bank Holiday) morning I went down there with V to see the video Gary Conklin, of Pasadena, California, sent of his *A Question of Class: English Literary Life 1918–1945*. This was somewhat confused affair. One would like to know who was responsible for the scenario. It seemed probable that Harold Acton had a chief hand in that as his name appeared among those on the masthead, as well as in the list of performers. Peter Quennell (with cat) also much in evidence, together with Jim Lees-Milne and Alan Pryce-Jones. I was the only subject shown with an interlocutor, Paul Fussell, tho' Paul seemed usually to have been the 'voice over' with the others.

All the above did their usual stuff, together with Stephen Spender, Christopher Isherwood and John Lehmann, the last two were caught

before The Reaper laid a hand on them. There was a good deal of Diana
Mosley (as usual called 'Lady Diana'), tho' what the Mosleys had to do
with literary life was inexplicable. The same was true of David Herbert,
the latter having changed from a relatively good-looking young man to a
depressing figure of the opposite sex. Nigel Nicolson was not very exciting
about his parents, how aristocratic they were (Vita Sackville-West's Spanish
hairdresser grandfather, or whatever he was, always forgotten).

A. L. Rowse also continually came on. I had not realized how parsonic
he is when speaking (pointed out by V), but he does his stuff, albeit all
too familiar, well, his genuinely proletarian background and Tory views,
welcome contrast to Spender & Co. Old Harold also says what he has said
(uninspiring as it is) well. Alan P-J's picture-of-Dorian-Gray side has at last
slightly caught up with him, and he does look as if he had had a fairly
rackety life. There were stills shown of various characters like Aldous
Huxley, the Sitwells, etc. belonging to an earlier generation, or George
Orwell, who were dead. If these (with others) certainly Cyril Connolly
should have been included, which he was not. This might have been due
to Harold Acton's intense hatred, had Harold, as I suspect, had a major
hand in it, tho' none of those shown were very keen on each other. All in
all it was a strange display, not always adequately captioned, without any
indication of what were individual claims to being shown. Georgia said
she thought Tristram would like to see it and not impossible that he might
not find some use for it, as Conklin hopes.

Mr Moss did bits of the drive (£200), including some of way to The
Stables. He had seen V on TV at the Inquiry, and 'gave her full marks'.

I reread *King Lear*. What an awful family the Lears were, Cordelia in her
way as bad as any of them. What happened to Lear's badly behaved Knights
whom Regan and Goneril jibbed at putting up? Were those who survived
the campaign with the French absorbed into Albany's retainers? or just
took to freelancing?

Friday, 29 May

A letter from Bruce Hunter saying he thinks *Some Poets, Painters, and a
Reference for Mellors* excellent title and project, so I shall continue to put it
together. *Under Review* had unusually intelligent notice in *The Scotsman* by
Colin Donald, to whom I sent a line. He asked to come here, which he
did today. Fantastically like the Waughs in appearance. I had not realized
quite to what extent they were hundred per cent Lowland Scots. Donald
better-looking than they and extremely bright, I thought, late twenties, on

his way to Thailand for six months (where he had already been for eighteen months as correspondent). He hopes to set up some form of news agency there, which John says are all the go now. He brought me *Halidon Hall: A Dramatic Sketch*, by Sir Walter Scott, a sort of pamphlet, 1822, First Edition. We had an interesting talk. He hopes to do a piece in *The Scotsman*. Donald had a great deal better manners than most of the journalists who come here, more intelligent, but I was a bit exhausted after. Snook took a great fancy to Colin Donald and insisted on sitting on his knee during the interview, then rushed out, killed a rabbit and brought it to Donald's feet when he was leaving.

Tuesday, 2 June

I read *The Big House at Inver* by Somerville & Ross (the latter dcd by the time this novel was written). Had been meaning to for some time, then galvanized by mild recommendation by John Bayley as well as V. Not a book of such depths as *The Real Charlotte*, but extremely well done it its way. Edith Somerville always knows exactly what every character she deals with is like, bringing a great many characters into play. She also knows to perfection her world, her own point of view, without the smallest hesitation. So few novelists possess these technical qualifications that she completely carries off by her dramatic sense (occasional) improbable moments. One also likes her unrelieved (except by quiet humour) pessimism.

Thursday, 4 June

Heinemann (Claire Hegarty) sent Sue M-S's roughs for *Venusberg, Agents and Patients* and *O, How the Wheel Becomes It*. I have only suggested that perhaps the colour of the uniform of the military figure in *Venusberg* should be changed from red to any other colour, as scarlet always carries the implication of a British uniform, tho' in fact the Danes use it too for their Royal Guards. A certain amount of telephoning with Heinemann took place, then I rang Sue herself, who perfectly understood, is taking steps, probably light blue.

Mr Mosley rang, the shadow of a new car hanging over us. He has left his former firm, now on his own again. The Maestro no longer in production. He suggests a Rover or Ford Escort, both considerably more expensive. He will leave details on Thursday afternoon.

Hilary Spurling rang. Their house is subsiding so that they have to evacuate it, may have to stay out until Christmas. Steps being taken to remedy this. It is 'against Nature', Hilary said. They are digging a hole all round, fortunately the insurance will pay. Meanwhile the Spurlings have been lent a house in Cornwall. She and Gilbert (fourteen) will lunch here on Thursday, 18 June (Waterloo Day). V very sweetly gave me an unbirthday present of the new Tiepolo book that has just come out. I am absolutely delighted by the Danes buggering up the EC. Quotations well up: 'What is a treaty that you forsake it' (Kipling: 'Harp Song of the Dane Women'); 'I'm none of those that took Maastricht' (Rochester).

Monday, 8 June

A Netherlands journalist, Johnaugust Jansen, came in the afternoon to interview me. Tall, young, very blue-eyed, good-looking, hippy clothes, green trousers. Immensely pleased with himself on these and other accounts. He brought a bottle of Bols. Brighter than expected, and knew Continental literature and my works well. He had done year and a half in Germany on a grant. He said *Dance* was spoken of there as comparable with Thomas Mann (*Buddenbrooks*, read from end to end by me comparatively recently, found distinctly heavy going). Jansen expatiated on the English and Dutch having a sense of humour as opposed to the Germans. When in Germany, a woman had brought a picture she had painted to show some people including himself. She remarked that she had nearly broken her leg while painting it. Jansen commented: 'A pity you did not break your leg.' The woman asked why. Jansen replied, 'You might have painted a better picture.' She thought this merely bad manners, owing to her lack of humour. He will do long piece on me for Netherlands monthly illustrated paper, recording for radio there of some of our conversation. He left soon after 5 p.m.

Tuesday, 9 June

Antonia Pinter and Alison Lurie to luncheon. Antonia in the car provided by her publisher for a general promotional visit to Bath to meet booksellers, driven by a black chauffeur of the Pinters' acquaintance, who fled from Kenya twelve years ago on account of being of the 'wrong tribe'. Antonia said he talks like Chokey in *Decline and Fall*, real name Charles, I think. Antonia gave Alison a lift to lunch here, Alison being over for her annual London visit. Alison in an unusual blue dress. Her hair, like Antonia's, is now a mild ash-blonde. This is an improvement in both cases,

Antonia is bigger than when last seen (rather than fat). Both of them were in excellent form.

Harold is negotiating about a movie of *Dorian Gray*. Americans suggested they should set it in the Twenties. One supposes the Twenties the furthest back in history people, anyway Americans, know about nowadays, anything up to that the Dark Ages, at least familiar only to academicians in the History Faculty. Antonia likes white wine, Alison is unpredictable what she drinks, so we drank two bottles (in fact about bottle and half) of English wine, Three Choirs (Gloucestershire, name from Gloucester, Worcester, Hereford Cathedrals), Pilton Down, from just up the road here. I thought the former better, tho' V (who anyway does not care for white wine) found it a shade sharp. Both girls drank wine as an aperitif. Melon, smoked Breton chicken with salami, salads, cheese. All pretty good. Enjoyable party. Antonia left us a book she edited which is about to come out, various writers' preference in reading. She did not ask Vidia Naipaul or me to contribute (rightly) as finding that too awful. Alison brought her traditional Black Magic chocolates. She is editing a collection of modern fairy stories, anyway children's stories, also about to appear. Apparently Chokey said 'Good Afternoon' to Mrs Lloyd. She said she jumped on her bicycle and pedalled away in a panic. I took photograph of Antonia, Alison and Chokey.

Wednesday, 10 June

The baroque French clock in the library stopped; the grandfather has not struck for several years, so in a reckless moment I wrote to Mr Jackman (who presented me with the clock he made himself some years ago) to ask if he knew anyone who could mend these. Before he replied the clock in the library recovered. By that time it was too late to stop Mr Jackman. He is seventy, extremely tall, with a fairly large neatly cut grey beard, and a great talker, a characteristic to which he himself referred. He possesses thirty-five clocks, but has a friend (who mends clocks professionally) who has thirty-seven in his sitting-room alone. I explained the situation. Mr Jackman examined the grandfather, said that if I wanted he would take the essential part to his friend, but he himself advised leaving it as it was, unless I thought the strike very important. I agreed, gave Mr Jackman a paperback set of *Dance*. He left the house, rather like a brief violent visit of the God of Clocks.

Later Mr Mosley left a lot of particulars about cars, which neither of us could understand a word of, but will hand them over to John during the weekend. I was mulling over the Tiepolo book (by William L. Barcham, Professor of Art History at Fashion Institute of Technology, NYC) for the second or third time in the evening, when I suddenly found my description of the imaginary Tiepolo in *Temporary Kings* quoted by Barcham in his account of *The Allegory of the Four Continents*, in the Archbishop's Palace at Würzburg. He said 'no better characterization of the stairway fresco could be expressed'. I am sending the Professor a line.

Thursday, 11 June

Bob and Liddie Conquest to luncheon. Bob perhaps a shade aged, I thought (his seventy-fifth birthday next month), he speaks in a very low voice these days and has always been a bit deaf, something I too now suffer from. Liddie (forty-nine) full of beans, looking charming if a trifle plumper. They had seen the Amis household, of which Bob brought a somewhat gloomy account. Hilly Kilmarnock has broken her hip (no doubt worked to death) getting out of a taxi. Sally, their daughter, keeps the household going. Kingsley said: 'I hope you will not think me a snob when I say that I cannot take her (Sally's) boyfriend to the Garrick.' The Conquest Baltic cruise was a great success. Lunch by Moura Dillon Malone: kipper pâté (excellent); Italian marinated chicken (eatable if a bit odd); strawberries on gooseberry fool (by V, excellent). Bob and I drank Christian Brothers (Californian Chardonnay type, not at all bad), Bob about three-quarters of the bottle, Liddie and V, Valdepeñas. Nice to see the Conquests again.

Saturday, 13 June

V and I watched Colour Trooping on TV. Primrose Palmer (daughter of Felicia Lamb), on her way to the young Asquiths, to tea. Nice, untidy girl in shorts, secretary to the MP, Dudley Fishburn.

Monday, 15 June

This hot weather makes me uncommonly stiff. A start on pasting up *Poets, Painters and Mellors*. Bill Pye rang, said he had sent the head to the RA, who don't usually accept his things, but the head has been put in the Octagon Room. My impression was that he was rather pleased about that, as, although not an academic sculptor, he no doubt likes to feel he can be represented in the Academy if he so wishes. Tessa Davies to tea to collect the video of the presentation of University of Wales Hon. D. Litt., which she is kind enough to want to see.

Thursday, 18 June, Waterloo Day

Hilary and Gilbert Spurling to luncheon on their way to Cornwall. Gilbert now is fourteen, not without charm. V says he ought to be a choirboy in a ruff. A good idea, but little prospect of that happening. Hilary in her usual form in spite of the disaster to the house, which was also broken into during the interregnum. This took place at 11 a.m. by just smashing a window. Crowds of neighbours came out, so only a box of rather battered toy soldiers was stolen. Hilary said Matisse would take ten years. Apparently he was born over the border not far from Van Gogh's birthplace. Some mystery about his parentage, which was humble. The French are utterly uninterested in biography, even hostile to it. Moura Malone did lunch: her speciality chicken pie, goodish, beans; excellent lemon pie, strawberries added. Bottle Château La Croix de Gay '78 (Pomerol), not much body but not bad. When they left Snook came and showed off. Katherine Sung, a fan now in England, sent two bottles of Californian red wine.

Monday, 22 June

I have been rather stiffer during last two or three weeks so V got Dr Irish to look in. He felt my lumbar regions. He said I was a bit creaky, and the trouble was that the base of spine not built for the age people live to nowadays. We agreed that on the whole it was better to take no action, pills likely to do more harm than good in the long run.

I reread *King John*, a curious play that does not quite come off, especially the Bastard, a powerful figure with no particular rôle, owing to the difficulty of making John's story a dramatic one. Shakespeare has a taste for Bastards who make general remarks, and seems to have brought this one in just for that reason. The latter half is better than the beginning. 'A module of confounded royalty', 'Which some suppose the soul's frail dwelling-house', cf. Waller's 'The soul's dark cottage, battered and decayed . . .'

Tuesday, 23 June

Archie talked of his English school (Blake to Eliot). He did not like Keats, the Romantics, but liked some Arnold, some Tennyson. His band (ten players) to perform in one or two places, including Manchester. He will hear results of his Finals in a week. Nice boy.

Thursday, 25 June

Archie departed with his 'household'. Yesterday they were fishing when Patricia Lomer, thinking they were trespassers, beckoned them from the bank. She was wearing, Archie said, 'yellow cooking gloves'. Archie revealed his identity. I am not displeased that she should keep an eye on who uses the lake. Stuart Preston (The Sergeant) wrote from Paris saying he would like to translate a selection from *Verdicts* and *Under Review* into French, and knew a publisher who might be interested. I sent his letter to Bruce Hunter, who must be away, as I have not heard from him about an earlier French translation letter I wrote.

Sunday, 28 June

Georgia and Toby Coke at The Stables for weekend. I read *Clever Hearts* (1990), a book about Desmond and Molly MacCarthy by Hugh Cecil (grandson) and his wife Mirabel. The title is regrettable, I think. I met MacCarthy once or twice. He was always agreeable, but I could never see the point of the enormous fuss made about him as a man and a critic. This book, not without interest tho' rather indifferently written, sets out to perpetuate the legend, but in fact showing how little there is to support it. MacCarthy was no doubt a better critic than some of the talentless hacks who were his contemporaries, also a much nicer man, but had no claims whatever to be more than a superior sort of hack himself, a gent, with some charm, without an idea in his head, lazy, slipshod, making no attempt to keep up with what was happening. It suited certain people's books, notably Cyril Connolly's, to crack MacCarthy up, as MacCarthy was an infinitely milder version of Cyril himself, in lounging about, borrowing money, sending in his copy too late; also an Etonian, it should be added, but not a patch on Cyril as a critic. MacCarthy had a fairly squally married life with his wife Molly, daughter of the redoubtable Mrs Warre-Cornish, wife of an Eton Vice-Provost. She suffered from deafness. We met her only once at dinner with Osbert Sitwell, who was rather apologetic about asking us with them both, as (it turns out from this book) she was liable to bawl her husband out for his unfaithfulness in front of other people. Desmond MacCarthy was a great patron of Cyril Connolly, but Molly did not like Cyril, saying he was Mr Hyde, an idea which rather took my fancy. If Cyril

were Mr Hyde, who was Dr Jekyll? Possibly Noel Blakiston, who was exceptionally well-behaved, with whom Cyril was at one time in love. So far as I
can remember, Mr Hyde was quite different from Dr Jekyll and did not
have the same characteristics and evil instead of good. In fact a really
excellent idea is never worked out by Stevenson as well as it might be, as
quite often happens with good ideas.

Tuesday, 30 June

Mildav working on scullery. The telephone has been out of order since
Saturday. John Piper obit. Nice man, good, if somewhat limited, painter.
I never knew him at all well. We used to go over to Fawley from the
Osbert Lancasters occasionally. He was a great friend of Osbert's, who was
distinctly in awe of him. I believe John collapsed during the last four or
five years of his life, and was a severe burden for Myfanwy to look after.

Henry Bath also packed it in. Henry and I were at the same private
school, then he failed for Eton (he had been ill for some time, also
teaching at our prep school was abominable), so went to Harrow, so I did
not see him again until Oxford, where, with Harry Stavordale and Michael
Rosse, he formed a group of peers, who did not have a happy effect on
undergraduate life in my opinion, leading to snobbishness of a tiresome
sort. We used to see quite a bit of Henry and Virginia here at one time.
Virginia is delightful, Henry was full of low cunning and had some humour,
but (as Henry Adams said of the Harvard students) ignorant of all that
man had ever thought or hoped. This handicapped him as a guest. Narcissistic, totally wrapped up in Longleat, he could barely take part in general
conversation. Henry had been extremely ill for a year or so, his passing
no great surprise.

Thursday, 2 July

Mr Mosley brought a Metro (3-door) for us to see and try what it is like
to sit in. The car seemed all right, so we told him to go ahead with 5-door
version. It will be smaller, which V wanted and may take month or two for
delivery. I am stiffish, as it has reverted to cooler weather, changes always
being inimical.

Saturday, 4 July

I rather weakly agreed to a Dutch photographer taking photographs for Jansen's piece, on condition he stayed only half an hour. He turned out better than might be expected, called Ravier, father (died when he was fourteen) French, looked much more French than Dutch. He was perhaps late thirties, not bad looking in saturnine manner. He arrived at 3 p.m., out of the house by 3.40, so I could not grumble. He is much taken with this part of England, which he had not previously seen, also the house, the Augustus John drawing, Caligula bust, the fact of it being Caligula particularly delighting him. He said I was like Charlie Chaplin when I laughed, also that I was a very good model.

Sunday, 5 July

Roland Gant rang. He had been in hospital for about a year, he said, but all right now, he sounded a bit tired. One gathers he nearly packed it in at least twice. They are returning to this country for a check-up in about two months' time when he will try to arrange a meeting. Archie got a 2.1 degree, with which he is pleased.

Monday, 6 July

Tessa Davies looked in to return the tape of the Welsh Hon. D. Litt. ceremony. She said the illegitimate son of the King of Denmark, called Count Something-or-other, lived a bit south of us, age about sixty-five. He has a Swedish girlfriend and spends his whole time saying how much he dislikes the Swedes. He formerly played the drums, but is now retired.

Friday, 10 July

Virginia to dinner. They had vile weather in Burgundy, but good food. Tristram is now in Scotland doing research on a new film. Artichokes (our own), Melton pie from Fortnum's John brought down, Léoville-Barton '82, good, light. The Thynne family (notably Alexander, Sylvie an exception) continues to fill the papers.

Monday, 13 July

Mr Moss called. He had some 'heavy bitumen', which I rather weakly took (£200 worth) for the drive. Mrs Merrit took away the 'bergère' chair to recover (green). John Saumarez Smith of Heywood Hill's bookshop rang. He has two or three of my First Editions inscribed to Colonel F. R. Packe, a Welch Regiment friend and contemporary of my father's, later Equerry to Princess Beatrice. Freddy Packe, who had been badly wounded in the war, became a stockbroker. He said: 'People are such snobs. They love doing business from Kensington Palace.' A very nice man. I told John SS all this, which delighted him for his catalogue. One (perhaps more books) had been reinscribed 'Mary from Fred', apparently Packe's sister-in-law. John told me (Sir) Alistair Grant, tycoon of some sort, is mad about *Dance*, and wants not only to collect all my First Editions, but create 'the world of Anthony Powell', i.e. all the books of people I have known, indeed everything to do with me. This seems rather a tall order.

I reread *As You Like It*. The beginning is very good, particularly the girls talking to each other, immensely real and even modern in its way. All this must have been exceedingly funny with boys camping about pretending to be a girl pretending to be a man. Shakespeare seems to have got bored at the end, finishing off with complete nonsense and a lot of songs. Touchstone I find unamusing.

Tuesday, 14 July

I finished the paste-ups of *Some Poets, Artists, and a Reference for Mellors*, as I think it may have to be called, too many odds and sods appearing, over and above Sculptors, in the section which was to be called *Painters*, more assonant. Now for the Introduction. I am exceedingly stiff in the joints.

Saturday, 18 July

The Stockwells at The Stables. Tristram came over before dinner. He and I had a talk. They had attended Archie's Graduation ceremony in Coventry Cathedral, long but impressive. Tristram brought Ben Sonnenberg Jr's autobiography.

Sunday, 19 July

Tristram and Virginia came over for a drink in the morning. We spoke of Sonnenberg's wildly inaccurate description of the Davises' house in Spain, La Consula. Also of what a bore Gerald Brenan was, whose biography has just appeared by Johnny Gathorne-Hardy. We talked too of rather mysterious figure of John Hope-Johnstone – Hope-J, Hopey, etc.

Monday, 20 July

I completed the Introduction (short) to *Poets, Artists, and Mellors*, and wrote telling Bruce Hunter, asking would he like John to deliver the MS. I am rather glad to have done this as aware during the process that from time to time my grip was not quite what it was, also apt to feel tired after less than a couple of hours' work in the morning.

I read Vol. III of Proust's *Letters 1910–1917*. These are quite interesting, giving good idea of the sort of personality he was to deal with, that is to say extremely difficult. Even allowing for the French being more formal than ourselves. Granting heavy weather made in any case seventy or eighty years ago, he must have been appalling for any publisher, not forgetting what French publishers are like themselves, even compared with British publishers. Among people he knew he completely accepts that they were familiar with all the characters in his novel and talks about them a lot. At the same time he was pleased at the most modest mention of himself or his books in the press. One also gets the extent to which he had cut himself off from all but aristocratic contacts. Proust's messing about with his stocks and shares, always unsuccessfully, is unbelievable. Proust's stockbroker must have had an awful time.

I am now rereading *Hamlet* in bed. The status of Marcellus and the rest of the sentinels on the ramparts at the beginning of the play has always interested me. I have come to the conclusion that they were a kind of Yeoman of the Guard, all more or less gents. You could get a short-term Territorial commission during the long vac from Wittenberg. Parents probably rather encouraged their sons to take these (like going into the Yeomanry), to keep them out of mischief, perhaps also to supply a bit of pocket money. This might account for the shocking discipline, sentries saying how fed up they were, and glad their relief had turned up.

Sunday, 26 July

Evangeline Bruce rang from London. She, with Tony and Marcelle Quinton, will lunch here on Thursday, 13 August. Evangeline said the woman who runs Albany asked if she were the Evangeline mentioned in *Dance*. The former turned out a great fan. She has entrusted a letter to Evangeline for me.

I reread *Bleak House*, a lot of good stuff, but one is never told who Lady Dedlock was, how she had the affair which resulted in the birth of Esther Summerson, or why Sir Leicester Dedlock never knew anything of it when he married her. Rather stiff latterly in the day.

Tuesday, 28 July

Haircut at Nunney (Sherry/Chérie). I have been corresponding with James Knox about people in Hypocrites' photograph for Oxford background of his Robert Byron book. James is in touch with Selina Hastings, trying to collate her Evelyn Waugh material. This is not easy. Evelyn had come up in a by-term in 1921, so he and Robert had 1922 (the year before I came up) together, then some of 1923, when Evelyn was living in a comparative withdrawal, with the idea of working. He went down at the end of the year. Evelyn's later incursions into Oxford life were done coming up at weekends, Robert being there the whole time, naturally.

James Knox is trying to show, an admirable intention, how largely through Robert the Hypocrites was turned from a rather jolly institution with an extraordinarily varied membership into a somewhat snobbish one, eventually closed down by the authorities. Robert's instinct for the main chance, getting on generally, was developed at an extremely early age, but it would be fair to say that he combined this with an absolutely relentless eccentricity and personal exoticism. Robert was immensely competitive, which made him jealous of everybody, including Evelyn, but Evelyn's ambition had not taken coherent form yet, nor did it, in my opinion, until marriage. All the same Evelyn certainly didn't care for Robert, while respecting him. I had an odd dream: some unknown people discussing whether there was a statue of Schiller at Oxford; they agreed one existed in some College quad.

Friday, 31 July

Ronald Manley rang to say his father, Edward Manley, died last night. V saw Mr Manley a few days ago and knew he had been moved to hospital. She thought he had looked very ill. He was a shade older, or a shade younger, than myself (eighty-six). He and Mrs Manley lived in The Lodge twenty years or more. Mr Manley was a quite exceptionally nice man. He was one of the few really 'good' persons one has known, I would say pretty well a saint, with none of the typical saint's forbidding characteristics. At least the characteristics that traditionally hang round the term. The Manleys could not have been better tenants of The Lodge. Ronald, the son, became quite a successful engineer. The Manleys' daughter, Heather, married a Frome vet and inherited the good qualities of her parents. She is unfortunately abroad at the moment (Germany).

Reading the Tiepolo book I was interested to find that when Tiepolo married Cecilia Guardi, her brother, Francesco, the renowned painter of Venice, was only seven. One had always imagined that Tiepolo came to know her through Francesco. However, she had another brother, Gianantonio, also a painter, so the connexion may have been through him, as her family was apparently not Venetian in the first instance. I think the luscious blonde who appears so often in Tiepolo's pictures (Cleopatra, etc.) was his wife.

Saturday, 1 August

I decided to take to a stick. William Barcham, author of the Tiepolo book, to whom I had written at a rather chancy NYC address after finding his mention of my name, rang from London. He turned out to have been as delighted at my writing to him as I was by his reference to the fictitious Tiepolo in *Dance.* He had only just received my letter as he had been spending a year in Italy with his wife (also an art historian) and children, now returning to what he called 'real life'. This presumably had been on a grant. Was astonished that I knew his New York address. Name of street being still only 'written up by hand'.

Stockwells down, Tristram came over in the evening. He pointed out that a stick gave status. He noticed that very much when he hurt his foot a year or two ago. The Pest Controller (cf. the Bee Boy in *Puck of Pook's Hill*) had been extremely whimsical about bees at The Stables, saying: 'Can't make any promises, bees are funny people', etc. Tristram brought a message from Barry Humphries that he had greatly enjoyed the two critical books, so, as Bruce Hunter had been gloomy about the prospects of *Poets, Artists and Mellors*, owing to the state of the market at present, I added a postscript to my letter saying that Dame Edna Everage had liked the last two.

Friday, 7 August

I now realize my stick, a malacca (reinforced with rubber tip), has always been mine (probably a present), dating back possibly to Melina Place days, which accounts for its familiarity.

I reread *The Great Gatsby* for about the fiftieth time, still finding it an immensely accomplished novel. Fitzgerald himself felt that he had failed in not saying more of how Gatsby's affair with Daisy was concluded, but that is one of the good points of the book. One knows exactly the sort of thing that happened. My own small criticisms would be that Gatsby's start as a boy (by being picked up by Dan Cody in his yacht) is a bit abrupt, might have been worked in earlier, but dare say that is more easily said than done. Also the amount of time, no doubt time and money, devoted by Carraway to clearing up matters after Gatsby's death was rather excessive for an impecunious young man. That is perhaps poetic licence.

I had not previously grasped that the main scene in the novel takes place at the Plaza Hotel, where various showdowns come about. I now remember I lunched at the Plaza with Naomi Thompson (Little, Brown's PR lady) and a high-grade journalist, Elizabeth Janeway (probably *New York Times*). I had the nastiest omelette I have ever attempted to eat. It tasted like an old woollen glove lightly flavoured with egg. I have a great dislike for leaving food on my plate (which Americans are rather apt to do), but could not manage more than about half, which caused comment.

Monday, 10 August

V attended Mr Manley's funeral at Nunney (Methodist Chapel). There was rain. I much regretted being too stiff for such ceremonies as I liked him enormously. It was very full. We drank Virginia's really first-rate Gran Reserva Rioja de Ramon Bilbao '81, she brought back from Spain for us.

Tuesday, 11 August

We lunched with Lees and Mary Mayall at Sturford. Both were in goodish form. Smoked salmon, roast beef, roast potatoes, summer pudding (from Marks & Spencer), all good. I had a glass of white burgundy.

Thursday, 13 August

Evangeline Bruce with Tony and Marcelle Quinton to luncheon. The weather began by being grey, then settled down to pelting rain. Evangeline, as ever immensely elegant, unimaginably thin, perhaps a shade *triste*. Marcelle (who brought a box of excellent chocolates) was in strange trouser-suit with a kind of turban, general effect like one of the pirates in *Peter Pan*. She and Tony in excellent form, Tony's prodigious memory is more striking than ever. Lunch by (Mrs) Philippa Witt was good: melon (supplied by V), chicken pie, individual chocolate puddings. Marcelle drinks nothing, eats very little; Evangeline had second helping of pie, so her thinness not due entirely to abstention. The rest of us drank a bottle of Léoville-Barton '84. Not a good year, but drinkable. Marcelle was severe about Tony not drinking too much as he was driving. They took Evangeline to Westbury to catch the London train, then proceeded, I presume, to Oxon. Enjoyable day, which I was rather dreading, on account of my stiffness, etc., but went off well. I gave Evangeline *Caledonia* and *Verdicts*, Quintons having both.

Sunday, 16 August

I reread *Fiesta* (*The Sun Also Rises*), which retains its unique qualities as a picture of the period, a new sort of novel. One never quite believes in the intensity of Jake's and Brett's love for each other, given the circumstances, nor in Brett's charm. I don't think that is entirely because I met her model, Duff Twisden, and thought her awful. The thread of the opening theme of Cohn is also rather lost. All the telegrams she sends at the end are a bit unconvincing. However, these are small grouses at Hemingway's book. I also reread *Our Mutual Friend*. After the splendid beginning of the Thames at night, Gaffer Hexam being 'in luck again' dredging up a dead body, the novel becomes unremitting rubbish. One is prepared to accept a certain degree of Dickens's unreality, but this passes all reason, also many loose ends are never tied together. It is difficult to see why the book is one of Dickens's best-known.

Tuesday, 18 August

Hazel Holt to tea. She is married, her husband retired from what I understood to be a fourth-generation family coffee business. They live in a
National Trust house (she calls it a cottage) in the Taunton–Minehead
direction. It is said to be haunted. The previous tenant (the usual earthy,
level-headed viewer of spectres) saw an old man in a square bowler, *c.*
1860, come from the house, straighten a hanging plant he had displaced
in passing, go into the garden. The ghost is thought to be the farmer who
had lived there in mid-Victorian days. Hazel Holt said she did not think
Barbara Pym ever truly contemplated marriage. She herself now writes
rather successful detective stories (as also does her son), which show hopes
of TV.

A Japanese paper called *Switch* wants to use my piece on Kilmartin's *A
la recherche* which (to me) seems of no startling interest; only possibility
because I object to Kilmartin's altering 'eyeglass' to 'monocle', and 'hat'
to 'trilby', both solecisms, anyway at Proust's date. Japanese may find this
an interesting social note.

Thursday, 20 August

Rachel and Kevin Billington to tea. Both in good form, Rachel becomes
steadily prettier as she grows older, wonderful legs. Kevin negotiating to
do one of her books on TV (Thames). Kevin was dressed rather as if he
had just landed from the Life Boat. I gave them *Verdicts*. Twenty-eight figs
to date.

Sunday, 23 August

Virginia to dinner. Snook made himself very agreeable to her. Spaghetti
Arabella (with whom Tristram and Virginia dined recently), the Wine
Society's Chianti, which I advantageously opened twenty-four hours before.
Virginia likes figs (now thirty-five). Barry Humphries sent his autobiography, so I wrote a line of thanks, saying I hoped he would come and see
Tristram at The Stables (something that had been suggested a year or two
ago), when I could show him my Conders. He replied that he saw Tristram
all too rarely, but hopes to bring this off some time. He said he was still
interested in 'old Conder', and had recently bought a Conder portrait of
Max Beerbohm, thought to have been lost. This appears to be the picture
of Max in a theatre box, painted in the Nineties (most of Conder's oils

were painted towards the end of his life). This one is reproduced in Frank Gibson's book on Conder (1914).

Wednesday, 26 August–Thursday, 27 August

Foul weather here, not too bad in London where V attended Antonia and Harold Pinter's party (Antonia's sixtieth birthday, etc., to whom I gave *Caledonia*). This V enjoyed, covering a mass of relations. The following day she went into Heywood Hill's. John Saumarez Smith sold *Agents and Patients* and *From a View* (with jackets), with inscriptions to Colonel F. R. Packe (friend of my father's also in Welch Regiment), to my American-Chinese fan Mrs Sung for £800, alleging that he gave £700 for them himself. John very kindly came down here to cook for me. I am extremely stiff owing to damp. V recalled that when we dined with Freddie Packe at his small house in Southwick Street (or Crescent), he said: 'Think pheasant gets rather boring in January, so we are having him boiled with oyster sauce.' Charming chap, Packe.

Friday, 28 August–Tuesday, 1 September

Tristram, Virginia, Georgia, Toby Coke, Christina Noble, her son Rau, at The Stables. Tristram came up for a talk. Among other things he spoke of John's great devotion to this place.

I am having second round of Barbara Pym, liking her much better. One has to get the hang of her own personality and comparatively limited range of characters, who are very funny when fully understood. She is one of the few novelists I regret never having met.

Tuesday, 1 September

David Moore reported a tree down by Dead Woman's Bottom partly blocking the road. I rang Lang Brown, who said he could do nothing until the following day. After a good deal of telephoning, it turned out tree not on my land. V went to have a look on returning from the dentist, and found it had been dealt with by ARC, who own the disused quarry on opposite side of the road, also what was originally The Chantry land sold by Barracloughs and the wood bought back by me. That was only after a bit had been reserved by Ted Evemy, who then owned the quarry, to make a roundabout for his lorries. Sixty-five figs to date.

Wednesday, 2 September

V had five teeth out, but survived this ordeal comparatively well. The police have ejected the New Age Travellers engaged on a 'rave' in the old disused quarry now owned by ARC, and have installed some large stones to prevent future trespassing. Three stolen cars are said to have been left behind, one burnt out. Lang Brown, contrary to what he told me, went out the same day to clear tree, so now slight muddle with ARC to decide who pays him, but I think this should be settled without too much difficulty. If David Moore had not seen the tree, and wrongly reported to me, there would have been no action on my part, accordingly no muddle.

Friday, 4 September

Higham rang to ask if I minded giving my number to an American, who wanted me to review a book, but would not reveal what, for *New York Observer.* I said they could if the chap rang me at once. This turned out to be Daniel Max who reviewed *Verdicts* (well, if not glowingly) for the *Washington Post.* He really wanted to talk about meeting Scott Fitzgerald, and suchlike. He also reviewed *The Fisher King* for St Petersburg paper, Florida, which he will send me. He said (I agree) that small US provincial papers are often goodish.

In his *Verdicts* review said I was the 'most famous obscure writer in England', 'now too late to get Nobel Prize'. I have never supposed the Nobel Prize very likely but I should have thought it was just as possible now that I have settled down to old age as when producing books. However, I was glad to have an American of thirty-one taking an interest, and we had at least half an hour's lively talk (*NY Observer* sells about 40,000, but respectable paper). Max wants the new editions of non-*Dance* novels sent him. The book he proposed for review was by Susan Minot (think I have vaguely heard of her), but I assured him I never reviewed novels, hadn't for years, eventually convinced him. He found this one good, possibly historical of some kind.

Saturday, 5 September

John bought me a pair of 'winter' trousers in Frome. It has now been ascertained that Snook spends his many nights out at Orr Farm, just across the field to our west, owned by the Rolfes, late of Chantry Cheese. Does he have a nostalgia for farm life, having been born on a farm?

From being merely tolerant of Barbara Pym as a novelist, I have now got into the swing of her style and characters, find the books very amusing.

I reread *Hamlet*. This is a piece of self-indulgence as I enjoy the work so much, find Hamlet behaving quite naturally, only too like many persons one has known.

> *Guild.*   The King, sir –
> *Ham.*   Ay, sir, what of him?
> *Guild.*   Is in his retirement marvellous distempered.
> *Ham.*   With drink, sir?

Monday, 7 September

Ania Corless of Higham says the French do want to do selection from *Verdicts* and *Under Review*. She will send the contract with Filleadeau & Corti. Their choice of names is interesting, sometimes quite unexpected. Mr J. M. Dutson of ARC came for talk. Rather like Gertler, the painter, in appearance. Very smooth, V thought nervous. He is a land agent, rather than working manager. This arose from the muddle about the tree across the road, but gave opportunity for him to broach larger matter regarding ARC's wish to install a contraption in Stanley Mead, the field across the road, to measure water table. He will pay Lang Brown (£100 + VAT) if I demand no payment for installation, ARC having its own machinery for forestry jobs. They would also pay legal costs. Obviously has to go to a lawyer, particularly as I do not want to prejudice any question of my being violently opposed to ARC's wish to close Mells Lane. Dutson will send me papers and agreement, in due course. Seventy-three figs.

Thursday, 10 September

Proofs of Philip Larkin *Letters* arrived for *Spectator* review, 700-odd pages. Informed Bob Conquest, who may want to do it for some paper. Bob is much represented, so could have been sent them. The book appears at the end of October. Eighty-two figs.

Thursday, 17 September

V saw Mr Rheinberg of Faulkners in Frome (with whom I propose to deal regarding ARC, Burgess Salmon being ARC's solicitors), who said ARC is making various try-ons in matter of the contraption they may want to

install in Stanley Mead, field across the road, but ARC themselves do not
yet know their own plans. Mr Mosley arrived unexpectedly wanting the
Insurance Certificate for new car, which should come next week. This was
produced a week or two ago for the old car's licence, seems to have
disappeared. Mr Mosley not at all worried. Said he could get copy from
Mr Edwards of CU in Frome.

   The Larkin *Letters* are rude to almost everybody, except perhaps Bob
Conquest. Larkin describes me as a 'creep', and 'horse-faced dwarf',
needing 'a kick in the balls for being too pleased with himself'. He had
asked himself to luncheon here with his enigmatic long-time girlfriend
Monica Jones (no Helen of Troy) some years ago (when in the
neighbourhood), the two of them eating more onion sauce than V and I
have ever seen two people eat, completely cleaning out the dish. In the
year of his death Larkin sent 'affectionate wishes to you both'. I was
surprised how little I minded Larkin's offensive remarks. Ninety-four figs.

Sunday, 20 September

Meredith Daneman (who turned out to be a woman) asked if she could
talk to me about Margot Fonteyn and Constant Lambert, as she is writing
a biography of Fonteyn. I agreed to this, and that her husband should
also come, as he drives, good at finding the way. I was rather dreading the
interview, but (as V, who remembers much more than I do, agreed) not
uninteresting. Meredith (known as Merry to her husband) originates from
Tasmania (about which I dropped a brick, when talking of Sidney Nolan,
Australians being far from laudatory about Tasmanians), a dancer herself.
I should have thought she was rather on the large side, pretty, middle or
late fifties. She has written several novels, one of which V knew by name.

   Paul Daneman, much older, perhaps early seventies, was an actor, Old
Vic, etc. and does a lot of voice-overs still. John was interested in this as
he collects voice-over names. Paul Daneman was rather jolly. One would
imagine both were married before. They arrived 2.30, left 4.45. They live
in the former Sidney Nolan house in Putney, which must be rather nice,
as its garden runs down to the Thames. The first Mrs Nolan (who did
herself in) was Tasmanian, which was why she consented to sell the house,
regarding which she was apparently very sticky. Paul Daneman said that
Bobby Helpmann (who made a rather minor element of the trio Freddy
Ashton, Billy Chappell and Helpmann), when he arrived from Australia,
was very anxious to make a career here. He found himself alone in a taxi
with Mrs Patrick Campbell, a formidable figure in the theatrical world.

Mrs Pat *de haut en bas* put a cigarette in her mouth looking straight ahead of her, expecting it to be instantly lighted. Bobby fumbled for a gold lighter from his pocket (given him by some adorer), clicked away with it, but nothing happened. Finally Mrs Pat snatched it from him, threw it out of the taxi window. Both V and I extremely exhausted after it all, but found a lot to discuss.

Wednesday, 23 September

Bob Conquest rang yesterday. He is just back from Moscow. Helen Fraser of Heinemann to luncheon today. Her train was an hour late, so we almost gave up hope of seeing her. Bruce Hunter had already adumbrated *Poets, Painters etc.* to her, also V's *Jane Austen Compendium*, in both of which she showed sympathetic interest. I had not grasped that three of my non-*Dance* reprints are already out. The rest will follow in December. Helen will send these to Daniel Max of the *NY Observer* as asked for. She knew about the paper, which she said was lively and literary. She will also send us the Stephen Spender biography about which he is making a great fuss, apparently merely from self-advertisement. I told her the story of Spender and Evelyn Waugh's gold watch. Much business done, an enjoyable visit. Moura Dillon Malone did luncheon: mackerel pâté (good), marinated chicken, chopped potatoes, broccoli (good, tho' I am not mad about broccoli), tartlets (good). Helen does not drink.

Friday, 25 September

V insists on my having an occasional check-up, so Dr Irish came in about 12.40 accompanied by a small female Oriental student of indeterminate origins, to whom Snook took a great fancy, sitting on her knee until she got up to follow Dr Irish's examination. Snook then found much to interest him in the Doctor's case. Report was 'splendidly fit'. Mr Mosley brought the new Rover Metro about 3.30, after John had arrived, so that he too could try it out. It seems a nice, neat little car, which we all like. Mr Mosley's final words were: 'Loyalty is very rare in the motor trade.' I think we first bought a car from him in 1968, since when he has had many changes. Now on his own, perhaps not finding things too easy.

I was cheered to see Christian Bourgois's ad in *TLS* for next two *Dance* volumes (*Valley of Bones, Soldier's Art*). Bourgois has left Les Presses de la Cité and is now on his own. Also an ad in the *PMLA Directory* (addresses of pretty well all US academics), University of Chicago Press ad for *Verdicts*.

Saturday, 26 September

Virginia to dinner for her birthday previous day. Dinner by Moura DM: chicken-liver pâté (which I happen not to like); navarin of lamb casserole, boulangère potatoes (excellent); De Courcy fizz, given me last birthday by Heinemann (perfectly all right, no taste following morning).

Tuesday, 29 September

Francis Watson obit. We had not seen him for years, tho' latterly he lived comparatively close, with a Chinese boyfriend, whom I rather think Francis had adopted as his son. Francis first appeared as boyfriend of the Widow Lloyd, good-looking, immensely vain, also extremely funny, their relationship very knockabout. Francis was able, knowledgeable, master of bluff, who, after a job at the Courtauld, eventually became head of the Wallace, knighted, many art jobs. He married a perfectly awful woman, Jane, plain, tactless, unequalled trouble-maker. However, Francis seemed to tick over quite happily with her, tho' her malice – that is not quite the word – was legendary. She died eventually, Francis returning to earlier tastes. His general familiarity with the arts was enormous, furniture, china, etc., if often totally inaccurate. When he 'did' the pictures at Whitfield, he attributed one to some unknown painter on the strength of a scrawl on the back. Mary (Clive) later pointed out that the letters were EBC – Edward Bolton Clive – referring to certain purchases. Francis having named some such painter as 'Ebick', or whatever he judged the scrawl to be. Francis was always totally unabashed on such occasions. When V and I with others were staying with The Squire at Woodgate, doing some newspaper quiz on Sunday, Francis was caught out cheating. He was good value, only age and decay preventing our getting him over when he came to live in Wiltshire. He always managed to give the impression of being several years younger than everyone else, but in fact turned out to have been eighty-five, about twenty months less than myself.

Wednesday, 30 September

Hilary Spurling to luncheon. She lost her way not far from here, arriving 1.45. The Spurling family is now returning to their London house, unexpectedly restored by local authorities, but painted the wrong colour. They had been staying in Cornwall at the house of their painter friend, Bridget Riley (née Gladstone), not far from Padstow, a pre-Conquest rectory.

Apparently there was a great tradition of Victorian intellectuals having houses in that neighbourhood, now in third or fourth generation. Hilary, as ever, in terrific form, immensely entertaining, stayed until after 5. I have to admit both of us rather cooked after this enjoyable flow on most subjects. Hilary has discovered all sorts of things about Matisse's origins on the Belgian border, among others that the name is sometimes spelt Matys, which immediately places him as a Netherland painter. I have done a fair amount of that sort of research myself in this country, but the thought of doing it in France/Belgium is exhausting even to think about.

Lunch by Moura DM: some sort of stew (excellent), beans, boulangère potatoes; chocolate cream in thin glasses; bottle of Château La Croix de Gay Pomerol '78 (not at all bad). I gave Hilary the three new editions (*Afternoon Men*, *From a View*, *Waring*), remarking on the difficulty of finding anyone who was any good at doing book jackets nowadays (as opposed to the Twenties and Thirties), how lucky to have discovered Sue M-S. Hilary pointed out the reason for this was the years during which students were not taught to draw from the figure. That had not struck me, but is obviously a profound judgement.

Thursday, 1 October

We celebrated our engagement (anniversary actually yesterday) with smoked salmon (excellent), the Society's fizz for dinner, the latter a shade rough, having been in the cellar some time.

Saturday, 3 October

Three copies of *La Vallée des Ossements* arrived, I suspect by the writing on the package sent by The Sergeant. Ninety-eight figs.

Tuesday, 6 October

Bob and Liddie Conquest to luncheon. We both thought them in better form than last time. I had hoped for Bob's views on the Larkin *Letters*, preferably with those of Kingsley Amis too, but Bob had only just got hold of the *Letters*, and done no more than have a rather muted lunch with Kingsley and some academic at Simpson's. Moreover, as Liddie said to V later, all former close friendship with Kingsley was now at an end owing to Kingsley's extraordinary behaviour in relation to Bob in his *Memoirs*. Bob had been (alone) to Moscow. They were now both on their way to

Berlin, Fiesole, Sofia, where Bob lectures. I gave them the new editions of *Afternoon Men*, *From a View*, *Waring*, sent on *La Vallée des Ossements*, as some more are arriving, Bob was interested in the copy I had.

Lunch by Moura DM: fish pâté (excellent), chicken with grape sauce (goodish), boulangère potatoes, lemon pie (excellent). Liddie had nothing to drink before, Bob sherry, at lunch Liddie and V split a bottle of Château Bernard Raymond '79 (V said not bad), Bob, bottle of Hungarian white Badacsonyi Keknyelu '88, of which I had a glass. I was rather uncertain about latter, as the cheapest white wine in the Wine Society's list, I discovered only at the last moment, but not too bad, Bob seemed to find it perfectly tolerable.

Saturday, 10 October

Georgia and Toby Coke at The Stables. I reread *Macbeth*, a favourite. I saw somewhere the other day the statement that all young men thought themselves Hamlet, all old men Lear. What rubbish. I never thought myself in the least like Hamlet (tho' I love the play), nor do I now look on myself as Lear. I do, however, find much fellow feeling with Macbeth, anyway in his ruminative moods. I am fond of Lady Macbeth too, an attractive woman. They were obviously a happily married couple. I discussed this with V. She said she was less pushy than Lady Macbeth (as I certainly am less pushy than Macbeth), but saw a slight element in telling me to get on with the job. The play sags a bit when Macduff, Ross, etc. discuss whether Scotland stands where she did, but the beginning and end are splendid. 'His spongy officers, who shall bear the guilt / Of our great quell.' 'Then fly, false Thanes, / And mingle with the English epicures.'

Sunday, 11 October

Georgia and Toby Coke to drinks in the morning. In afternoon everyone watched the cassette Seventh House (Anglia) sent of the programme on L. P. Hartley (Clive Swift and Edward Storey, called rather fatuously *Bare Heaven*). I appeared occasionally. On the whole not bad, tho' always something rather absurd about actors doing somebody known to one. In this case Clive Swift looked reasonably like Leslie physically, but actors never have the least idea what writers are like temperamentally, especially a complicated figure like Leslie. His curious loves were suggested, mainly his own menservants, it would appear, even then possibly platonic, as were certainly his two or three female emotional interests, women of mature age Leslie said wanted to marry him.

At about 9 p.m. V answered the telephone, then returned to say she had been talking about the film to Jonathan Cecil, who played quite a part in it. Now that Jonathan would like to discuss it with me. 'What a charming voice you have,' Jonathan began, I suppose a compliment from a professional, then we talked for the best part of forty minutes. I agree with Jonathan that Leslie was probably in love with Jonathan's father, David, a friend from Oxford. David played some part in Leslie's development as a writer too, tho' David younger. Jonathan produced a story about some henchman of Leslie's who stuck a knife into his pillow, with a prayer-book containing references to death underlined, which I had not heard. I told the story of the cook, who, on the day she left, with her small daughter, entering the room where Leslie was writing, said: 'Take a good look at him, Emily, an Oxford man and a cad.' Also then on the night we arrived at the Bathampton house and were greeted by Leslie with the words: 'I don't know whether we shall get any dinner. Roger is crying on the stairs.' Jonathan is now playing Sir Andrew Aguecheek. Anna, his wife, also in the production.

Wednesday, 14 October

Vidia and Pat Naipaul to luncheon. Vidia looked very trim, in spite of recent operation on spine, not to mention the loss of MSS and books in an accident at warehouse. Pat also well, arguing the toss with Vidia sometimes, which we had never seen her do before. V thought this due to a certain domination Pat established over Vidia while in hospital. He is at work on a new book. Vidia drank a glass of sherry before lunch, Pat nothing, not even a soft drink, Moura DM produced one of the best curries I have ever eaten (vegetable) with lots of trimmings, bottle and half of Côtes du Rhone Villages Valréas '89 (not bad). Enjoyable party.

Tristram to dinner, just back from filming of *The Long Roads*, begun in Skye, working down through Glasgow to London. Tristram was in excellent form. He and Virginia are going to a Film Festival in Ghent, then for a trip to Taormina. He might get *Middlemarch* in six parts, but others in competition. Moura DM chicken casserole (done with grapes, the rice from curry added). Bottle Saumur (domaine D'Heretière), light after heavy wine at lunch.

Monday, 19 October

Mr Moss called, put some more chips in front of the garage and did minor repairs to drive. He was rather tedious when I told him he could have £200 to do these two jobs, when I grew cross saying, 'Don't hit me with your stick.' I said, 'I shall if you go on like this.' V in fits of laughter.

Tuesday, 20 October

V drove me to have my hair cut in Nunney, done by Sherry (Chérie, in fact it turns out Cherry). Afterwards we returned by Dead Woman's Bottom to see the fencing John had put in to discourage trespassers. It has grown up a lot since I was last round there, the woods looking marvellous in the wet autumn afternoon.

Sunday, 25 October

Archie, with two of his band, at The Stables for working weekend, Sarah Holland and Malek Hyde-Smith. After rereading John Bayley's *Characters of Love* I decided to have another go at *The Golden Bowl*, and finished it after a bit of a struggle. Then reread John again on the subject.

I am prepared to accept Mr Verver and Maggie, especially their love as father and daughter. I am not prepared to accept the Prince, nor to a lesser degree Charlotte. As an impoverished Roman Prince, Popes in his background, the Prince would surely regard marrying for money as a necessity. If it happened that he then fell in love with Maggie, such a comparatively surprising event should have been Henry James's theme, but that would have left James in difficulties about Charlotte. Again, I am prepared to believe the Prince and Charlotte were mutually in love during their affair in Rome before they both married, where Charlotte seems to have been an adventuress, presumably with some sort of an income. Again, I am prepared to believe she may have had a father (dcd) in the background, and for that reason fell in love with Mr Verver, but again I think James should have done some explaining if that were so. It seems much more probable that she married Verver (finding him reasonably agreeable) for his money. In other words, I don't think James altogether delivers the goods as far as 'love' is concerned in all four cases. The trouble as usual is James not being familiar with what my former Balliol tutor, Kenneth Bell, used to call the wish to put your arm round a girl's waist.

Monday, 2 November

Reviews of the Larkin *Letters* have their comic side, because reviewers who would like to applaud Larkin as a poet, while prepared to overlook his attacks on individuals, have also to stomach a good deal of comment like 'the first thing to do is to get rid of all the niggers', not to mention:

> I want to see them starving,
> The so-called working class,
> Their wages weekly halving,
> Their women stewing grass.

The BBC critics do the best they can by saying Larkin didn't really mean it, he liked playing the curmudgeon. There is nothing on earth Larkin meant more. With regard to individuals, Hilary Spurling put her finger on it in her review, saying he hated everyone who showed themselves in the smallest degree in competition with himself, in fact Larkin was not a very nice man. That is the case with many poets. We had two additional telephones installed (the library, my dressing-room), which will be a great amelioration, I think.

Wednesday, 4 November

After replying that Henry James was simply a matter of what he, James, stated, John Bayley said Larkin was a comedian in his *Letters* (also to some extent in his poems). Very gloomy letter from Billy Chappell. Clinton won the US Presidential Election.

Thursday, 5 November

As V had a check-up at the Bath Clinic yesterday, thought she might be late back, Moura DM did lunch. It appears that her sister-in-law was George Gale's second wife, accordingly she knew Kingsley Amis quite well. On some occasion (presumably between Kingsley's parting from Jane and fixing up to live with the Kilmarnocks) Moura and Kingsley were both staying with the sister. Everything that went wrong in the house was always attributed to Moura's small son, Daniel, then aged three or four, one imagines. Among various other adjuncts of Kingsley's neurasthenia is stopping up his ears with cotton-wool in bed in order not to be frightened by bogies and beasties and things that go bump in the night. While they were all having breakfast, Kingsley eating muesli, a large piece of cotton-wool was seen in the bowl and Kingsley about to eat it. Moura's sister cried out: 'Daniel has put some cotton-wool in Kingsley's muesli,' but the truth was then revealed. The cotton-wool fell out of Kingley's other ear into the muesli.

The Maastricht treaty approved by three votes in House of Commons. To my great satisfaction the signed contract arrived from the French publisher Corti for the selection from *Verdicts/Under Review* edited by The Sergeant (Stuart Preston), all his doing, for which I am very grateful.

Saturday, 7 November

I had written to the National Library of Scotland saying I had a copy of *Caledonia* available for presentation (for which they asked many years ago, when I had not), to which they replied that they had already bought a copy, inscribed to 'Poiuscznik Auberon Herbert', which I take to mean Private or Ensign, as Auberon was then in the Polish Army in Exile. I was amused at this.

At 2.20 Frank (Longford) rang. V answered. After a conversation that was obscure to me she said: 'Well, you'd better talk to Tony about it.' Frank began a long rigmarole about his 'being' Widmerpool. I began to explain that he was not, but he cut me short, saying: 'Authors always say that.' After a bit I began to understand that he *wanted* to 'be' Widmerpool (the fact that Frank does not interest me in the smallest degree as a character in a novel being naturally impossible to explain to him. Indeed a subject so subtle that it is difficult to explain to anyone why certain people are good models, others not). It seemed that some TV programme was being arranged for people who had 'appeared' in novels, and Frank was willing to be included.

Sunday, 8 November

I watched the Cenotaph ceremony (V went to church), which I always find moving. The Stockwells are down. When they came over Tristram threw some light on Frank's telephoning. There is indeed a TV programme on the agenda, of which Hilary Spurling seems at the root. So far as I could gather this is on the general subject of 'real people' in novels, but, in practice, mostly about *Dance*. As far as I could gather, Frank would actually appear *in propria persona*, also Barbara Skelton, which certainly might be funny. Frank takes everything (especially himself) with deadly seriousness, brushing aside my words 'Love to all' when he rang off. This was not in the least because he was angry but because I was not being sufficiently serious.

Saturday, 14 November

A letter from Bruce Hunter saying the University Press of Chicago want to do *Under Review.* This pleases me very much. I also had a letter a day or two ago from Christian Bourgois saying he had been in touch with Corti, the French publisher doing a selection from the two critical books, and hopes to arrange that the latter comes out simultaneously with one of the volumes of *Dance,* a good idea, I think. Very stiff in the joints these days.

Thursday, 19 November

I sent *Caledonia* to Janet Adam Smith, who wrote amusing letter of thanks. I had previously offered one to the National Library of Scotland (see Saturday, 7 November) who replied that they had bought a copy some years ago, inscribed to (whatever the Polish for Second Lieutenant is) Auberon Herbert. Janet had been on the committee when this happened. She said the Librarian was then a Welshman, who greatly relished the purchase (£500). Janet's son, an authority on Africa, recognized the long-forgotten references to Macintosh, Macnamee, and Tchekedi. Today I sent copies to Alison Lurie and John Monagan, tho' not sure how much it will mean to Americans. True, the high saleroom prices are usually American. I reread *Henry IV.1*, a favourite. I am struck how, to someone reading the play, Shakespeare clearly intended Falstaff and Prince Hal to be recognized as the pair of scoundrels they obviously were, something not at first apparent.

Thursday, 19 November

I reread the Larkin *Letters* in the bound edition, doing this slowly, which made the relations with women much clearer, also drew attention to the important point that to the end of his life Larkin's real ambition was to be a novelist. At the period when his poetry had dried up (which after all happens to most poets) he regarded his life as a failure in spite of the inordinate public acclaim and good sales he attracted as a poet. This seems extraordinary because Larkin's two novels that were published are about as uninspired as novels could be. He clearly had no talent whatever as a novelist. He did not read many novels himself, nor was he interested in other people, only himself. Interest in other people is the one absolute *sine qua non* for a novelist in my opinion.

The *Letters* give a vivid picture of him. He hated anyone he felt competed in the smallest degree. Latterly his unfriendly comments on myself are all but insane. They are obviously inspired by jealousy (to which one dislikes having to attribute people's behaviour), but to object to my writing to Kingsley Amis before I knew him 'because he was younger, and had said something nice about him' is patently absurd, especially as my Memoirs state plainly that I had no idea who had written the piece (thinking 'Kingsley Amis' might well be a *nom de guerre*), and what Kingsley said was not particularly laudatory, only compared my style to something under review, so far as I remember. Incidentally, Larkin also wrote to at least one person younger than himself even in the 'Who's Who' at the beginning of the book. All Larkin's life was lived as a provincial librarian, so that perhaps inevitably his point of view, notwithstanding his gifts, was 'provincial'. In fact the letters, as such, are not particularly interesting, only in relation to Larkin's own character, tho' it might be said that they have an interest in being so purely provincial.

Friday, 20 November

Jeremy Lewis, arriving about 2.40 p.m. He came to talk about Cyril Connolly, whose biography he is writing, Deirdre (Connolly) having finally given in as opposing that. This all seems to have come about in a most haphazard manner. Lewis has not even met Deirdre, who, with Peter Levi and Jim Lees-Milne, is to be present tomorrow at luncheon at the Bradys (Terence and Charlotte Bingham) near Bruton where Lewis is staying. Lewis is enthusiastic, big (V said like a floppy labrador), jolly. Fifty with a daughter of twenty-one. He has spent most of his life in publishing with various firms, now involved with Alan Ross in running the *London Magazine*. Lewis was going on to stay with Humphrey Ellis, who had been twice passed over as Editor of *Punch*, when Malcolm took over. That naturally did not lead to particularly easy relations with me as Malcolm's henchman when Literary Editor. Ellis wholly bound up in *Punch* (which as far as it went he did pretty well) wrote a book about a comic schoolmaster, which Jeremy Lewis thought immensely funny. I cannot conceive anything Cyril would find less sympathetic, but Lewis seemed already to have mugged up all the Connolly stuff pretty well, might not be too bad as a biographer.

Personally I liked him. The situation was at one moment complicated by *Mervyn* Lewis arriving on the doorstep with the Fishing Syndicate's present.

Monday, 23 November

Jeremy Treglown arrived at 2.30 to talk about Henry Yorke (Henry Green) on whom he seems to be writing a piece and doing Introductions to some of Henry's books. Treglown, forty-six, scholarly type, married twice, edited *TLS* (Ferdie Mount took over from him), has done various academic jobs. I admitted I had never been very keen on Henry's books, tho' recognizing that people did admire them. Treglown said neither had he (just what Paul Bailey said, who recently threw up the sponge for writing a Henry Green biography), so one doesn't quite know why either took the job on. Treglown had mugged up a lot of the stuff pretty well, but, perhaps inevitable, didn't appear to have grasped a lot of the 'snobbish' material, without some knowledge of which it is impossible to attempt to grasp Henry's personality and behaviour, although I could admit that in spite of knowing him since we were both eleven I can never satisfactorily explain him even to myself to this day.

Without being deficient in humour, Treglown had to have jokes rather rammed in until he understood them. I asked if he were Cornish. His parson father was the first of the family to leave Cornwall. Treglown had arranged to catch the early afternoon train, so left about 3.40. This is certainly less tiring for me. He gave me a book he had edited of R. L. Stevenson's Essays. I was glad to have this, but on investigation find they are quite unreadable. Apparently Sebastian Yorke objected to his father being called a drunk, but did not mind him being termed a heavy drinker. Treglown said, 'They say that Yorke had affairs, but where did he have them?' He also asked what Henry and I did when I stayed at Forthampton. What can one think?

Thursday, 26 November

The French advance for Selection arrived from Corti via Higham. Mr Fricker came to check the wires. All OK. Mr Moss called. He was told I could spend no more on the drive until the spring.

Friday, 27 November–Sunday, 29 November

Tristram, Virginia, Georgia, Toby Coke at The Stables. Tristram talked of projects. He had hoped for *Middlemarch*, but that had fallen through.

Tuesday, 1 December

Fifty-eighth anniversary of our wedding. A lot of cards at breakfast, including a splendid one of two seals from Bob and Liddie Conquest. When writing back I shall refer to the Darley poem:

> In his green den the murmuring seal
> Beside his sleek companion lies.

We had smoked salmon and bottle of fizz for dinner (Veuve Clicquot Ponsardin '82, given, I think, by James Sandilands).

Saturday, 5 December

Tristram brought down Barry Humphries to luncheon, more specifically to see my Conders. This dates back a long way, when Humphries, far less well-known, gave a TV talk on Conder, after which I wrote a fan letter. Since then he has become famous as Dame Edna Everage, and to a lesser degree, Sir Les Patterson, the Australian Cultural Attaché, a rôle I really prefer. The Dame slightly gives me the creeps. Barry Humphries, in his late fifties, heavily built in the manner of Australians, is dark, with that slightly melancholy air of all great comics. One might add that it is perhaps slightly a characteristic of Australians. I remember Kenneth Bell once saying that in connexion with Anzac troops. One imagines he was primarily interested in Charles Conder from the Australian connexion, but he is very well up on the Nineties, indeed on all the arts. He brought V some jonquils. We had a lively time talking about this and that, and I think he was impressed by the number of Conders we possess. He made one very aware how rarely one meets anyone remotely to be described as 'cultured'.

He was to some extent introduced to London by John Betjeman, whether on account of Betjeman's visits to Australia, I don't know. His first appearance at a club called The Establishment, which I never visited. After this he went on to a party of Betjeman's where he met Osbert Lancaster. Osbert, not recognizing Humphries, said: 'I've just been to a new club called The Establishment and seen the worst turn I've ever watched in my life.' However, later they met again and became friends. When playing Sir Les Patterson, Barry Humphries liked to enter through the audience and make a disturbance. On one occasion the doorman would not let him in, thinking he was just a drunk. He brought down the two critical books to sign and I gave him *The Fisher King*. He is married (thirdly, I think) to Lizzie Spender, who rang up after he had gone to ask some trivial question. V wondered if she were just checking up on him. Luncheon was cooked by Moura DM (a great fan of Barry Humphries, as was Pat Moore at The Lodge, the latter extracting a signature and sentence): guinea fowl, excellent Moura potatoes, profiteroles. Barry Humphries, ex-alcoholic, perhaps just laying off, had soft drink, John of course never drinks, Tristram, V and I a bottle of Côte Touraine. Enjoyable party. Luckily decent weather after weeks of rain.

Monday, 7 December

In the evening Peter Parker (by arrangement) rang to talk about Harold Acton for article-obit commissioned by Selina Hastings for *Harpers & Queen*. This he did for an hour. Seemed reasonably bright. Parker is writing a biography of Christopher Isherwood, about whom he also asked a few questions, i.e. did 'intellectuals' at the time share my view that Auden and Isherwood leaving the country when they did was deplorable? It is impossible to explain that, so far as I was concerned, I don't seem to have lived in a group of 'intellectuals'. Anyway, I was almost immediately in the Army when war broke out, where I remained for six years.

Friday, 11 December

The *Daily Mail* rang to ask my views on the separation of the Prince and Princess of Wales. I said I had none. They added, 'Constitutionally?' Said I had none on that either. They will have to sort it all out without my help. Actually, I think the Princess has no rights whatever. She was born a lady, came into the world in her right mind, ought to have known what was implied by marrying the heir to the throne, and accordingly put up with whatever befell her. In fact, duty. Archie is at The Stables for one night, as he is to see some people in connexion with his band tomorrow. He came to dinner. We had a bottle of Beaujolais.

Monday, 21 December

My eighty-seventh birthday. I can't say I feel particularly grand, mostly owing to stiffness and lack of mobility. It is fairly sunny weather after weeks of rain. V is going to give me a new *Who's Who* when it appears, pending that, pants and chocs. She arranged luncheon by Moura DM, who kindly gave me some liqueur chocs. We gave her a *Fisher King.* John, hankie, film; Tristram, postcards; Virginia, caviar; Archie, a bottle when he arrives; Georgia rang. They all rang; at least a call at 9.15 a.m., which rang off as I was rather slow in answering, feel pretty sure was Tristram from his car. Congrats telegram from Hugh Massingberd. A letter in *DT* from a lady named Flavia Lambert, who said I ought to have the OM, as no one left representing the arts. Vidia and Pat Naipaul rang, also Marcelle and Tony Quinton. Marcelle talked for some time, Oxford group etc. Sheila Rhys, also born herself today, but mainly to talk to V. Frances Lloyd-Jones wrote, adding she was enthralled by *John Aubrey and His Friends.* Card of greetings from Georgina Ward in Mexico. Lunch, salmis of pheasant, Moura potatoes, cabbage, very excellent cheesecake/tart, half a bottle (rest at dinner), Léoville-Barton '86, bit thin, not bad flavour. Enjoyable birthday.

Tuesday, 22 December

Henry and Jane Mee turned up about 4.30, bringing the catalogue of the large Sickert show, which I was glad to have. Henry and I have been out of touch because he never told me whether or not he got the house in Lloyd Square he was after. He is doing some sculpture, plenty of work, some through Mrs Thatcher. Jane seemed a very nice girl. I gave them a set of my new paperbacks. Virginia to dinner. Bottle of one of half-dozen (Roederer Brut) Heinemann gave me for my birthday. Excellent.

Wednesday, 23 December

Tessa Davies to tea. Very elegant. She said Isfahan was full of dwarfs. Jonathan Cecil rang to thank for *Caledonia.* He had been playing *Twelfth Night* (Aguecheek) with Anna (Maria) in Liverpool, where Tristram and Virginia had gone to see them.

Friday, 25 December, Christmas Day

Misty. Felt unable to face The Stables party of ten (all the Mounts) so had luncheon alone here. As a matter of fact V served it early, so she was present for most of mine, I thereby having best of all worlds. Then I passed into a coma in the library, fitfully persecuted by Snook. In the morning Virginia brought up an open oyster for elevenses, one of some she had from Johnny Noble. Delightful idea. Presents included Lafite Rothschild '86 from Tristram; Château Belgrave '83 from Archie; La Mission Haut Brion '87 from Ferdie. Would have been an enjoyable Christmas had one not been so bloody stiff.

Saturday, 26 December, Boxing Day

Mary Mount came up from The Stables where the Mounts are staying. Dark, saturnine, unsmiling. After her being in room a minute or two one realizes she is very good-looking in that sort of way. She is at Oxford (Magdalen).

Monday, 28 December

Lees Mayall died. He had been ill, but all the same this was sudden. In the night, certainly the best way to go. Lees was a friend, the nicest man I knew in the Foreign Office. He ended as Ambassador to Venezuela. He was son of an Eton beak, Monkey Mayall, a fairly boring man. Sympathetic as one found Lees, occasionally one came up against a difference from what, for want of a better term, I call 'bohemian' friends, though some of these could not in a way be less 'bohemian'. We shall miss him, even tho' I have pretty well ceased to 'go out'. V reports Mary M as naturally very cut up.

Wednesday, 30 December

Hilary Spurling rang. We talked for some time (Matisse, etc.). Devoted as I am to Hilary I find long conversations, telephonic or others, rather tiring these days.

Thursday, 31 December

Last day of what I would not dissent from HM the Queen's view in calling a 'horrible year'. 'Envy and calumny and hate and paint' cover it pretty well. I realize more than ever how much I depend on V, and on the rest of my immediate family.

Index

Acton, Sir Harold 6–7, 191, 192, 224
Acton, William 7
Adam Smith, Janet 220
Adams, Henry 67, 72, 199
Adlard, Ken 46
Allen, Edward Heron 102
Althorp, Northamptonshire 29
Amis, Sir Kingsley: *Amis Anthology* 9; *Folks That Live on the Hill* 17, 24, 26, 45; *Green Man* 74, 76, 77–8, 82; *Memoirs* 96–103 *passim*, 107, 117, 122; *Old Devils* 116, 130, 132, 142, 144, 176; *Russian Girl* 183; *We Are All Guilty* 153; other refs 35, 71, 72, 95, 176, 178, 196, 219, 221
Amory, Mark 41, 44, 78, 97
Anderson, Eric 68, 185–6
Anderson, John 68
Annan, Noel, Lord 10, 103–4
Anthony Powell Society of Toronto 51, 160
ARC (quarriers) 55, 56, 57, 61, 113, 154, 174, 182, 183, 189, 190, 208–9, 210, 211
Argyle, Pearl 28, 37
Ashton, Sir Frederick 212
Assouline, Pierre 126–8
Aubrey, John 147, 150, 167
Auden, W.H. 98, 103
Autrement 84, 120
Avon, Clarissa, Countess of 84, 98

Awkward Age, The (James) 110–11

Bacon, Francis 186
Bailey, Paul 95, 172, 174, 222
Balliol College, Oxford 90, 113, 129
Balzac, Honoré de 14–15, 77
Bangor, Edward, Lord 37
Barcham, William 196, 204
Barnaby Rudge (Dickens) 108
Bath, Henry, Marquess of 199
Bath, Virginia, Marchioness of 199
Bayley, John 69, 137, 175–6, 189, 191, 193, 217, 218
Baylis, Lilian 70
Beaufort-Palmer, Diana 69–70, 140
Beaufort-Palmer, George 70
Beerbohm, Sir Max 48, 173, 208
Bel-Ami (Maupassant) 59
Bell, Kenneth 129, 218, 223
Bennett, Alan 94
Bennett, Arnold 20, 21
Benson, E.F. 116, 187–8
Berlin, Sir Isaiah 120
Bernard, Jeffrey 152–3
Bernstein, Henri 80–81
Berry, Lady Pamela 186
Betjeman, Sir John 7, 17, 46, 98, 101, 155–6, 176, 224
Big House at Inver, The (Somerville & Ross) 193

Billington, Lady Rachel (niece) and Kevin 87, 207
Bingham, Charlotte 53, 85, 222
Birkenhead, 1st Earl of 73
Bisalta, La, Frome 169, 177
Blakiston, Jeremy 189
Blakiston, Noël 199
Bleak House (Dickens) 203
Blunt, Wilfrid Scawen 91, 104
Bodleian Library 166
Bourgois, Christian 4, 11, 136, 138, 140, 164, 213, 220
Bourgois, Dominique 136–7, 164
Bowden, Gerald 27–8, 60
Bowlish House, Shepton Mallet 44
Bowra, Sir Maurice 10, 37, 56, 62, 103, 120, 170
Boxer, Mark 160, 162
Boyd, Alice, Lady (niece) 46, 51
Bozkova, Polya 90
Bradford, Anthony 37, 41
Bradford, Sarah 37–8, 41
Brady, Terence 53, 85, 222
Brenan, Gerald 202
Brennan, Neil 152
Bridge House, Nunney 29, 42, 119, 121, 165
Briggs, Michael 22
Brooke, Jocelyn 123, 150, 156
Brooks's Club 151, 161
Brotherton-Brackley, Isobel 136
Brown, Harry 63–4, 65
Bruce, David 96–7, 146
Bruce, Evangeline 22, 54, 58, 89, 96, 103, 131, 136, 138, 146, 160, 203, 206
Buccaneers, The (Wharton) 31
Buddenbrooks (Mann) 194
Bulgaria, books sent to 122–3, 129
Burgess, Anthony 68
Burgess Salmon (solicitors) 65
Butler, Lucy 17
Byron, Robert 7, 17, 142–3, 203

Caccia, Harold, Lord 75
Calder-Marshall, Arthur 184–5
Campbell, Mrs Patrick 212

Campbell-Orde, Eleanor, Lady 154–5
Canfield, Tess 29
Capel-Dunn, Denis 151, 162
Caraman, Fr Philip 98
Carcasonne, Manuel 4, 5
Carpenter, Humphrey 104
Carter-Ruck, Peter 124
Casson, Sir Hugh 117
Castlerosse, Lord 151
Cather, Willa 147
Cats 9, 54, 84, 99, and see Snook
Cavendish, Lady Elizabeth 156
Cecil, Lord David 20, 78, 80–81, 86, 88, 91, 93, 173, 216
Cecil, Hugh 198
Cecil, Jonathan 80, 88, 93, 94, 167, 216, 226
Challis, John 45
Channel 4 TV 10, 13, 39–40
Chantry, The: burglary 18, 19; The Stables 73; farmland 24, 40, 129, 135, 166, 168, 175, 217; forestry 8, 10, 11, 14–15, 29, 33, 34, 39, 46, 47, 57, 65, 66, 83, 149, 188–9, 191, 208; quarrying, see ARC; walls 112
Chantry church 108
Chappell, Billy 61, 212, 218
Charney, Ellen 7
Charrington, Richard and Mary Anne 22, 27
Chatwin, Bruce 33
Cheshire, David 188
Chicago, University Press 146, 220
Chichester-Clark, Emma 164
Church, Denis 157
Churchill, Randolph 98
Claire, William 16
Clanmorris, Lord and Lady 53
Cleever, Martin 12
Clive, Lady Mary (sister-in-law) 213
Cobb, Richard 59
Cocteau, Jean 150
Cohen, J.M. 53
Coke, Toby (grandson-in-law) 104, 140, 150, 161, 191, 198, 215, 216
Colville, Joan 190
Colville, Robin 190

Colvin, John 162
Compton-Burnett, Dame Ivy 130, 132, 134
Conder, Charles 208, 223
'Congressman, The', see Monagan
Conklin, Gary 191
Connolly, Cyril 20, 43, 54, 135, 156, 169, 187, 198, 199, 221–2
Connolly, Deirdre 221–2
Conquest, Robert and Liddie 26, 33, 103, 107, 117, 122, 139, 144, 146, 149, 170, 183, 191, 196, 210, 212, 215, 223
Conrad, Joseph 22, 59, 94, 105, 114, 127, 153, 186
Contarini Fleming (Disraeli) 8
Cooper, Jilly 65, 66, 67
Cooper, Leo 65, 66, 68
Cooper & Tanner 175
Corless, Ania 4, 210
Correggio 113
Corti (publishers) 210, 219, 220, 223
Cousin Pons (Balzac) 16
Coward, Noël 40
Cox, Frederick J. 142
Cranborne, Hannah, Lady 78, 80–81
Cross, Paul 160
Crowley, Andrew 32

Daily Mail 224
Daily Telegraph 6, 40, 78, 129, 148, 152, 163, 165, 166, 167, 169, 172
Daneman, Meredith 211
Daneman, Paul 211–12
Dardis, Tom 101–2
Dauncey, Dick 162
Davies, Joff 27, 99
Davies, Tessa 22, 34, 48, 55, 97, 99, 120, 178, 197, 200, 226
Davis, Bill and Annie 50, 59, 186
'Deacon, Mr' 48
Debrett's People of Today 109, 135
Delafield, E.M. 20
Democracy (Adams) 67
Denning, Lord 5, 12–13, 39–40, 60
Denning, Mrs (Halkin Gallery) 35–6
Deschamps, Pierre-Olivier 127–9

Desert Island Discs 22, 39, 179
Devonshire, Andrew, Duke of, and Deborah, Duchess of 51, 54, 58
De Winton, Gerald and Prudence 109
Dickens, Charles 107–8, 203, 206
Dietrich, Marlene 189
Digital Company of Canada 7–8, 183
Dilworth, Thomas 8
Disher, Eve 101, 159–60
Disraeli, Benjamin 4, 8
Dodo (Benson) 187–8
Dog at Clambercrown, The (Brooke) 156
Donald, Colin 192
Donaldson, Frances, Lady 47
Donna's (hairdressers) 93, 100, 126
Dostoevsky, Fyodor 82, 108
Dracula (Stoker) 115–16
Driberg, Tom 36, 189
Dru, Alick 98, 180
Duggan, Hubert 10
Dulac, Edmund 73
du Maurier, Gerald 109
Durrell, Lawrence 118
Durrell, Sappho 118
Dutson, J.M. 154, 210
Dymoke, John 59, 108–9, 126

Eastwood (bookseller) 68
Education of Henry Adams, The 67, 72–3
Eliot, T.S. 72
Elizabeth, H.M. Queen 227
Ellis, F.H. 222
Elton, Margaret, Lady 159, 160
Empson, William 180, 181
English Heritage 29, 33, 34, 65, 66, 83
Erskine, Derek 19
Eton College 90, 166
European Community 194, 219
Evening Standard 78, 121, 126, 162, 175
Everett, Barbara 54

Falkner, John Meade 180, 181
Fallowell, Duncan 19
Faulkner, William 27
Faulkners (solicitors) 211
Feltrinelli (Italian publishers) 6
Fergusson, Sir Ewen and Lady 49

'Ferrand-Sénéschal, Léon-Joseph' 137
Feuchtwanger, Lion 118
Fielding, Henry 11
Fiesta (Hemingway) 206
Fille aux yeux d'or, La (Balzac) 15
Finney, Albert 74–5, 77–8
Firbank, Ronald 57
Firminger, Enid 97
Fitzgerald, F. Scott 117–18, 205, 209
Fleming, Ann 79
Fleming, Peter 174
'Flitton, Pamela' 137–8
Florence, Alan 13
Flying Casserole (caterers) 41, 54, 55,
    66, 68, 74, 108, 118–19, 121, 122,
    123, 131
Flynn, Jane 106, 119–20, 121, 124
Folks That Live on the Hill, The (Amis)
    17, 24, 26, 45
Fonteyn, Dame Margot 95, 211
Ford, Ford Madox 54
Forster, E.M. 38–9
Foster, Sir John 41
Fraser, Lady Antonia, *see* Pinter
Fraser, Benjamin (great-nephew) 134
Fraser, Helen 68, 91, 118, 137, 145,
    146, 147, 181, 164, 168, 170, 212
Friede, Donald 102
Frome, secondhand bookshops 4, 10
Frost, Laurie Adams 61
Fuller, Roy 34, 39, 144, 146, 149, 151,
    176
Furbank, P.N. 38–9
Fussell, Paul 191

Gant, Roland, and Nadia 34, 38, 84,
    147, 182, 200
Gardner, Evelyn 130, 133, 153, 154
Gargantua and Pantagruel (Rabelais) 53
Garland, Nicholas 29, 147
Garland, Patrick 167
George VI 38
George, Bishop Ian 116
Glashan, John 158
Glenconner, Lord and Lady 100–101,
    165
'Glober, Louis' 102, 142

Godden, Rumer 116–17
Golden Bowl, The (James) 217
Good Books Guide 45
Good Soldier, The (Ford) 54
Gorbachev, Mikhail 139
Gotlieb, Sondra 56
Gowing, Sir Lawrence 46, 94
Graham, Alastair 19
Grant, Sir Alistair 201
Gray, Cecil 102
Green, Henry 17, 53, 91, 95, 168–9,
    170–1, 172, 188, 222
Greene, Graham 54, 74, 79, 85, 105–6,
    157
Greenfield, Sister Kate 91, 151, 165,
    167
Green Man, The (Amis) 74, 76, 77–8, 82
Gruffydd, Geraint 165–6
Gray, Tasha 102
Great Elm Literary Group 108
Great Gatsby, The (Fitzgerald) 205

Hackett, Gen. Sir John 151
Haggard, H. Rider 114
Haggett, Tim 88
Hall, Sir Peter (Edward) 63
Hamilton, Patrick 175
Hammond, Norman 157–8
Hancock, Graham 145
Hangover Square (Hamilton) 175
Hardy, Thomas 104
Harlech, Pamela, Lady 30–31, 133
Harlow, Jean 102
Harpers & Queen 130, 135, 153, 224
Harris, Wilson 106
Hart-Davis, Sir Rupert 34, 173
Hartley, L.P. 112, 118, 141–2, 216
Hartley, Norah 141–2
Hastings, Max 41, 133, 148, 152, 163,
    167
Hastings, Lady Selina: researches on
    Waugh circle 31, 110, 130, 153, 154,
    164, 187, 203; other refs 30, 50, 61,
    119, 121, 133–4, 224
Hayek, Friedrich 180
Hayward, Miranda 13
Healey, Dennis, Lord 56

Heinemann, William (publishers) 23,
    38, 68, 88, 118, 137, 140, 145, 146,
    147, 167, 193, 225
Hellstén, Frank 103
Helpmann, Sir Robert 212
Hemingway, Ernest 72, 206
Henley, W.E. 4, 9, 18
Henry Brulard (Stendhal) 157
Herbert, Auberon 187, 219, 220
Herbert, David 192
Herbert, George 23
Herbert, Susanna 78, 162
Heygate, Sir George 154
Heygate, Sir John 129, 143, 154
Heywood Hill (booksellers) 172, 201,
    208
Higham, David & Co. (literary agents)
    4, 63, 118, 156, 209
Hill, Lady Anne 30
Hillier, Bevis 44, 46
Hobson, Anthony 30–31, 34, 49, 57, 58,
    65, 66, 144
Hobson, Charlotte 144
Hobson, William 144
Hodgkins, Irene 97
Hoggart, Simon 163
Holloway, David 165
Hollyer, Belinda 44, 63
Holmes, Sherlock 120
Holroyd, Michael 141, 172
Holt, Hazel 91, 139, 207
Hope-Johnstone, John 202
Horrocks, Gen. Sir Brian 44
Houghton Mifflin (publishers) 12
Housman, A.E. 189, 191
Howard, Elizabeth Jane 57–8, 144
Hudson Prize 94
Hughes-Onslow, James 121
Hughes-Onslow, Neil 91, 94
Huish, Sister Bobby 167, 178, 182
Humphries, Barry 116, 204–5, 207–8,
    223
Humphries, Jasper 162
Hunter, Bruce (literary agent) 8, 12,
    28, 44–5, 63, 88, 146, 148, 164, 190,
    198, 202, 205, 220
Huntingdon, Jack, Earl of 50

Hyde, H. Montgomery 140
Hypocrites Club, Oxford 203

Independent 171
Irish, Dr W.T. 158, 169, 197, 212
Irvine, Rev. Gerard 84
Isherwood, Christopher 191, 224

Jackman, Doug 195
Jacobi, Dr 142
James, Henry 3, 16, 31, 110–11,
    112–13, 116–17, 127, 132–3, 217
Jansen, Johnaugust 194, 200
Jefferson, D.R. (great-uncle) 90
Jenkins, Dame Jennifer, Lady 66
Jenkins, Roy, Lord 34, 65–6, 138, 185
Jennings, Elizabeth 176
Jew Süss (Feuchtwanger) 118
John, Augustus 102
Johnson, Celia 174
Johnson, Frank 81
Johnson, Paul 184
Jones, David 8
Jones, Lewis 6
Jones, Monica 55, 91, 211
Jones, Steve 179
Jourdain, Margaret 134
Joy, Richard (dentist) 76, 179
Joyce, James 66–7, 73
Joyce, Michael 175
Jullian, Philippe 137

Keble, Louise 4, 5
Keegan, John and Suzanne 52–3, 59
Kemp, Alan 169, 177
Keraudrin, Capt. Jean 136
Ker-Seymer, Barbara 14
Ketton-Cremer, Wyndham 104
Kilmarnock, Ali, Lord, and Hilly, Lady
    122, 130, 176, 196
Kilmartin, Terence 207
Kingsmill, Hugh 59, 81, 141
King Solomon's Mines (Haggard) 114
Kinnock, Neil 164
Kipling, Rudyard 9, 43, 130
Kislinger, Peter 3–4
Kitson, Gen. Sir Frank 46–7, 181

Knott, Herbie 171
Knox, James 17, 203
Kooperstein, Jonathan 156–7
Koran 189

Lamb House, Rye 116–17
Lamb, Lady Pansy (sister-in-law) 78,
  165, 167
Lambert, Constant 14, 36, 76–7, 95,
  115, 211
Lambert, Flo 77
Lambert, Isabel 169
Lambton, Antony, Viscount 86, 88, 91,
  93, 94
Lancaster, Anne, Lady 17
Lancaster, Sir Osbert 199, 224
Lane, Margaret, Countess of
  Huntingdon 50, 60
Lang Brown (land agents) 16, 33, 57,
  83, 208–9, 210
Lankford, Nelson D. 96–7
Larkin, Philip 55, 71, 91, 148, 156, 210,
  211, 215, 218, 221
Larrett, John 24
Lawson, Dominic 94, 113
Lawson Dick, Oliver 150
Lees-Milne, Alvilde 54, 84, 133, 134
Lees-Milne, James 54, 84, 133–4, 167,
  191
Lehmann, John 191
Leith, William 30, 63
Lennox-Boyd, Charlotte 151, 181
Lernet-Holenia, Alexander 3
Levi, Peter 221
Levin, Bernard 85, 86
Lewis, Jeremy 221–2
Life at the Centre (Jenkins) 138
Lilley, George 65, 81, 160, 169, 171
Lire 126, 128, 142
Lister, Charles (dentist) 49, 52
Liveright (publishers) 102
Lloyd, Innes 139
Lloyd, John ('The Widow') 8, 115, 213
Lloyd, Mrs 19, 59, 180
Lloyd-Jones, Frances 225
Lloyd-Jones, Sir Hugh 156
Lomer, Patricia 182, 198

London Library 67, 142
London Magazine 144
Longford, Elizabeth, Countess of
  (sister-in-law) 100
Longford, Frank, Earl of (brother-in-
  law) 87, 100, 173, 219–20
Lopat, Bruno 145
Lorca, Federico Garcia 28
Lord, Graham 152
Lowry-Corry, Mary 91, 95
Lucan 184
Lucarini (Italian publishers) 6
Lucas, Audrey 110
Lurie, Alison 42, 121, 194, 195, 220
Lycett Green, Candida 155–6, 170
Lycett Green, Rupert 155
Lygon family 98
Lyon, Lady Mary 91

Maastricht, Treaty of 219
Macannock, Claudia 97
Macartney-Snape, Sue 161, 164, 165,
  170, 178, 179, 184, 190, 193, 214
MacCarthy, Sir Desmond, and Molly,
  Lady 198
McCraith family (kinsmen) 21, 22
McEwen, Neil 152
McIndoe, John 78
Mackenzie, Sir Compton 3
Mackenzie, John 176
Maclaren-Ross, Julian 28
Macmillan, Harold, Earl of Stockton
  32, 96
Macmillan's Dictionary of Art 46, 62
Macnamara, Robert 160
Major, John 83, 155, 182
Malone, Moura Dillon (caterer) 150–1,
  159, 196, 197, 212–19 passim, 224,
  225
Mandy (hairdresser) 93, 100
Manley, Edward and Marion 49–50,
  204, 205
Manley, Ronald 204
Mann, Thomas 194
Manning, Olivia 26
Manningham-Buller, Reginald, Lord
  Dilhorne 162

Marmion, Sally 172
Massie, Allan, 86
Massingberd, Hugh 6, 29, 34, 39, 120,
    133, 165, 167, 170, 175, 225
Matisse, Henri 97, 197, 214
Maupassant, Guy de 59
Max, Daniel 212
Mayall, Alex 30, 125
Mayall, Sir Lees and Lady 10, 30, 41,
    99, 116, 125, 129, 150, 178, 226
Mayall, Robert 125, 157, 178
Meacher, Michael 60
Mee, Henry: bookjacket design 118,
    173; 'Eminencies' exhibition 12, 30,
    39–40, 48, 76, 107; exhibition
    catalogue 45, 50, 56, 60, 61, 63, 65,
    68; marriage 106, 119–20, 124, 225;
    portrait of AP 13, 23–4, 58–9, 181;
    other refs 4–5, 12, 46, 110, 176
Meredith, Michael 90
Merleaŭ-Ponty, Maurice 137
Merriman, Henry Seton 105
Methuen, Lord 69
Mildav (builders) 19, 22, 57, 58, 145,
    199
Millard, Christopher 140
Mills, Sir John 12, 40
Milne, A.A. 109–10
Milnes, Rodney 144
Minns, Amina 85
Minot, Susan 209
Mitchell, Brigitte 84
Mitchell, Charles 161, 181
Mitford, Nancy 98
Mizener, Arthur 27, 117, 121
Mockler, Anthony 83
Modern Painters 23–4
Moisey, Clifford Urwin 88, 90, 96
'Molly, Lady' 56
Monagan, Senator John ('The
    Congressman') 11, 30, 74, 131, 147,
    160, 220
Monkman, Phyllis 38
Montgomery, F.M. Viscount 37
Montgomery-Massingberd, Hugh, *see*
    Massingberd
Moonfleet (Falkner) 180–1

Moore, David and Pat 16, 110, 208, 224
Mortimer, Raymond 115
Mosley, Diana, Lady 192
Mosley, Mr (motor car dealer) 59, 193,
    195–6, 199, 211, 212–13
Moss, Mr (drive-repairer) 25–6, 74,
    106, 152, 192, 201, 217, 223
Mount, Ferdinand (nephew) 30, 80,
    222
Mount, Harry (great-nephew) 101
Mount, Mary (great-niece) 226
Mount, William (great-nephew) 101,
    131, 132, 185
Moyne, Brian, Lord 181
Moynihan, Rodrigo 76
Muggeridge, Kitty 80, 87
Muggeridge, Malcolm 36, 78–82
    passim, 85–7, 90, 97, 106, 222
Mumford, Peter (land agent) 10, 11,
    34, 39, 66, 83, 143, 149, 166, 191
Murch, Fiona 13
Murdoch, Dame Iris 64, 137
Murphy, Patrick 21–2, 25
Murray, Jock 156

Naipaul, Sir Vidia, and Pat, Lady 30,
    31, 43, 57–8, 75–6, 137, 138, 182,
    189, 195, 216
Najda, Z. 127
National Library of Scotland 219, 220
National Library of Wales 166
Nelson, Katie (publisher) 63–4
New Statesman 115
New York Observer 209, 212
Nicolson, Nigel 192
Nightingale, Evelyn, *see* Gardner,
    Evelyn
Noble, Christina 104, 208
Nokes, Philip 11
Nolan, Sidney 211
Norman, Frank 186
Norton, W.W. (publishers) 63
Nostromo (Conrad) 114
Nunney Castle 12–13

Old Devils, The (Amis) 116, 130, 132,
    142, 144, 176

On the Black Hill (Chatwin) 33
Orchid Trilogy (Brooke) 150
Orwell, Eileen 135
Orwell, George 86, 110, 135, 137
Orwell, Sonia 100, 135, 137–8, 186
Our Mutual Friend (Dickens) 206

Packe, Col. Freddy 201, 208
Packer, K. Harvey 76–7
Pakenham, Thomas (nephew) and
    Valerie 46–7, 87
Palin, Michael 104, 105
Palmer, Primrose (great-niece) 196
Paravicini, F. de 170, 174
Parker, Peter 224
Parsons, Bridget 37
Parsons' Pleasure, Oxford 170, 171,
    174
Partridge, Frances 57
Pastors and Masters (Compton-Burnett)
    132
Peel, John 39
Perrick, Penny 32–3, 87, 94, 114
Phillips, Stephen 148–9
Phipps, Henrietta (niece) 165, 178
Phipps, Mrs Paul 70
Pickthorn, Sir Charles 67, 130
Pinter, Lady Antonia (niece) 123,
    194–5, 208
Pinter, Harold 123, 134, 195, 208
Piper, Sir David 62, 90
Piper, John 199
Pitter, Ruth 176
Point, Le 4, 5
Pope-Hennessy, James 58
Possessed, The (Dostoevsky) 82
Powell, Anthony: cooking 120;
    dentistry, *see* Joy; dreams 10, 41, 48,
    100, 109, 110, 122, 124, 131, 136,
    143–4, 158, 169, 203; fan mail
    181–2; health 40, 88–9, 91, 93, 94,
    99, 119, 151, 158–9, 165, 169, 179,
    197, 212; papers 107, 113, 165;
    portraits, *see* Mee, Pye
        Works: *Afternoon Men* 6, 14, 30, 36,
        184; *Agents and Patients* 28, 30;
        Caledonia 89, 90, 120, 160, 167,

206, 208, 219, 220, 226; early
    novels 29, 146, 147, 161, 165,
    168, 190, 209, 214; *The Fisher
    King* 56, 63, 75, 131, 147, 209,
    224; *The Garden God* 167; *Infants
    of the Spring* 59; *John Aubrey and
    His Friends* 11, 32, 91, 150, 156;
    Miscellaneous Verdicts 5–6, 12, 14,
    16, 25–6, 28, 34, 38–43 *passim*,
    54, 59, 118, 146, 147, 148, 198,
    207 209; *O How the Wheel
    Becomes It* 14; 'Poets, Painters
    &c; 192, 196, 201, 202, 205, 212;
    Under Review 88, 91, 118, 137,
    140, 143, 148, 160, 167, 168,
    173–182 *passim*, 192, 198;
    Venusberg 22
    A Dance to the Music of Time 3, 4, 5,
        11, 16, 22–3, 26, 63–4, 65, 71, 82,
        83, 103, 112–13, 126, 131–2, 139,
        140, 145, 171, 179; *Books Do
        Furnish a Room* 11, 81; *Hearing
        Secret Harmonies* 24; *Valley of Bones*
        79, 82, 214
Powell, Archie (grandson) 9, 26, 28,
    42, 101, 131, 132, 142, 146, 160, 178,
    185, 197, 200, 201, 217, 225
Powell, General Colin 11, 110
Powell, Georgia (grand-daughter) 9,
    23, 42, 56, 74, 101, 129, 131, 139,
    140, 141, 150, 178, 191, 198, 215
Powell, John (son) 8, 30, 64, 68–9, 85,
    90, 93, 101, 107, 108, 112, 160, 161,
    164, 165, 168, 176, 181, 188, 202,
    208, 212, 217, 227, and *passim*
Powell, Col. Philip (father) 73, 114,
    152
Powell, Trevor 94, 124
Powell, Tristram (son): on David Cecil
    80–81, 94; on Barry Humphries
    207–8, 223; on AP adaptations 65;
    films: *American Friends* 27, 51,
    99–105 *passim*; *Count of Solar* 97, 170;
    Kremlin Farewell 25; *Long Roads* 217;
    Old Devils 130, 132, 142, 155, 176,
    180; other refs 13, 75, 78, 116, 139,

160, 173, 178–9, 180, 186, 189, 192, 200, 201, 204, 220, 227, and *passim*
Powell, Lady Violet (wife): on Jane Austen 212; birthday 178; health 5, 69, 76, 78, 147, 180; on M. Muggeridge 79; lecture on AP 108; on B. Pym 174; other refs 15, 79, 92, 93, 95, 101, 112, 127, 128, 143, 168, 174, 188, 208, 225, 227 and *passim*
Powell, Virginia (daughter-in-law) 42, 54, 69, 75, 145, 151, 161, 176, 178, 200, 213
Powell, William 102
Poyntz, Newdigate 12, 14
Preston, Stuart ('Sergeant') 49, 198, 214, 219
Preview (Sotheby's) 44, 46
Pritchard, William 49
Prothero, Dr David 93
Proust, Marcel 51–2, 59, 94–5, 202, 207
Pryce-Jones, Alan 191, 192
Punch 78, 79
Pushkin 62
Putt, S. Gorley 117
Pye, Susan 117, 159
Pye, William 54, 113, 117, 130, 148, 152, 158, 159, 164–5, 167, 173, 196–7
Pym, Barbara 72, 91, 139, 174, 207, 208, 209

Quennell, Marilyn, Lady 133
Quennell, Sir Peter 17, 28, 133, 162, 191
Quinton, Tony, Lord, and Marcelle, Lady 56, 131, 136, 160, 203, 206, 225

Rabelais, François 53
Rackham, Arthur 73
Radio Times 94–5
Ramsden, George 140
Raphael, Frederic 39, 90
Rawlins, Dr David 99, 108–9
Real Charlotte, The (Somerville & Ross) 76
Reef, The (Wharton) 43

Rees, Goronwy 37
Rees-Mogg, William, Lord 125
Reitlinger, Gerald ('The Squire') 35–6, 44, 46, 62–3, 143, 154, 213
Rhys, David and Sheila 116, 119, 120, 165, 190, 225
Richmond, Tim 166, 173
Riley, Bridget 214
Roberts, Cecil ('Bobby') 69–70
Robinson, Bill and Virginia 60, 117–18
Rocca, Octavio 12, 14, 30
Rogers, Michael 46, 62
Rolf, Mr (sweep) 180
Roman Fever (Wharton) 46
Rose, Kenneth 151, 161–2
Ross, Alan 130
Ross, Jennifer 130
Rowse, A.L. 192
Royal Literary Fund 119–20
Royds, Debbie and Poppy 179
Rush, John (literary agent) 22, 26, 63, 64, 112, 118, 167
Russell, Erik 153
Russian Girl, The (Amis) 183
Rylands, George ('Dadie') 139

Sabbat, Le (Sachs) 150
Sachs, Maurice 150
Sachs, Richard 86, 87
Sackville-West, Vita 20
St James' Club 151, 161–2
Sandilands, James 223
Sassoon, George 145
Saumarez Smith, John 201, 208
Scotsman 192
Scott, Paul 32, 54, 68, 69, 84, 114
Scott, Sir Walter 4, 14, 18
Scriven, Marcus 125–6
Seitz, Raymond 93–4
Select Suppers (caterers) 190
Selig, Robert L. 92
Septimius Severus 11, 61
Seventh House Films 112, 141, 216
Seven Types of Ambiguity (Empson) 180
Seward, Desmond 151, 161–2
Shakespeare, Nicholas 4, 40, 109
Shakespeare, William: AP's critical

comments on 106; *All's Well that Ends Well* 134–5; *Antony & Cleopatra* 147–8; *As You Like It* 24–5, 201; *Hamlet* 119, 202, 210; *Henry IV* pt 1 171, 220–1; pt 2 179; *Julius Caesar* 139; *King John* 197; *King Lear* 7, 192; *Love's Labour's Lost* 76; *Macbeth* 157, 215; *Measure for Measure* 85–6, 129; *Merry Wives of Windsor* 70; *Midsummer Night's Dream* 14; *Pericles* 10; *Romeo & Juliet* 32, 174; *Tempest* 86, 108; *Timon* 151; *Troilus & Cressida* 45, 185; *Twelfth Night* 65

Shearer, Moira 28
Shelden, Michael 110, 135, 137, 191
Sheppard, Sir John 139
Sherry, Norman 74, 83
Schrijver, Herman 134
Simmonds, Posy 161
Singh, Rau 104, 208
Sitwell, Dame Edith 36, 42, 72, 171
Sitwell, Georgia, Lady 28, 37, 41
Sitwell, Sir Osbert 21, 72, 198
Sitwell, Sir Sacheverell 28, 37–8, 41, 72
Skelton, Barbara 220
Smith, Stevie 135
Snook (cat) 5, 13, 18, 40, 66, 120, 128, 139, 149, 171, 187, 192, 197, 207, 210, 212
Soames, Sally 34–5
Somerville, E.Œ, and Ross, Martin 76, 130, 193
Sonnenberg, Ben Jr 201–2
Southwood, William Frederick Walter 34
Sparrow, John 168
Spectator 41, 59, 69, 78, 86, 93, 96, 109, 113–14, 122, 135–6, 165, 167
Spender, Lizzie 224
Spender, Sir Stephen 175, 186, 191, 212
Spoils of Poynton, The (James) 132–3
Spurling, Gilbert 197
Spurling, Hilary: biography of Ivy Compton-Burnett 132, 133–4; biography of Paul Scott 32, 54, 68, 69, 84, 114, 197, 214; biography of Henri Matisse 97, 197, 214, 227;

commissioning of Pye head of AP 113, 130, 148, 152, 158, 159, 163, 164–5, 172; other refs 29, 34, 40, 41, 61, 90, 107, 141, 179, 193–4, 218
Spurling, John 41, 159
'Squire, The', *see* Reitlinger
Stannard, Martin 110, 184, 186, 187, 188
Steegmuller, Francis 150
Stendhal 82, 157, 159
Stevenson, Robert Louis 18, 123, 222
'Stockwells, The', *see* Powell, Tristram and Virginia
Stoker, Bram 115–16
Ston Easton Park 125, 126, 127, 128–9, 142
Storey, Edward 112, 118, 141, 216
Stroheim, Erich von 64, 189
Summers, John 43
Sunday Express 152, 176
Sunday Telegraph 29, 32, 39, 81, 132, 167, 175
Sunday Times 32, 34–5, 39, 42, 87, 171, 175
Sunnucks, John and Lucinda 22, 99
Surtees, Robert Smith 53, 68, 130, 167
Sutton, Denys 93
Swift, Jonathan 98
Sykes, Christopher 184
Sykes, Christopher (Simon) 34
Symons, A.J.A. 140

Tabner, Helen 174
Tatler 30, 34, 63
Taylor-Martin, Patrick 16, 28, 39, 42
Teakle, William 166
Temple, Shirley 157
Thames TV 22, 26
Thatcher, Sir Dennis 86
Thatcher, Margaret, Lady 82, 149
Theocritus 27
Third Ear 172, 174
Thomas, David 78
Thomas, Stuart 176
Thwaite, Ann 109, 110
Thynne, Lady Lenka 101, 103
Tiepolo, Giovanni Battista 196, 204

Time Out 19
Times Literary Supplement 38–9, 80
Tom Jones (Fielding) 11–12
Treasure Island (Stevenson) 18
Treglown, Jeremy 38, 39, 222–3
Trevor-Roper, Hugh (Lord Dacre) 142
Trotman-Dickenson, Sir Aubrey 169, 171
Trueheart, Charles 6, 11
Turn of the Screw, The (James) 112–13
Turnball, Mr (typewriter agent) 55–6
Twiston Davies, David 172
Tylden-Wright, David 147, 150, 156
Tylee, Edward 61–2

Ulysses (Joyce) 66–7
Umpleby, Mr (consultant) 147
Updike, John 168
Urquhart, F.F. ('Sligger') 168

Van Gogh, Vincent 139
Varda Bookshop 69
Vaughan, Henry 23
Vicosa, University of 113, 114, 138
Vincent, Wayne 34

Wade, Jane 29, 33
Wake, William 45, 46
Wales, Prince and Princess of 224–5
Wales, University of 158, 160, 164, 169, 177, 197
Waley, Arthur 175
Walker, Lt-Gen, Sir Anthony 65–6
Walker, Suzie, Lady 57, 65
Wallace, Tom 155
Washington Post 6, 11, 12, 14, 16, 22
Washington Times 11–12, 30
Watkins, Alan 60, 81
Watson, Sir Francis 213
Watson, Jane, Lady 213
Watts, Eleanor 154–5
Watts, James 154–5
Waugh, Alec 164
Waugh, Evelyn: and Bowra 120; and R. Byron 203; and Driberg 36; and Greene 106; and Spender 212; and

A. Wilson 119; and Wodehouse 47; Stannard on 184, 186–8; *Diaries* 100–101; *Letters* 95, 98–9, 164; other refs 7, 19, 31, 35, 43, 97, 125, 143, 154
Waugh, Evelyn, *see* Gardner, Evelyn
Waugh, Laura 98
Waves, The (Woolf) 20–21
We Are All Guilty (Amis) 153
Weaver, James 171
Welch, Colin 115, 122
Wellesley, Anne 116
Wellesley, Mary 142
Wells, John 142
Wells-Dymoke, Lionel (grandfather) 15, 58, 81
Westminster, Duke of ('Bendor') 37
Wharton, Edith 31–2, 43–4, 46, 48–9
Wharton, Kate 175
Wheatcroft, Geoffrey and Sally 133
Wheeler, Sir Mortimer 61
Whistler, J. McNeill 122
White-Spunner, Maria 178
Whiteford, John 40
Whitfield, Herefordshire (Clive family seat) 167, 213
'Widmerpool, Kenneth' 34, 71, 151, 161–2, 163, 189, 219–20
Wigan, Juliet 50
Wilson, A.N. 41, 44, 46
Wilson, Sir Angus 119
Withers, Mr (driver) 145
Wodehouse, P.G. 47–8, 110
Woolf, Leonard 21
Woolf, Virginia 19–21
Worsthorne, Sir Peregrine 133
Wrecker, The (Stevenson) 123

Yorke, Adelaide ('Dig') 91, 95, 169, 171, 172
Yorke, Henry (*see* Green)
Yorke, Matthew 168
Yorke, Sebastian 168–9, 171, 222
Yorke, Vincent 187
Years, The (Woolf) 21

Zielcke, Alexander 6–7

—